GYPSIES

IN CONTEMPORARY EGYPT

GYPSIES

IN CONTEMPORARY EGYPT

On the Peripheries of Society

Alexandra Parrs

The American University in Cairo Press
Cairo   New York

First published in 2017 by
The American University in Cairo Press
113 Sharia Kasr el Aini, Cairo, Egypt
420 Fifth Avenue, New York, NY 10018
www.aucpress.com

Exclusive distribution outside Egypt and North America by I.B.Tauris & Co Ltd., 6 Salem Road,
London, W2 4BU

Dar el Kutub No. 14621/16
ISBN 978 977 416 830 7

Dar el Kutub Cataloging-in-Publication Data

Parrs, Alexandra
        Gypsies in Contemporary Egypt: On the Peripheries of Society / Alexandra Parrs.—
Cairo: The American University in Cairo Press, 2017.
        p.   cm.
        ISBN: 978 977 416 830 7
        1. Romanies—Egypt
        305.8191497

1 2 3 4 5   21 20 19 18 17

Designed by Adam el-Sehemy
Printed in the United States of America

CONTENTS

INTRODUCTION

In a busy street of central Cairo, I was once approached by a woman dressed in a long black *abaya* selling packs of paper tissues. She had tresses of very blond hair coming out of her dirty headscarf, and she was looking intense and desperate. The Egyptian friend I was with gently pulled me away from the woman: "Be careful, she is a Ghagar. She is a thief." Later, I learned that Ghagar are considered a tribe of Middle Eastern Gypsies. Their women like to dye their hair yellow. Most of them are supposed to be beggars or thieves. They are fortune-tellers or dancers or prostitutes. It is better to avoid them, as they will not bring good fortune to anyone, and they will ask for extravagant amounts of money to rid you of the evil eye.

So much of this first encounter and the discussions that followed illustrate the perceptions and misconceptions associated with Gypsies in general, and Egyptian Ghagar more specifically. Interestingly, Ghagar seem to be ascribed an alienating alterity—as if they were *others* by essence while at the same time being denied any kind of history or even the right to own a precise identity. They may be that dangerous *other*, from another tribe, or from another social class (a deep underclass). As the ethnomusicologist Kevin Holmes cynically noted about Egyptian Ghagar: "No one really knows where they are from, and no one really cares." Somehow, this ignorance cruelly reminds one of the ignorance of medieval Europeans who attributed Egyptian roots to the 'Gypsies,' dark foreigners coming from some place in the Orient—scary and fascinating *others*.

1

Middle Eastern Gypsies are called the Dom, as a mirror name to the European Roma and the Armenian Lom, but that name is mostly used by scholars and rarely by Egyptians or by members of the Dom communities themselves. They are also called Ghagar, Nawar, or Halebi in Upper Egypt. In urban centers, they are called Hanagra when referring specifically to members of the community who commit crimes. The terms all have negative connotations in Arabic.

Many stories circulate about the Egyptian Ghagar, which is the term I will mostly use as it is the most widely acknowledged one in Egypt, particularly in the urban centers of Cairo and Alexandria. There are stories of Ghagar training their monkeys to steal from unsuspecting Egyptians or to kidnap Egyptian children, as well as stories about Ghagar women traveling to the holy city of Mecca in Saudi Arabia to rob pilgrims, or of Ghagar disrupting public order during *mulid*s, the popular saint festivals in Egypt. There are also stories about their origins: Ghagar may have descended from one of the lost tribes of Israel, or perhaps they were slaves who arrived with Roman legions more than two thousand years ago and then stayed in Egypt to form a lower class, akin to a caste. They may also have been the thieves who stole some of the large nails used to crucify Jesus Christ: according to some narratives, this brought them good luck because they alleviated his suffering; according to others, it brought them bad luck and turned them into eternal, rejected wanderers. There is a plethora of stories, legends, stereotypes, and very little else. The Ghagar, the 'Egyptian Gypsies,' seem largely invisible in academia, forgotten in public policy, and perhaps only existing as parcels in popular imagination. *Or are they?* My initial goal in starting this research was to answer that question and to explore who the Ghagar are and why they seem, at least superficially, so strikingly socially absent in Egypt.

The Paradigm of Diasporic Identity

It is a conspicuous fact that talking about Gypsies or Gypsiness is in itself controversial, as the group(s) bears many origins and possesses flexible boundaries and subclassifications. Establishing a framework of analysis is also a complex task. Scholars have sometimes tried to use the paradigm of 'diaspora' to show both that Gypsies actually do not constitute a diaspora in the classical sense of the term and also that some more constructivist dimensions of the concept of diaspora can nonetheless be used for analytical purposes (Toninato 2009; Renard, Manus, and Fellman 2009; Willems and Lucassen 2000). The primordialist definition of diaspora given by William Safran (1991, 1999) attributes to diasporas a few essential traits: they are dispersed groups that suffered from a traumatic departure, have constituted collective memories that serve as an anchor for the group identity, create strong boundaries that prevent their full integration into the host society, rely on a myth of return to the (often-idealized) homeland, and engage in certain political actions such as those of long-distance nationalists (as defined by Benedict Anderson [2011]). While some of these attributes fit Gypsies—departure from a homeland, dispersion among many other nations, and the creation and maintenance of boundaries between Gypsies and outsiders—the groups also lack some of those crucial features, and it would be dangerous and unproductive to try to fit them into a model that their very existence seems to negate. For instance, the notion of trauma in the departure from a homeland, which could be a basis for diasporic identity, may be absent. The departure may not have been brusque but progressive, made up of successive waves and motivated by a variety of elements such as war, poverty, entertainment, and religion, not necessarily persecution or violence.

Secondly, the 'homeland' is traditionally not a core part of Gypsy/Romani identity. Linguistic research may point toward India as a possible country of origin—nearly a millennium ago—of at least part of the contemporary Gypsy population. But that does not mean that all the Gypsies of this world live in awareness of a homeland from which they once moved or were dispelled and suffer all the traumatic consequences: "There is no collective, cherished memory, no developed or documented mythologization of an ancestral home to which they hope to return one day" (Willems and Lucassen 2000, 268). The homeland is not a clear component of Gypsy/Romani identity itself, either. While differences are not anchored in a precise nation-state which would contribute to fostering diasporic practices in their most traditional definitions, their perceived foreignness still anchors Gypsy groups in an

'elsewhere' (which is not in the land where they live), and the identified Indian origins serve to unify the group and give substance to its
otherness, more than they legitimately create a true Indian origin. The
concept of collective memory is not associated with a homeland, even if
some cultural traits distinguish members of the group from the cultural
majority of the countries where they live—for instance, the use of the
Romani language and to a lesser extent the Domari language, or some
essentialized cultural characteristics.

The theories of a migration out of India were mostly established by
non-Gypsy linguists who attempted to connect Gypsies to a specific point
of departure in order to make sense of the group in a European context,
where the construct of the nation-state was something fundamental, a
unit of analysis necessary for scientific research. In more recent years, the
notion of Indian origins has been appropriated by some Romani organizations with the objective of giving an understood or normative meaning
to the group and to use it as a basis for the creation of an ethnic minority.
Some scholars have pointed out that, ironically, when Roma present themselves as an ethnic minority, they actually give the ethnic majority and the
nation-state the power to model Romas' self-representations (Acton and
Gheorghe 2001). In the same vein, Paloma Gay y Blasco noted that the
diasporization of the group may actually be a sign of the internalization of
the concept of nation-state more than an act of resistance. Other scholars
continue to describe Gypsies as living in the present rather than in the
past, representing them as a people without a nation or history. All in
all, and despite the politicization of narratives, Gypsies are not associated
with the notion of a desired return to a homeland, be it real, mythical, or
instrumentalized. They are not involved in any political participation in
that homeland, which is the traditional goal of diasporic long-distance
nationalists (Anderson 2011). As a matter of fact, one commonality among
Gypsies may have actually been that their very existence challenges the
hegemonic modern thinking that uses the concept of the nation-state as
an undisputed unit of analysis, and on which national/ethnic identities are
built. Wim Willems and Leo Lucassen have tried to apply the concept
of diaspora to Gypsies specifically to engage in a general critique of the
concept itself. They conclude in these terms:

Our critique of the diaspora concept, however, transcends the
Gypsy case. Although Cohen, Safran, and most historians who use
the concept make perfectly clear that they reject outright its essentialist connotations and stress its metaphorical and heuristic value,
the danger of primordial notions creeping back is still considerable,
especially in the work of politically motivated scholars who identify
with such victim groups as Gypsies, Jews, Armenians, and former
African slaves. (Willems and Lucassen 2000, 269)

While the substantialist definition of diaspora (Safran 1991; Cohen 1996)
is not a satisfying frame of analysis, William Rogers Brubaker's constructivist definition of diaspora provides more guidance. Brubaker, distancing
himself from primordialism, identifies three salient dimensions to diasporas, or perhaps three diasporic practices: orientation to homeland,
dispersion, and the maintenance of boundaries vis-à-vis the host country.
These dimensions need not all be present—certainly not in any kind of
reified fashion—to contribute to creating diaspora-ness. Diasporas are no
longer defined as a bounded entity, but as stances or claims: "To overcome these problems of groupism, I want to argue that we should think of
diaspora not in substantialist terms as a bounded entity, but rather as an
idiom, a stance, a claim" (Brubaker 2005, 7).

Gypsies have certainly dispersed but, in doing so, they have constantly
contested and negotiated their identities, while keeping certain attributes
relevant, such as their social marginalization and their association to a set
of stereotypes and practices that seem to be prevalent, albeit constantly
changing. Perhaps many Gypsies are nomads, but not all. Perhaps some
Gypsies engage in characteristic occupations as peddlers, entertainers,
animal trainers, but some do not. Perhaps some Gypsies adhere strictly to
their traditions such as endogamic practices, certain taboos, and specific
gendered roles, but some may not. In each region where they have settled,
Gypsies have absorbed many of the local practices and redefined their
identities within the realm of the cultures that surround them. Gypsies
are strangely very predictable and unpredictable. The most predictable
element surrounding their identity may be the positions of host societies
toward them, which have often oscillated between rejection and forced

assimilation. These practices, interactions, and identity constructions have been very carefully studied in Europe, and much less in the Middle East. Gypsies have also often been symbolically the local other that serves as the buffer and that somehow allows the creation of a unified identity against them. In other words, while often marginalized, they also have been integrated in a fragmented manner, economically and symbolically, in many host societies, as noted by Judith Okely: "Unlike most nomads, Gypsies are directly dependent on the economy of another society which is usually sedentary, around which they circulate supplying goods and services" (Okely 2005, 60).

The classical concept of diaspora, although ambiguous when applied to Gypsies, is nonetheless useful, as it tells us what to look for and what *not* to look for. The association of the Dom (and in this case, I am using the more scholarly accepted term purposely) with the European Roma and to a lesser extent the Armenian Lom is important, as it informs us about the creation of the group, in its original similarities to the Roma, foreign and perhaps of Indian origins, but also in its differences: the language and the habitus of some groups differ, and the time of migration and the routes may have varied. The concept of a dispersed group may help us answer the question: Who are the Dom? Or how are the Dom constructed? To do so, it is essential to make a close study of the origins of the European Roma in order to understand the evolution of the study of the Dom, because a large portion of the scholarly work on Gypsies' origins has been conducted by linguists, most of them non-Gypsy. Starting in the eighteenth century, when the Romani language became scientifically constructed as the main repository of Gypsy history, the theory of the emigration of Gypsies out of India became prevalent, mostly built on linguistic proximity between Romani and Sanskrit. Many linguists and scholars then focused on the paradigm of the trilogy of Rom/Dom/Lom as constituting the main dispersed Gypsy subgroups, differing in their trajectories to distinct geographical locations: the Roma into Europe, the Dom into the Middle East, and the Lom into western Asia. The claim of a common origin or identity is based on linguistic similarities between Romani, Domari, and Lomavren, respectively spoken by the Roma, the Dom, and the Lom.

Do these dispersed subgroups constitute nonetheless an encompassing 'Gypsy' entity? As a matter of fact, the very essence of the similar origin can be contested, and has been.

The question of the relationship between Roma and Dom, similar to the question of an encompassing Gypsy identity among Roma, remains controversial and can be approached from many angles. Is there even an actual group subsumed under the name 'Gypsies,' or is this just, as some scholars have argued, a European construction that was about five centuries in the making and has relied on fears, legends, folklore, and popular assumptions first, linguistics and occasionally racial studies later, and DNA analysis more recently? David Mayall has identified two contrasting views on Gypsy identity, one being ethnic/racial and the other a sociohistorical construct. While the idea of an ethnic/racial identity builds on the notion of Indian ancestry and considers that the members of the group display specific rigid characteristics, maintaining their language and lasting cultural practices and often racializing the group, the sociohistorical approach combines "way of life with low socio-economic and social status," and social and cultural practices such as nomadism appear as more crucial identity markers than confirmed common origins (Mayall 2004, 93). For authors such as Michael Stewart or Gay y Blasco, the notion of collective memory is not part of the Romani community as it can be for other diasporic groups, and therefore, they do not have a sense of ethnicity (Matras 2015). Okely has famously challenged the link between ethnicity/Indian origins and language, suggesting that the origin of the Gypsies was "mythical or only apparently empirically proven" and that the Romani language developed "along the trade and pilgrim routes," which does not imply definite Indian origins (Okely 1984). While anchoring a Gypsy identity in Indian roots leads to its essentialization, social practices can also be reified, and nomadism or a stubborn refusal to incorporate host societies' norms can become innate characteristics of *the* Gypsy identity.

More recently, another representation of Gypsies has emerged, which is that they embody a 'social problem.' This un-ethnic or even un-cultural representation portrays Gypsies as a problematic, deviant social group, the consequence of a set of social factors (Kabachnik 2009; Belton 2005).

Gypsy groups can also become political entities with specific goals. Roma in Europe have in recent decades appropriated their history and their destiny, creating the International Romani Union, trying to fight for their rights in different ways, which, of course, sometimes contributes to self-essentializing their group. The Roma activist Paul Polansky assumes that nobody knows for certain the origin of the Gypsies, and Mayall notes:

> What we are faced with is a complex and multi-layered Gypsy identity—or rather identities, as we are talking not of a single identity but several—and also a high degree of difference and confusion in the application of labels, images and boundaries. (Mayall 2004, 54)

Even more thought-provoking, according to Donald Kenrick, Egyptian Dom may not even be of Indian origins.

> Today in Egypt we find the Halebi, possibly a million in number, living mainly from casual farm work, though some men work as veterinary surgeons and some women tell fortunes, as well as the Ghagar and some families of Dom (Nawwar). The Ghajar speak European Romani and it is thought they were deported to Egypt from the Balkans. The men work as blacksmiths and the women traditionally as rope dancers, singers and tattooists. The Halebi are said to have come originally from Aleppo, hence their name, and they do not speak Romani. They speak Arabic using a large number of words which are jargon. *They are perhaps not of Indian origin.* The same three groups appear in the Sudan but all seem to have lost their original language and speak only Arabic. (Kenrick 2004, 87; emphasis added)

Kenrick concludes: "If the general impression . . . is that there are a large number of clans in the Middle East and Asia who in some ways resemble the Romanies of Europe, who may not have come from India, that reflects our knowledge at the present time" (2004, 87).

The classical concept of diaspora therefore encourages us to look at the creation of historical, and possibly cultural, proximity between different subgroups, and makes us question why and how a seemingly encompassing identity may have been created, as well as whether this adjacency is indeed meaningful, not only for scholars of Gypsy identity, but also for non-Gypsy/Dom populations (Egyptian in this book), and for the Dom themselves. Preconceptions and knowledge about the Roma and their practices will constantly be a point of reference in my research. It is essential to examine the production of knowledge about the Roma to understand how research about the Dom was conducted in Egypt, perhaps mimicking certain European reflection mechanisms motivated by linguistics and an acute interest in 'race' and racialization. It is also instructive to ask whether certain characteristics and practices are depicted or constructed as belonging to both Roma and Dom identity and what this can mean: Are the different dispersed groups indeed engaged in practices that show similarities? Are the processes of othering those groups following similar paths, or possibly some mirror constructions of others?

The constructivist notions suggested by Brubaker also address the orientation to a (real or imagined) homeland, and the maintenance of boundaries vis-à-vis the host country. The notion of orientation to a homeland is not a core aspect of Romani identity, but could it be an important one in Dom identity? Do the Dom perceive their potential differences to be anchored in a different national origin? Do they see themselves as simply culturally or tribally different? This leads to the question of contextualization, and particularly the nature of the markers of belonging in the Egyptian national identity construction. For instance, is nomadism an exclusionary practice? Do linguistic and religious identifications serve to incorporate or exclude? What is the role of tribal identification?

Lastly, the notion of boundaries is a well-tested approach to the study of group identity formation. As a concept, it was largely developed in the seminal work of Fredrik Barth (*Ethnic Groups and Boundaries*, 1969 [1998]), in which he focuses on the frontiers of ethnic groups, the interconnectedness of ethnic identities, and the continuity of ethnic groups. In the same line of thought, Stuart Hall contends that identity goes beyond the recognition of a common origin or shared characteristics; instead, the construction of identity is an ongoing process. Identities are the names given to the various ways in which we position ourselves within narratives from the past; "far from being eternally fixed in some essentialized past, they are subject to the continuous play of history, culture and power" (Hall 1990, 225). Hall suggests that cultural identity is seen as "unstable, metaphoric and even contradictory—an identity marked by multiple points of similarities as well as differences" (1990, 236). Identity consists of becoming as well as being. A stagnant identity is unthinkable under the circumstances of movement, displacement, and relocation in which we live. Identities are constantly being transformed; they are not an essence but a positioning, and every single angle of the positioning needs to be observed.

Boundary creation as well as identity formation and transformations are compelling elements in the study of Gypsies, and constitute more and more the main paradigm of analysis. The use of boundaries when looking at any ethnic or cultural group is probably one of the safest tools to avoid essentialization; furthermore, it informs us about the group itself and about the non-group which tends to project much of its fear onto the building of boundaries. It is perhaps the best initial building block when analyzing Gypsy identity as something created, negotiated, and contested. Boundaries can also be instrumentalized, and the use of boundaries has served, for instance, to analyze strategies of survival in hostile environments (Smith and Greenfields 2013, 10). Indeed, they can become marginalizing elements: "the common theme of Gypsy identity, across differing economic, social and political structures is one of contestation, and often, but not always, one of marginalization" (Marsh and Strand 2006, 16). The study of boundaries shows that they are not rigid entities, but flexible and constantly renegotiated, even if they can certainly be reified or occasionally broken. Furthermore, the construction of boundaries not only involves interactions among different actors, but also needs to be approached from a multiplicity of levels of analysis, from interactions that happen at the micro level to the role of institutions, politics, economics, and the nation-state with its own philosophies of integration, as well as the impact of globalization and modernity. In this way, the use of boundaries permits a multidimensional and fluid perspective on identity.

This research is based on examining the various mechanisms of formation and transformation of Ghagar identity from a multiplicity of angles. On an individual level, the Gypsy is often the embodiment of the useful pariah, the one who never totally integrates into society, who shows the limits of the socially acceptable, and whose existence allows non-Gypsies, by way of contrast, to inject prestige into their own identity and cultural practices. At the national level, creating boundaries against Gypsies has often helped to create the a-national other and therefore reinforced a sentiment of national belonging. Gypsies have also often illustrated the "torments of society" (Charnon-Deutsch 2004). Discourses also contribute to creating identities; knowledge production from academia on the Dom is scarce, but what Foucault calls *le savoir des gens* is very present and both shapes and is shaped by those identities. To what extent are Ghagar becoming Ghagar simply because they are defined as such? This is particularly salient, first because of the fact that many people who are defined as such will deny they are Ghagar, or will change their narrative. Additionally, the definition of Ghagar varies so widely that it seems that the only reality is the discourse itself, a production constantly modified, about the group.

Essentialization

When looking at the Dom of Egypt, specific factors need to be taken into consideration. First, our limited current knowledge leaves an intimidating space to be filled. It would be easy, metaphorically, to fill up that emptiness with reified constructs that would then somehow add a few features to the landscape. In other words, since we know very little about the Dom, the temptation to come up with a few certainties is high: the Dom live here, the Dom engage in this type of activity, their traditions are such and such, and of course "they come from that precise place." Such an approach would probably be more gratifying, as it would give the researcher the impression of producing something tangible: facts and certainties. However, precisely because of the current voids in this field, it is crucial to proceed with caution and avoid essentialization and assumptions. The temptation of exoticization is, however, less pernicious than other more subtle mistakes, such as taking for granted what is being said—in interviews, but also in the very fluid media production—and ignoring the impact that discourses have on identity constructions.

The second element is contextualization. An initial comparison to Europe is helpful because the study of Gypsies started in Europe and that knowledge needs to be used, not only because it gives us some direction on how to proceed or not to proceed, but also because the European approach in studying the Roma has already spilled into the Middle East. Roma have been racialized, given specific origins, and ascribed meaning in the context of the traditional construct of the European nation-state: fixed and exclusive at times, liberal and diverse in other instances. Racialist discourses sugarcoated in scientificism have done their share in contributing to Gypsies' identity construction. In the case of Egypt, however, the nation-state may be anchored in different philosophies, not only distinct from the European ones, but also constantly evolving historically. The relationship to nomadism, for instance, is different; even if nomadism is more and more constructed as an archaic practice, it may still hold a certain space in the national imaginary. Ethnic diversity may also have another meaning, as the current Egyptian national identity narrative actively builds on homogenization.

In his groundbreaking book *Orientalism*, Edward Said (1978) traces the origins of the power of representation and the normative agency it entailed to the colonial hubris that carried a militant band of mercenary merchants, military officers, Christian mercenaries, and European Orientalists around the globe, enabling them to write and represent the people they tried to rule (Dabashi 2009, xi). Orientalism has been at the root of the study and creation of the Orient. Post-Orientalism, or the destruction of Orientalist constructs, has prevailed since the enlightening work of Said. But to what extent is it necessary to go beyond that dichotomy? Understanding Orientalist constructs and deconstructing them is still very important, but it is equally important to look for perhaps less rigid paradigms. One of the critiques of Said's thesis was that it reduced Orientalism to a unilateral action from the West, and denied agency to the 'Orientals,' in production of self-knowledge or knowledge of others. But could it be that Egyptians followed those mechanisms and applied them, proceeding to the Orientalization of the Dom in mimicry of the European Orientalization of Egypt? There still persist some fragments of Orientalism, and there are many fragments of post-Orientalism studies that need to be taken into account. Particles of imagination of the West have been appropriated and reused to construct the Dom, but these particles have themselves been changed in the process.

Particles and fragments appear as important concepts in the study of Egyptian Dom. I realized early in my research that I would not be able to get a complete picture. I would have to look for fragments and try to piece them together, keeping in mind that they are indeed pieces and may not lead to an integrated, final picture. I will look at fragments of boundaries and fragments of identity, composed of a variety of actors. The lack of a complete picture is perhaps closer to reality; it is also more of a component of Egyptian Gypsies, who have not yet been fully created as a finished entity with recognized characteristics. Fragments not only represent different parts of Dom identity, they are also rooted in different elements, such as mimicry of Orientalism, tribalism, nation-state identity construction, scapegoating, self-representations, stereotypes, and the like. Since little research has been conducted on Middle Eastern Dom, it is difficult to predict the types of constructs that will predominate. The Dom themselves have not created any type of politicized structure like the International Romani Union—they have not even formally decided on an appellation. They seem to have been disengaged from knowledge production. As a matter of fact, as I mentioned earlier, the term 'Dom' itself is seldom used—occasionally in scientific literature, and again predominantly in contrast to the Roma identity. The Dom have occasionally been constructed as Eastern Gypsies, mostly by European scholars imitating the study of the Roma, as we will see in later chapters. In Egypt, more often the Dom have been represented as members of tribal structures, a type of structure that makes sense in the Middle Eastern context. They have been, and are still, identified by their tribal appellations: Ghagar, Halebi, and Nawar in Egypt; Halebi in Syria; Ghajar in Iraq; or "Barake, Nawar, Kaloro, Koli, Kurbat, Ghorbati, Jat/Zott and Zargari" in different Middle Eastern countries (William 2000).

Could the Ghagar— and I am using the term I will mostly use in this book as it is the term primarily used in Egypt, then be nothing but what people say they are? At one point, I came to ask myself if there was indeed a group called Ghagar, or if under that appellation (which also has a negative connotation in Arabic, such as 'thug' or 'marginal') came anyone who appeared a pariah, the roots of the pariah-ness historically varying between social, ethnic, and moral. I came to wonder if this was not all the product of the imagination of nineteenth-century European Orientalists who had created the Dom, in contrast to the Roma, and who have assigned this role to a group of marginalized outcasts, declaring them the Oriental cousins of the well-known Roma, both identifying in them and applying to them some of the typical Roma characteristics: origins rooted in India, a gift for fortune-telling, belly dancing, and natural criminal instincts. Perhaps this is all the illusion of an identity. I cannot prove that there is such an individual as a true Ghagar; I cannot prove that the Dom are indeed related to the Lom and the Roma. And most importantly, I do not intend to. But I can look at representations, interactions, and discourses, as well as practices and power relations. The last aspect, of course, draws from Foucault's uses of the term "power/knowledge" to signify that power is constituted through accepted forms of knowledge, scientific understanding, and 'truth.'

Literature on Middle Eastern Gypsies

Among the Middle Eastern Dom, the Egyptian Dom may be the least researched. Two important articles in English that mention Gypsies were written in the nineteenth century. The first one, written by Captain Thomas Newbold in 1856 for the *Journal of the Royal Asiatic Society of Great Britain*, is entitled "The Gypsies of Egypt." Newbold focused on Gypsies and their subgroups, seeking to attribute specific traits to each of them: the Halebi are described as horse and donkey dealers who "pretend great skills in the veterinary art" (286) while the Ghagar are individuals with "vagabond habits" who wander about the cultivated portions of Egypt in tents (292). They are also described as tinkers and blacksmiths, while the women were "excellent rope dancers" (292). The second article, less than ten years later, was written in November of 1864 by the Austrian consul in Cairo, Alfred von Kremer, for the Royal Anthropological Institute of Great Britain and Ireland. His article started with this statement:

> Excepting the Jews there is no people so scattered over the earth as the gipsies. Homeless and yet everywhere at home, they have preserved their physiognomy, manners, and language. Everywhere they support themselves as tinkers, musicians, fortune-tellers, and everywhere have they but loose notions concerning the rights of property. (1864, 262)

He then explained that the tribes in Egypt were the Nawar and the Ghagar and associated them with occupations that made them travel throughout the country, such as "tinkers, rope dancers, monkey show-men, and snake charmers" (262). Both scholars provide interesting accounts of the Dom in the sense that they still are among the rare writ-ers to actually address the existence of Egyptian Gypsies. Their accounts are, however, deeply tainted with Orientalist and essentialist tones that need to be contextualized.

The main Egyptian contributor to the study of Gypsies in Egypt is the late Nabil Sobhi Hanna, who in 1982 published "Ghagar of Sett Guiran'ha: A Study of a Gypsy Community in Egypt." It is a unique work that provides an ethnographic account of the community and focuses on some of its rituals. He described the lives of the Ghagar fifty years ago, leading a seminomadic lifestyle in rural settings, often liv-ing in tents and engaging in peripatetic activities. Cultural identities are, however, subject to transformations triggered by economic, social, and political forces, and while the Ghagar described by Hanna lived seminomadic lifestyles in the Delta region, it would appear that many of them, like other poorer communities, were forced to move to urban areas, where they then settled.

More recently, the Dom Research Center has published articles on the Egyptian Dom. Adrian Marsh (2000) wrote a piece on the sedentary Gypsies in the City of the Dead in Cairo who live alongside the Cop-tic Zabbalin, and Kevin Holmes (2002) wrote on the music and folklore associated with Egyptian Gypsies. The fact that the literature review encompasses less than ten papers is revealing of the profound denial of (or lack of interest in) the existence of Gypsies in Egypt.

The literature on the other Dom in the Middle East is also very scarce, aside from Meyer's (1994) study of the Dom living in Damascus and linguistic analyses of the variety of Domari spoken in Jerusalem (Matras 2000, 2012) and Aleppo (Herin 2012). Very recently, a few arti-cles have focused on the Gypsies of Lebanon and the Gypsies of Iraq. Zeidel's (2014) article on the Gypsies of Iraq reflects on the landless-ness of Iraqi Gypsies and the loss of their language. What is particularly interesting in the article is the role of the state, particularly under

Saddam Hussein, in defining the position of Gypsies within Iraqi society. Zeidel explains that while in most of the world the state policy tends to be dichotomous (expulsion or assimilation), in Iraq, up until the late 1950s, expulsion or segregation was the rule, as Gypsies were usually stateless. The sedentarization of Gypsies, however, started gradually after 1958, officialized in the mid-1970s with the construction of Gypsy settlements. Those centers, however, turned into prostitution hubs hosting "other shadowy activities such as the selling of alcohol (always a problem in Iraq), gambling, contraband and the like" (Zeidel 2014, 38). Those 'pleasure cities' were nonetheless tolerated, and "only when there was an extraordinary outcry by influential social or religious factors was police force used to disband Gypsy encampments. Normally, their presence and activities were tolerated" (Zeidel 2014, 39). The state actually benefited from the existence of those peripheral camps, which moved prostitution out of the center of cities and allowed these 'entertainment' activities to be concentrated in one place, permitting better management and simplifying the logistics of attracting wealthy visitors, mostly from the Gulf states. The article argues that "things were positive for Gypsies under Saddam Hussein." He gave them citizenship shortly after ascending to power in 1979. They also became entitled to purchase land (a new Gypsy settlement started in Abu Ghraib), and the number of nomadic Gypsies decreased. But the Gypsies were not assimilated; on the contrary, "Gypsy entertainment was monopolized by the State and Gypsy concentrations, now branded 'pleasure towns,' mushroomed" (Zeidel 2014, 79), mostly for tourists from Gulf countries, replacing war-torn Lebanon as a destination for 'pleasure.' Of course the backlash of all of these advantages was, first, that since they benefited from the support of the regime, they also had to give back. Many had to enroll in the army or the police, which made them hated by the rest of the population, who saw them not only as morally depraved (because of the pleasure centers) but also bought out by the Hussein regime. In the collapse of the Ba'th regime, concludes Zeidel, "Gypsy concentrations were attacked everywhere, both Sunni and Shia hated them, and by 2012, many Gypsies had fled to other parts of Iraq, including the Kurdish north" (Zeidel 2014, 84).

Official Invisibility

Zeidel's case study of the Iraqi Gypsies leads us to question the role of the Egyptian state in the articulation of Dom social and political identities. There is virtually no research on the topic, aside from the reflection of the nineteenth-century Captain Newbold, who explains: "The present energetic ruler of Egypt would appear to be a severer taskmaster than its old kings; for he has compelled the gypsies to pay a species of poll-tax, to elude which they practise every kind of deception: hence the difficulty of arriving at a faithful approximation of their numbers" (1856, 291). Newbold then estimates that the Gypsies consist of four different tribes, each ruled by a sheikh and comprising about forty families. Regarding the Ghagar, he contends:

> It is impossible to obtain from the Ghagar a true statement of their numbers, as they, too, like the Helebis, are subjected to a poll tax. When the tax-gatherers are on the prowl, they take themselves off, and, ostrich-like, hide their heads in the sand of the desert. After paying a first visit to them in the Hosh-el-Ghagar, I returned the following day, but, to my surprise, found the quarter quite deserted. Suspicious of such unusual attention bestowed on them, they had quietly absconded, and, as I afterwards learned, had crossed the Nile to some village on the skirts of the desert. (Newbold 1856, 293)

The role of the state in creating collective identities within its borders can take different forms. One of them is the census and its categorizing of a population, dividing it according to different races, ethnicities, religions, or languages. These categorizations not only reflect societies but also create them, by constructing a specific reality (Kertzer and Arel 2002). In Egypt, the main categorizer is religion: it is taken into account by the Census Bureau questionnaires, in the form of an optional question. The other bureaucratic element that influences the construction and maintenance of collective identities is the national identity card, which identifies the religion of its holder, offering a choice among three religions: Islam, Christianity, and Judaism—and more recently an 'other' category. Not only is religion the main social marker, but the limited number of options leads to a denial of the social existence of individuals outside of the spectrum of official religions. Since religion is the official marker, other markers, such as ethnicity, are not used, and groups whose identity would be ethnically based are socially ignored. This is the case for the Bedouins, the Nubians, and, of course, the Dom. The existence of identity-based categorizations and statistical representation, besides constructing a specific social environment and promoting the social absence or overwhelming presence of certain constructed groups, triggers additional phenomena: a relatively reliable estimation of the size of the minority groups and, sometimes, a need for promotion, control, segregation, eradication, or forced assimilation of the members of the identified group. All of these phenomena are absent for Gypsies in the Egyptian context.

Because of their official absence, it is difficult to estimate the size of the Gypsy population in Egypt, and the estimates are mostly provided by evangelical organizations. *People Groups* estimates the Domari to have a population of 1,745,000, with most of them "Sunni Muslim" ("Domari Gypsies of Egypt" 2017). According to *Idlewild*, there are 270,000 Dom in Egypt and 99 percent of them are Muslim, but with a growing Christian population ("Unreached" n.d.). According to the U.S. Center for World Mission, there are 1,653,000 Dom in Egypt. According to their documents, the Halebi live near the Nile Delta and consist of four tribes that migrated from Yemen. Some live on floating islands, built on the Nile. They raise horses and practice folk medicine and fortune-telling; the Halebi are "not citizens, nor reliably counted in any Census data. [It] has been estimated that the Gypsies in Egypt may number 3 or 4 times their present estimate (or as high as four million people)" ("Romani, Domari in Egypt" 2017). Finally, according to the website *Ethnologue*, there are 1,080,000 Muslim Gypsies in Egypt, or 2 percent of the population, including 864,000 Halebi and 216,000 Ghagar ("Domari" 2017). The Dom Research Center published an article in 2000 that estimated the population of the Halebi or Nawar of Egypt in the range of 864,000 to 1,067,000. In the absence of an official category, there is room for interpretation, and the estimates vary not only in number but also in the description of the groups, as well as the boundaries of each group.

The question of their citizenship also needs to be raised: according to the Dom Research Center and some newspaper clips, some Egyptian Gypsies may actually be stateless and have been so for many generations. The question of statelessness is ambiguous. It should be addressed in more depth and treated carefully. Their uncertain nationality status seems to keep them in an identity limbo and deprived of political, economic, or cultural rights, as is also the case for some other minorities. Based on the interviews I conducted, most Ghagar now seem to have an Egyptian identity card. However, since the only information on the identity card is the religion, the card does not serve to identify them as members of any specific ethnic group.

Rural and Urban Dom

Since the publication of "Ghagar of Sett Guiran'ha" in 1982, things have changed and the Ghagar have followed a path of urbanization. Rural Ghagar were relatively well-known figures to villagers, mostly because they provided them with entertainment during ceremonies such as weddings, engagements, or circumcisions. Ghagar men would recite poetry and play the *rababa*, a small string instrument. Some of my Egyptian interlocutors recalled seeing, when they were younger, Dom entertainers singing and dancing during weddings that would usually take place in the streets. Dom, under various tribal appellations, were clearly very present in villagers' lives, within certain limits, as illustrated by a well-known Egyptian proverb that says that you can certainly have a Dom at your wedding, but never as the groom. Generally, their traditional occupations were similar to those in which the Roma engaged, such as blacksmiths, tinkers, wool traders, shearers, saddlers, musicians, and dancers (Marsh 2000). Traditionally, Dom, like European Roma, rarely engage in large-scale agricultural activity. However, they may engage in small-scale operations, such as herding goats and sheep (Holmes 2002).

The focus of my research is on urban Dom established in Cairo and Alexandria. Since very little has been written on them, and the little that exists often focuses on communities in the countryside, the information I initially obtained on Dom in urban settings is largely based on the scarce material I came across (mainly Marsh and Holmes) and some assumptions based on discussions I had with Egyptian interlocutors. It would appear that many Dom left rural environments to settle in large urban centers during the second half of the twentieth century. In Cairo, they appear to have established themselves in specific areas such as Sayyida Zaynab, Dar al-Salaam, Helwan, and Giza, as well as the City of the Dead, Cairo's vast necropolis. Many of these areas are relatively poor and marginalized. In Alexandria, many Dom are established in the area of Muharram Bek. While some Dom still live in Dom enclaves, many have also dispersed throughout the cities, and more often larger Dom communities have been replaced with smaller and more socially integrated clusters. The changes are due in part to government interventions, in clearing the canals next to which they customarily settled, but also because many of the trades they traditionally engaged in, such as blacksmithing or tinkering, have slowly disappeared (Holmes 2002).

As a result of their urbanization and the general modernization of the country, many of the traditional Dom occupations have in fact been lost. While they used to be peripatetic peddlers or tinkers in villages, they now engage in more sedentary occupations in urban neighborhoods, such as metalwork, saddle-making, and fortune-telling. Some Dom sell items or offer horseback rides to tourists near the Giza pyramids. Some have established themselves in the Cairo market of Khan al-Khalili. Dom are also identified during the *mulid*s. The *mulid* of Sayyida Zaynab is one of the largest and most famous of all. Traditionally, one subgroup, the Ghawazi (although not always recognized as part of the Dom) used to perform belly dancing, but this practice seems to have largely stopped, partly because the Ghawazi themselves are becoming less prevalent and partly because *mulid*s have become more conservative and scantily dressed dancing females are frowned upon. The Dom have therefore modified their occupations during *mulid*s, and tend to sell items for children, run small attractions, or provide bizarre entertainment, such as shows that feature five-legged cows and other extraordinary creatures. Ghagar also used to engage in specific activities such as snake-catching in both rural and urban environments. The snake-catcher would, as described by von Kremer in the nineteenth century, "give a few knocks on the walls and floors, play a short tune on his reed pipe, and the snakes made their appearance, which is explained by the fact that there are in most of the old houses of Cairo many snakes, most of which are, however, quite harmless" (1864, 263). I was told that the snake-catchers would come to houses in affluent neighborhoods of Cairo, such as Maadi, up until a few decades ago to rid homes of their snakes. Nonetheless, while the vast majority of Ghagar are de facto sedentary, their contemporary activities still comprise an element of mobility and temporariness; while they are not peripatetic anymore, neither are they fully settled or integrated into the Egyptian society. They occupy intermediary, short-term jobs; they mostly rent their houses; and they may move from place to place within a neighborhood. Above all, according to the most widespread representations, the Dom predominantly exercise their talents as beggars and as thieves.

Methodology

This book is the result of over two years of research in Cairo and Alexandria. In order to obtain a wide understanding of the representations of Egyptian Dom, by outsiders, institutions, and finally by themselves, I looked at different levels of their identity formation. I used the writings of early Orientalists (mainly Newbold, von Kremer, Lane, and Burton) who depicted them in the nineteenth century, as well as more recent literature, mostly from Nabil Sobhi Hanna (1982) and articles from the Dom Research Center written by anthropologists, ethnomusicologists, and journalists. I examined the official representations, or lack thereof, using the Egyptian Census questionnaires, which since the late nineteenth century have not collected ethnic and racial data of the Egyptian population. I explored the representations of the Dom in art, focusing particularly on Egyptian movies depicting Gypsies, from Stelio Chiarini's 1928 *Suad the Gypsy* up to the most recent production, the 2014 Ramadan television series *Women's Prison* (*Sign al-Nessa*).

At the individual level, my research began by interviewing non-Dom Egyptians. A vast majority of the individuals I met had no knowledge of the Dom and told me that Gypsies only "existed in Europe," or they linked Gypsies with "Romania or Spain." A few Egyptians established connections between the terms "Gypsy" and "Egypt" but were oblivious to the presence of Gypsies in Egypt. Some suggested that Gypsies were mostly unknown to the "Egyptian upper classes," who never had to inter-act with them, but that they were better known to the lower class, mostly because of their geographical proximity in poorer neighborhoods or the fact that lower-class Egyptians attend *mulids* more frequently. Proximity creates awareness, and in the poorer areas, the existence of Gypsies is known. Often they are feared as untrustworthy criminals, a cliché similar to the one held by many Western Europeans. The prevailing perception of absence, in itself, is crucial to illustrate the invisibility of Dom in the Egyptian context. Interestingly, however, when asked more precise ques-tions, many interlocutors admitted having encountered glimpses of Dom as fortune-tellers or as beggars. They also recalled having heard about their mischief or read an article "in passing" about their criminal actions. Some also "remembered" having seen a movie depicting a Dom, usually the classic *Tamr Henna*, or more recently *Women's Prison*. It seems that although Gypsies are not fully identified, they nonetheless reside on the margins of people's consciousness, and they can suddenly materialize, in specific contexts, by fragments.

The individuals who were aware of the presence of Ghagar can be divided into two groups, the 'wise' and the 'normal,' a distinction inspired by Erving Goffman's (2009) *Stigma*. Goffman distinguishes between the stigmatized, the normal, and the wise. The stigmatized bears the stigma. The normal does not, but may contribute to it. The wise, situated in an intermediary category, does not bear the stigma but is accepted by the stigmatized as 'wise' about their condition. In this research, the wise are non-Dom Egyptians who have come into regular contact with Dom because of their professional occupation or their interest, as well as their geographical proximity. 'Wise' persons typically presented themselves as "knowing and understanding" the Dom, displaying a certain empathy.

I interviewed four main individuals that qualify as 'wise.' One 'wise' woman is a social worker who works with Ghagar (the term she uses) in the downtown Cairo area of Sayyida Zaynab; her organization offers them micro-loans, mostly financed by religious groups. She has been engaged in this activity for more than ten years and she interacts with Ghagar daily, which has led her to form very distinct opinions about "her Ghagar." One 'wise' man is from Alexandria; for many years he collected Coke bottles from Ghagar that he then sold to a factory for recycling. He also owns a small van and sporadically uses it to drive Ghagar families to run errands or deliver messages. The last two 'wise' persons are a man and a woman who work for an organization that provides training for working children, some of them Ghagar. Their office is set up in Umraniya, a Cairo neighborhood with a high concentration of Ghagar, and they interact socially with them on a regular basis. I conducted extensive interviews with these four individuals and occasionally met Ghagar in their company, which allowed me to observe the interactions between the Ghagar and the 'wise' and contrast those interactions with the narratives of the 'wise,' collected during one-on-one interviews.

I also interviewed non-Ghagar Egyptians who have interacted sporadically with Ghagar, typically because they have used their services as fortune-tellers or entertainers, or otherwise participate in *mulid*s, or because they had seen them beg. Sometimes Ghagar embodied familiar figures linked to the interlocutors' childhoods. Often those distant silhouettes were tainted with both nostalgia and angst. Some people had seen movies involving Gypsies or had an idea of who they were. The level of abstraction between what the Gypsies represent and the recurrence of contact is significant.

The hardest part of this research was to find Ghagar to interview. As a vulnerable population, they tend to be distrustful of outsiders. Many Ghagar are happily invisible (at least superficially) and initially met my curiosity with intense suspicion. I used different strategies to approach them. The most successful was to be introduced to Ghagar communities by an intermediary (including the four 'wise' identified earlier), which happened in both Cairo and Alexandria. Typically, I would meet the 'wise' who described the Ghagar community we were scheduled to meet and his or her relationship to them. We then visited them together, and I occasionally scheduled more visits, with or without the 'wise.' Either I went to Ghagars' homes or we met in a coffeeshop.

The other, less successful, strategy I used was simply to go to places frequented by Ghagar. On one occasion, I decided to survey a specific area called Hosh al-Ghagar, which had been described both by nineteenth-century Orientalists and more recently by a journalist as a Ghagar sanctuary.

I went there with a female translator, unannounced, and encountered resistance: despite the fact that they displayed what I had constructed as Ghagar traits, no one in the Hosh admitted being Ghagar. As a matter of fact, most people argued fervently *against* it. The denying narratives were nonetheless telling about the way in which the Ghagar identity is negatively constructed and rejected. That experience also shows that it is very easy for the researcher to essentialize the object of study. I also engaged in conversation with Ghagar in the City of the Dead and at the Giza Zoo, where Ghagar fortune-tellers practice their art. In those instances, initial denial of identity was usually followed by acceptance.

Many power relations were at play. I was a foreigner, talking to one of the most marginalized groups in Egypt. Often, Ghagar interlocutors did not understand what I was looking for. Most had never met anyone with a genuine interest in their cultures and traditions. They sometimes initially asked that we not talk about politics or crime; when I told them I was not interested in those topics and instead interested in their traditions, certainly a more approachable term than 'identity,' they would usually be happy to discuss these, and occasionally would then offer a few commentaries about crime and politics, perhaps precisely because they had been asked not to do so. The narratives may have been influenced by the desire for social acceptability, and often their Gypsiness may have been specifically reinvigorated precisely because I was asking about it. This was particularly palpable when addressing gender relations. According to a deep-rooted stereotypical representation, Ghagar communities are structured as matriarchies, in which females play a leading role as breadwinners (thieves, belly dancers, fortune-tellers) and intermediaries between Ghagar and non-Ghagar communities. Many interviewees seemed to perform a role inspired by the stereotype: women would claim that their communities promoted 'women power,' and men would pretend to be exaggeratedly submissive. After the formal interviews were over, those roles would sometimes be reversed. One woman called me to explain that in reality her husband did not grant her any of the freedom they had talked about; another man called to ask if I could help him find a job since he had to be the breadwinner in his family, despite the claims that females supported everyone in the community.

This research is qualitative in nature, and I have focused on lengthy interviews with a small number of individuals. Most of the interviews were based on open-ended questions, as my approach was deductive, simply because I was not sure what I was looking for, since the 'world of the Dom' is still largely unknown. I never used formal research techniques, such as questionnaires and structured interviews; as other ethnographers have remarked, when studying communities that suffer from social and economic marginalization, like Gypsy and Roma groups in Europe, formal research methods hold little empirical value (Okely 1983, 40–46). I did not record any of the interviews because participants were opposed to it. I usually took notes during the interviews, which everyone agreed to. All the names have been changed.

The interviews were almost always conducted in Arabic and translated simultaneously by my translator. The small amount of time between the moment when interviewees spoke and my translator translated allowed me to grasp valuable information about the body language of the interviewees and the reactions of other participants if the interview took place in the presence of other individuals, as was often the case. The problem with translation is that a lot may be lost in the process: much depends upon why one word may be chosen over another and the implicit meaning of that choice. My translator was instrumental in guiding me through what was being said, often indicating if correct Arabic was used, or if a pejorative term was chosen. Of course, the subjective interpretation of the translator cannot be ignored. One advantage of using a translator was, however, that the issue of social desirability could sometimes be avoided. Interviewees would occasionally ask, "Why on earth is she asking that?" or make jokes that were occasionally offensive and that they might not have made to me directly if we had spoken the same language. Many times people said things about non-Ghagar that were negative and that they might never have said in English or if they had spoken to me directly. My regular translator was an Egyptian man who managed quite well to engage interlocutors in somehow mundane talk, taking away from the process the academic aspect, which can be intimidating. I sometimes decided to withdraw from the conversation and let him meet some interlocutors alone at a subsequent meeting, particularly when it was supposed to be a men's talk about marriage and relationships. Another time, I met a group of Ghagar in a coffeeshop in Sayyida Zaynab. After we sat for about fifteen minutes, eating copiously and drinking coffee, the owner came and asked us to leave because we were taking too many tables—we were six individuals spread across two small tables. We left and the Ghagar said it was probably because they were Ghagar and I was a foreigner. When they met again with my translator, they met in a coffeeshop that was owned by a friend, but they had deemed it more appropriate that I should not come.

Interestingly, I never conducted a one-on-one interview with a single Ghagar. All the 'discussions' took place in group settings; typically, one person was talking and about three or four people sat silently in the room. On one occasion, one interlocutor brought his cousins to the coffeeshop where we met. He explained that he was "scared to meet a foreigner alone," but it seemed as if the presence of his cousins served as much to protect him as to observe him. When I met people in their homes, family members would always come to the meetings; they had heard about it and were usually curious. Most of the time, they would sit silently around the person being interviewed but intervened very rarely. It seemed clear that one person performed as the principal interviewee and the others were mere spectators, each knowing their role. The silent spectators would often acquiesce to what was being said and, rarely, softly counsel the person interviewed not to say too much. The collective setting seemed rather natural and never appeared problematic for the person being interviewed. Sometimes, after the interview, one person who had been silently present in the room would follow us to the car and share a few furtive comments. Occasionally, one person would call after the meeting and propose another meeting where they could be the main speaker. One woman from Alexandria called me on numerous occasions to set up a "secret meeting" in Cairo, without the knowledge of her family. She called me repeatedly but would always cancel the meeting the day before it was supposed to take place.

My overall impression was that the collective meetings were definitely a control mechanism, preventing anyone from saying something that would not have been group-approved, but it also became, perhaps unintentionally, an opportunity for the group to reflect on their Ghagar identity. It was also an opportunity to witness interactions between the different participants, both the speaking and the silent ones, displaying what was explicitly described by participants as their codified language, or their silent language, constructed on looks of agreement and disapproval and small gestures meaningful for the whole group (like touching an earlobe). Finally, being a foreigner was somehow an advantage as well, as many interlocutors admitted they felt free to talk about their relationships with Egyptians without being afraid of offending me.

Naming of the Group

I will use different names for the group, based on the context. The scientific appellation is 'Dom,' as a parallel to 'Rom' or 'Lom,' each of them meaning 'man' in their respective language—Domari, Romani, and Lomavren. I have never heard anyone using the term 'Dom' in Egypt. This may be because the production of knowledge about the Dom and Domari is so limited that none have been labeled that way by researchers. In Jerusalem, the role of Matras' linguistic analysis of Domari may have very well contributed to making the Dom of Jerusalem a more tangible object of study. The term that is used more consistently in Arabic is 'Ghagar,' which is the translation of 'Gypsy.' Calling someone a Ghagar is an insult. The other term occasionally used is 'Nawar,' which is another negative term. The terms 'Nawar' and 'Halebi' are used for communities in rural environments but rarely in Cairo. The only time I met someone consciously defining herself as a Halebi was a fortune-teller who said that the Halebi were "the one with the gift of predicting the future." The other term that I heard in Cairo during my interviews that I had never heard before nor seen written in English is 'Hanagra.' The term may be linked to Hungary, and some theories postulate that Ghagar left Egypt to migrate to Hungary, then came back under the new appellation 'Hanagra'. Newbold (1856, 293) mentions that the Ghagar speak of coming from "Hongarieh" (Hungary), which could be an etymological explanation for the origin of the word 'Hanagra.' Often, however, Hanagra are described as criminals. Perhaps unsurprisingly, then, I never met anyone who defined themselves as Hanagra. I met many Ghagar who "knew of" Hanagra and described them as thieves, or rarely distant relatives. As one Egyptian interlocutor explicitly put it: "The Hanagra are the Ghagar who are thieves and criminals."

The term 'Gypsies' is controversial. I have decided to use 'Gypsies' when talking about how the group has been constructed by Orientalists to convey the implicit characteristics that have been ascribed to the group. I also occasionally use the term to look at the parallel construction of Gypsies of Egypt in contrast with Gypsies of Europe and how some features are transferred from one group to the other.

Outline of the Book

This book is constructed to look at Ghagar from different angles: from the historical search for roots based on Orientalists' accounts of their encounters with Gypsies and the representation of Gypsies in popular imagination and cinema, to discussions with non-Ghagar Egyptians and Ghagar themselves, as well as an analysis of media discourse.

In the first chapter, "The Eternal Quest for Roots," I examine how European scholars have used language (Romani) to assess the origins of the Roma, a group deemed foreign but whose 'origins' have never been scientifically proven. When links started to be drawn between Romani and Sanskrit, which happened when theories of 'race' began to be developed, European Gypsies became racialized and different levels of 'Roma purity' were established. I look at how this phenomenon affected the production of knowledge about and construction of the notion of Egyptian Gypsies, and I ask if nineteenth-century European Orientalists transferred European racialist theories to Egypt by looking for 'foreign roots' for Egyptian Gypsies using fragments of their language, and thus contributed to an Orientalization of Gypsies in Egypt. I then examine alternative narratives used to establish the Dom's origins.

The second chapter, "From Belly Dancers to Thieves," focuses on how popular culture and the Egyptian cinema have represented the figures of the Ghawazi and Ghagar, who seem to have embodied the torments of Egyptian society at different periods of time. While in the 1950s they symbolized mostly a romanticized exotic 'other,' embodied in beautiful female belly dancers and *baladi* attributes, more recent representations of Ghagar have lost much of their romanticism and revolve around a sordid condition of poverty and marginalization. They have become social outcasts more than cultural exoticisms or remnants of a traditional past. Furthermore, while marriage between Ghagar and non-Ghagar (symbolically representing the union of past and present, tradition and modernity) was possible in the 1960s and 1970s, in later decades, as the Ghagar started to exemplify criminality, such unions became inconceivable because they were too impure. This transformation can be interpreted on two levels. One is the continuous closure of Egyptian identity to heterogeneity, and the other is the further entrenchment of Gypsies in marginalized spaces, combined with the limitation of their interactions with non-Gypsies to purely economic ones. I also look at female representations and ask why traditional plot lines tend to involve a male non-Gypsy and a female Gypsy (in a reproduction of the Carmen-like archetype). I reflect on how, in many Orientalist discourses, females are the ones who engage in relations with males of the dominant society, and while females are often over-sexualized, as embodiments of masculine fantasies, males are emasculated.

The next chapter, "Uncrossable Boundaries?," is the first of a series of chapters based on fieldwork. It examines how non-Ghagar Egyptians present their interactions with Ghagar and how both the interactions and the meanings attributed to those encounters contribute to constructing fragments of Ghagar identity. Although the identification of Ghagar in an urban setting is problematic because of a lack of visible identity markers, I examine how the creation of boundaries nonetheless materializes by fragments, by emphasizing the Ghagars' intrinsic inability to integrate Egyptian norms and values, or their slightly inaccurate practice of cultural or religious conventions. The cultural boundaries are based on the fact that unacceptable social behaviors are routinely attributed to Gypsies: they steal other people's children or sell their own; they do not have origins (which is detrimental in a kin-based society); they are dirty; and so on. I also look at how racial boundaries are erected in a process of 'racialization' of Gypsies by attributing to them certain physical traits, both positive and negative (males with "dangerous eyes," women with "animal sensuality"). I finally look at spatial boundaries and how, even in marginalized neighborhoods, Ghagar seem to be relegated to the margins of the margins.

The following chapter, "Identity Negotiation: Ignoring, Passing, Changing, and Exchanging," is based on Ghagar narratives and ethnographic observations: I examine the strategies used by Ghagar to 'pass' in different ways. They may pass as genuine Egyptians either because they perceive themselves as such or because they want to hide any other origins. Another passing strategy is evasiveness in providing others with in-group information and offering alternatives to the person they interact with, from simple denial to partial admission. The decision to do so is made by weighing the benefits of being perceived as a Ghagar or not in the immediate situation. Ghagar engage in a denial of identity in certain contexts, for instance to obtain employment or housing, or overemphasize their identity when they engage in certain 'specifically Gypsy' occupations such as fortune-telling. I also look at impression management and concepts such as passing to grasp some of the identities and strategies deployed by the Ghagar themselves when they perform differently according to the audience and, again, the context. Using the theme of performativity, I look at gender performativity (Butler 1990), since many of the Ghagar performances, from Ghawazi to female thieves, are genderized. I also look at ethnic performativity when ethnicity, or what is expected of a certain ethnicity, is either over- or underemphasized. Scholarship on Gypsies has highlighted that Gypsies tend to be segregated from non-Gypsies but simultaneously constantly engage in short-term economic relations. I reflect on the multiplicity of roles that Gypsies use, not only in their economic interactions with non-Gypsies, but also in their (perhaps not so) occasional social interactions.

The fifth chapter, "Underground World: Crime in the Blood and Secret Language," looks at the criminilization of Ghagar identity. It confronts the media discourse of Ghagar practices and how Ghagar position themselves within the limited space allocated within the stereotypical discourse. It also addresses fragments of Ghagar language, known as Sim, and its different usages, as well as the meaning associated with its usage.

In the last chapter, "Matriarchy and Bride Price: Ghagar Traditions?," I examine the characteristics that Ghagar tend to think differentiate them from non-Ghagar Egyptians. One area appeared to be of special importance: marriage practices. Gypsies pride themselves on what they construct as different marriage practices, particularly the role given to women, sexual practices, and the distribution of labor within households, which vary strikingly from traditional Egyptian cultural and social practices, as well as from practices found in other Gypsy groups in Europe and some Middle Eastern countries. However, despite the proclaimed egalitarian gender structures, patriarchy remains very present. I ask whether narratives that actively proclaim 'women power' are trying to pervade traditional norms in order to create some sense of difference, or whether these narratives could be the result of an internalization of the representation constructed by outsiders, of Gypsies as a feminized group.

1

THE ETERNAL QUEST FOR ROOTS

Language and Roots

"[What] is certain, is that the Gipsies are strangers in the land of Egypt," wrote Captain Thomas John Newbold in 1856. Newbold was a British officer in the East India Company, fluent in Persian and Hindustani, who served as the interpreter for his regiment. An amateur scholar who meticulously collected information about the different groups he encountered during his expeditions, Newbold wrote more than forty-six scientific papers for the *Royal Society of Great Britain* and the *Journal of the Asiatic Societies of Bengal and Madras*, covering the geology of India, as well as a host of other eccentric topics, from the Chinese triads to the Chenchawar, "a wild tribe inhabiting the forest of the Eastern Ghauts" (1844, 271). From 1845 to 1847, Newbold took a leave of absence from his post in India and spent two years in Egypt; among the objects of his investigation then were the geology of Egypt and the Gypsies of Egypt, Syria, and Persia. He died at Mahabaleshwar, India, May 29, 1850, aged forty-three, "too early for his fame," lamented Sir Francis Richard Burton, whom he had met and convinced of the Indian origins of the Egyptian Gypsies. His findings concerning the Gypsies were published posthumously, in January 1856, in the *Journal of the Royal Asiatic Society*, in a short article, "The Gypsies of Egypt," in which he described the mysterious tribes, assessed them as strangers in the land of Egypt, carefully reported their cultural practices, and tried to uncover their roots.

The Romani scholar Adrian Marsh uses the term "soldier-scholar" (Marsh and Strand 2006, 46) to describe Colonel John Harriott, also of the East India Company, who submitted a treatise to the Royal Asiatic Society on the "Oriental Origins of the Romanichal." The term can also be applied to Burton and to Newbold. All three of these men were exposed to different cultural practices because of their position in foreign lands, usually with the British army. Their mastery of the language of the country where they were stationed gave them the illusion of a more intimate understanding of their environment and offered both the excitement of pioneering the penetration of exotic cultures and the privileged means to engage in philological investigation. The soldier-scholars' observations, Marsh cautions, need to be "seen in the complex light of European Orientalism and part of the process Said has described as 'all the knowledge collected during colonial occupation with the title "contribution to modern learning"' when the natives had neither been consulted nor treated as anything except pretexts for a text whose usefulness was not to the natives" (Marsh 2006, 47).

Along with Newbold, other European travelers, soldiers, translators, explorers, consuls, and lexicographers wrote about the Dom, though they never used that term, preferring the universal 'Gypsy/Gipsi' or 'Ghagar,' a common term in Egypt to this day. They also used distinctive tribal names: Halebi, Nawar, or Ghawazi. Their accounts scrupulously described the Egyptian 'Gipsies,' usually detailing their occupations and some cultural practices, with an uncanny focus on their physical appearance, along with attempts at interpreting the political organization of the groups. Toward the second half of the nineteenth century, the amateur scholars also compiled glossaries and studied the grammar of the language(s) spoken by the Gypsies, chronicled sometimes as a single language, Sim, or as a variety of dialects spoken by the different Gypsy tribes, referring to the Halebi or Ghagar languages. Language was a crucial element in the Orientalist scholars' investigation of the Gypsies' origins, and those origins were also constructed as a crucial part of their general study.

Why were Orientalist explorers so intrigued by the origins of the Egyptian Gypsies and determined to use language as their main tool of analysis to assess them? The most compelling explanation for this specific quest is probably rooted in a transfer of the European obsession with discovering the roots of the Roma. When eighteenth-century linguists discovered correlations between the Romani language and Sanskrit, scholars started to speculate on the roots of the mysterious group, which had historically been deemed foreign but rootless. Since DNA tests had not yet been developed, language started to fulfill the role of blood as a core element in the determination of racial origins; unlike intuitive deductions and physical descriptions, philology and linguistics had the legitimacy of science. In other words, language became the test of race, and most nineteenth-century writers on Gypsies became convinced that their language was indeed the key to identifying their race (Mayall 2004). The attempts to uncover Sanskrit roots of the Romani language and the development of comparative philology need to be contextualized within a more general vogue for Orientalism that was sweeping Europe; hordes of scholars studied the 'other' in the foreign Orient and, within European borders, the Gypsy embodied the local other.

Another contextual element was the development of the concept of 'race' itself, as a scientific category. The concept of race is a modern one, albeit historically prefigured in various ways by ethnocentrism and the oppositions of concepts such as civilization versus barbarity, or the citizen versus the outsider (Winant 2000). The idea of race in its recent form is a "by-product of Darwin's work," evolving from the principle of different species that "cannot produce fertile off-spring when crossed with a representative of another species," and whose primary characteristic is "consistency of character" within the group (Isaac 2004, 29). However, unlike many animal groups, the human group does not possess subcategories such as species, so the human subcategories became biological 'races.' As soon as the attribution of race became situated in biology, resting on physiological traits such as skin color, eye color and shape, hair color and texture, shape of the nose, and so forth, impermeable groups were created, ascribed moral and mental characteristics, and placed in hierarchies. Spencer's Social Darwinism applied Darwin's theories to show that the hierarchy of races was an evolutionary hierarchy: the lower races were less evolved, stuck in the past, biologically and culturally simpler than the highest race, the Caucasian race. Race as a scientific and biological concept was born out of racism, and while differences had always been attributed to certain groups by other groups, the perceived biological objectivity of races helped to rigidify those differences and to legitimize them under the banner of science.

Historically, Gypsies had always been considered non-white; they were the exotic others, differentiated by their occupational characteristics as entertainers, peddlers, and thieves, or by their appearance (dark eyes, dark hair, sensual women, or threatening men), but lacking specific origins. Without any objective or scientific proofs of their difference, they were often seen as a people without history and without roots. With the surge of the scientific racialization of groups, the study of language became crucial to establish the roots of Gypsies and to elucidate the course of their journey from India (or some other foreign point of departure) to Europe. Their language served to anchor them to a specific place and to unearth the successive steps of their journey, for the degree of purity or corruption of their language was an indication of how long the group had remained in a particular area. While the claims for Indian ancestry "did not stem from the Gypsies themselves" (Mayall 2004, 121), many Gypsies have more recently come to accept and embrace this explanation, to assert their identity in a differentialist manner. However, in eighteenth- and nineteenth-century Europe, vocabularies and glossaries of Gypsy words were mostly compiled by outsiders to the group and were of questionable accuracy.

The earliest attempts to analyze the Romani language date from 1542. Andrew Borde, an English physician, who was also a traveler and a writer, collected and published thirteen sentences of Romani speech, under the title "Egipt Speche." He mostly tried to transliterate sounds collected from 'Egyptians'/Gypsies and to translate them, a first and hesitant attempt which, as a 1907 article from the *Journal of the Gypsy Lore Society* warns, needs to be viewed with caution.

> Dr. Borde was noting down sounds, the exact meaning of which he did not know, and his notes were printed after his death, many mistakes have been made in the Romanes, but it also seems probable that his informant was a British Gajo, who consorted with Gypsies, and whose knowledge of Romanes was imperfect. (1907, 164).

In 1562, Johan van Ewsum, a Dutch nobleman, published a Romani word list presented as "The Speech of Little Egypt"; in 1691, Job Ludolf published a Romani word list. Other scholars, linguists, and amateur scientists compiled lists of Romani vocabulary, but none of the lists were used to establish connections with other foreign languages until the year 1777, when Johann Christian Christoph Rüdiger, professor at the German University of Halle, wrote a letter to a colleague suggesting that Romani, "the Gypsy language," was related to the languages of India. In 1782, Rüdiger published an article, "On the Indic Language and Origins of the Gypsies," that established links between the Romani language and Hindustani (Romani Project at the University of Manchester). Rüdiger had initially gathered from his mentors, Christian Büttner and Hartwig Bacmeister, that the Gypsy tongue might have some roots in India and Iran. He later obtained a copy of a grammatical description of Hindustani and worked with an illiterate Gypsy woman, attempting to connect her Romani dialect to Hindustani. Rüdiger identified matching words and grammatical structures. He concluded that Romani was rooted in Indian languages and had preserved much of the Indian vocabulary and grammatical structures. However, while claiming that the Roma had come to Europe as migrants from India, he did not speculate as to why they had left. He also called for fair treatment and protection of Romani people in Europe (Matras 2015), which was a unique stance among early Romani scholars.

Later research built on Rüdiger's findings, as "within the scholarly community, Rüdiger's thesis and the linguistic facts that point to the Indic origin of the Romani language remain undisputed" (Matras 2015, 133). The focus became the exact period of departure from India, the reasons that had triggered emigration, and the group's premigration identity. August Friedrich Pott published a historical comparative grammar of Romani varieties; he linked the Roma to the Indian caste of the Domba, a caste of service providers mentioned in medieval texts from Kashmir (Saul and Tebbutt 2005, 62). Much of the discussion focused on which Indian groups the Roma had emerged from: were they a specific Indian caste, as suggested by Pott, or were they camp followers providing service to military populations who eventually reached Europe with retreating armies, as suggested by M. de Goeje in 1875? Ralph Turner, a British philologist affiliated with the School of Oriental and African Studies at the University of London and a prolific writer on the Romani language, proposed in 1926 that Gypsies had in fact originated from a population indigenous to central India (Romani Project at the University of Manchester).

Scholars of Romani history highlight the interest of "hordes of scholars" in the Romani language and explain its motivation by the fact that "analysis of the structures of a language is able to unfold a series of hidden facts about the history of its speaker population" (Matras 2015, 134). Aside from providing a sense of adventure through the discovery of facts revolving around what was perceived as a mysterious group, the linguistic exploration of Romani also embodies uneven power relations, since research has mostly been conducted, until very recently, by non-Roma. Speculating on the origins of the group helped to essentialize it: not only was the Roma's otherness rigidified by scientific linguistic evidence, but the Roma also became an object of study. The study of objectified Gypsies developed as 'Gypsylorism,' what Adrian Marsh conceptualized as "a new discipline and area of specialization, a means of categorizing 'natives' in the colonies and at home" (Marsh and Strand 2006, 47).

Thus, nineteenth-century philologists used language not to understand the intimate structure of their new object of study, the Gypsy, in its linguistic representations, but to explore its connections to other foreign languages. That approach is emblematic of how Gypsies were constructed as an object of study: primarily from the outside and mostly as foreign bodies. Undoubtedly, the discovery of the origins of a cultural group by outsiders participates in the creation of a relationship of power, between the active scholar and the passive object of study. The Gramscian concept of hegemony, which explains that the ideology of the ruling class is normalized to the extent that resistance seems absurd, helps explain how the processes of construction of the other and the self-attributed role of the observer/analyst who owns and controls knowledge further marginalized Gypsies, in who they were and in how they related to their identity. Furthermore, a normalized reality is based on elements (dichotomy between national belonging and foreignness/

otherness, the perceived scientific reality of race, and a set of norms and values constructed as national values) deemed obvious by the powerful researcher who looks for foreign origins of the Gypsies, via their language. But these elements are only a hegemonic creation that managed to become 'common sense' and embody an idea of normalcy, against which others are built. The construction of foreign, a-national Gypsies started largely in Europe, in a context of racialization, an interest in scientific research, and the desire to form national identity based on who is to be included and who is to be excluded.

Orientalists' Perceptions of Gypsies in the 'Orient'

Bonaventura Vulcanius was one of the last Renaissance humanists. He was born in Bruges in 1538 and eventually became a professor of Greek and Latin literature in Leiden. Displaying an avid interest in languages, he edited and translated many rare texts. In 1597, he gave one of the first descriptions of Gypsies in Egypt in his book *De Literis et Lingua Getarum*. After a very succinct analysis of a collection of a few Gypsy words, probably around forty, he concluded that Egyptian Gypsies were Nubians, without any etymological analysis to support his claim. Evidently, at the time of his writings, no European linguist had yet connected the Gypsy language with Sanskrit, and therefore no scientific account of their origin had been suggested. Consequently, Vulcanius had plenty of space in which to establish suppositions and derive conclusions.

Also among the first Europeans to explore the language of Oriental Gypsies is Ulrich Jasper Seetzen, the first collector of data on the Domari language. Seetzen was a German explorer who had studied medicine. He traveled extensively in the Middle East: Palestine, Mecca, Medina, and finally Yemen, where he was poisoned by his guides on orders from the imam of San'a, and where he died in 1811. His diaries were edited posthumously by the publishers Kruse and Fleisher, between 1854 and 1859. His descriptions of Gypsies of the region depict a group living in very poor conditions, even more marginalized and less pious than Bedouins. They were particularly numerous in Egypt, where they were mostly known under the name 'Nawar.'

Seetzen later remarked that their physiognomy was precisely that of modern Egyptians. He collected some of their vocabulary, obtained from the Palestinian Domari language in 1806, which was published in 1854. His linguistic material was collected among the metalworkers of Nablus, before he continued his journey toward Jerusalem. His glossary covers "body parts, food, landscape, animals, plants, fruits, expressions of time, material, person and numeral" (Matras 2012, 5–6). Seetzen noticed at that time that the language contained many Arabic words, but maintained a grammar close to Sanskrit.

Edward Lane, another scholar–traveler, is the author of the seminal *Manners and Customs of the Modern Egyptians*, a best seller in Europe, a book described by Edward Said as "an authority whose use was an imperative for anyone writing or thinking about the Orient, not just about Egypt" (1978, 23). Lane was a British Orientalist, as well as a translator and a lexicographer. He came to Egypt in 1825 and spent about two and a half years in Cairo, mixing with the locals, to become a self-proclaimed expert on Egyptians' comportment, an expertise which he translated into a book. As proof of his unconditional love and understanding of the country, he abandoned his European dress code and wore exclusively Egyptian clothes; he spoke mostly Arabic and sought to explore every layer of Egyptian society. One segment with which he could hardly interact, however, was the local females, and many of his depictions, for instance those of entertainers, are colored by his own imagination. The lack of direct interaction with any of them left room for speculation. Their social inaccessibility was perhaps one of the reasons he took such an interest in Egyptian dancers and entertainers. He particularly described the Ghawazi, a group of belly dancers who may have been members of a Gypsy tribe (the Ghawazi tribe, the name alluding to both a group of people and an occupation), and to a lesser extent, the Gypsy fortune-tellers.

Fortune-telling is often practised in Egypt, mostly by Gipsies. There are several small tribes of Gipsies in this country, and they are often called collectively "Ghagar" or "Ghajar" (in the singular "Ghagaree" or "Ghajaree"), which is the appellation of one of their tribes, who

profess themselves descendants of the Baramikeh, like the Ghawazee; but a different branch. (Lane 1871, 97–98)

The definition of the 'Baramikeh,' in Lane's words, is a descendant of
the "famous family of that name who were the object of the favour
and afterward of the capricious tyranny of Ha'roo'n Er-Rashee'd and
of whom we read in several of the tales of the 'Thousand and One
Nights'" (1871, 89). However, while other writers (Newbold and von
Kremer, for instance) associated the Ghawazi with Gypsy tribes, Lane
looked further back when he speculated that "perhaps the modern Ghawazee are descended from the class of female dancers who amused the
Egyptians in the times of the early Pharaohs" (1871, 89). As for the
Ghawazis' language: "[it] is the same as that of the rest of the Egyptians;
but they sometimes make use of a certain number of words peculiar to
themselves, in order to render their speech unintelligible to strangers"
(1871, 90).

It was Captain Newbold and the Austrian consul Alfred von Kremer who focused their attention most carefully on the Gypsies of Egypt
during the late nineteenth century. Each of them, in different ways,
inserted many of his preconceived ideas about how Gypsies were represented in Europe and applied some of their perceived characteristics
to groups in Egypt that were deemed similar. Both engaged in a series
of speculations as to who those groups were and, of course, as to where
they could possibly come from, since Gypsies had to come from an
alienating foreign place. Newbold looked for the origins of the three
main tribes he had identified: the Halebi, the Ghagar, and the Nawar.
About the Halebi he wrote:

[They] pretend to derive their origins from Yemen or the Hadra-
mat; and assert that the early history of their race is chronicled in a
written record called the *Tarikh ez Zir*, which as far as I can glean,
is an obscure and unsatisfactory document. . . . from Yemen they say
their tribes were expelled by the persecution of Zir, a king of the Taba
race; and wandered over Syria, Egypt, Persia and Europe. The seven
brother chiefs of the tribes which migrated into Egypt obtained from

its sovereign the privilege of exemption from taxes, and of wandering about the country without molestation. (Newbold 1856, 291)

Newbold's descriptions of the Ghagar are much less extensive; he mostly mentions their linguistic similarities with the Halebi, specifically in "[some words] apparently of Indian origin, such as *pani*, water; *machi*, fish; *bakra*, sheep" (1856, 293). In the following paragraphs of his article, however, he inserted a few additions, commenting that the Ghagar "speak of having brethren in Hongarieh, who have preserved their original language in much greater purity than the mingled jargon they now speak in Egypt" (1856, 293). He then compared the "jargon" of the Ghagar, Nawar, and Halebi in these terms:

It will be observed that there is a marked difference in the three dialects or jargons. That of the Ghagar most assimilates the language of the Kurbats, or gypsies of Syria, and the gypsy dialect on Borrow's work: it contains also more words of Indian origins than the Halebi and Nawar jargons. (Newbold 1856, 294)

He added that the Halebi language "comprises a large number of words of Arab roots, indicating a long sojourn in Yemen or other parts of Arabia," alluding to the earlier mention of Yemen, not necessarily as the place of origin, but most likely as a place of sojourn. He compared numerals in the three dialects, noting that both Halebi and Ghagar numerals bore strong marks of Indian or Persian linguistic roots, though usually "the Halebi adopt the vulgar Arabic numerals" (1856, 295). He concluded confidently:

I have been informed by a Copt, that they have secret symbols which they sedulously conceal. It seems to me probable that the whole of these tribes had one common origin in India or the adjacent countries on its Western frontier, and that the difference in the jargons they now speak is owing to their sojourn in the various countries through which they have passed. *This is certain, that the Gipsies are strangers in the land of Egypt.* (Newbold 1856, 296; emphasis added)

Newbold also provided his readers with comparative lists of vocabulary in English, Halebi, Ghagar, and Nawar, without further analysis (1856, 296–97):

English	Halebi	Ghagar	Nawar
Father	*garubi*	*balo*	*bayabi*
Mother	*ammamri*	*kuddi*	
Brother	*huwjji*	*burdi*	
Wife	*kudah*	*gaziyeh*	*gud*
Sister	*khawishti*	*semah burdi*	
Husband	*el baraneh*	*marash*	*maras*
Sun	*shomas*	*kam*	*shmos*
Moon	*kamr*	*Kano*	*mahtaweh*

In his next chapter, on the Gypsies of Syria, Newbold adds:

Since my visit to the banks of the Indus I am more than ever convinced that from the borders of this classic river originally migrated the hordes of Gypsies that are scattered over Europe, Asia, and the northern confines of Africa. (1856, 307)

A few years later, in his book *The Jew, The Gypsy and El Islam*, Sir Francis Richard Burton reflected on his travels and the knowledge he accumulated on different groups he encountered, particularly Oriental Gypsies. The book, posthumously published in 1898, integrates many of Newbold's observations and analyses of Gypsies' practices, languages, and origins, both in India and in Egypt. One section of his book focuses on the Gypsy in Africa, "The Egyptian Ghagar or Ghajar."

If there is anything persistent in Gypsy tradition it is the assertion that the Gypsies originally came from the banks of the Nile—that Egypt in fact, gave them a local habitation and a name. Yet, curious to say this is the country, and the only country, where a tribe of the Roma, preserving their physiognomy and the pursuit of its ancestors has apparently lost its old Aryan tongue, or rather has exchanged it for a bastard argot, mostly derived from Arabic. (Burton 1898, 233)

Burton reports the findings of Newbold regarding the "Indian origins" of Gypsies, which seem to satisfy him. He notes in his opening paragraph the paradox of encountering Gypsies in Egypt, a country that had "erroneously" given them a name (referring to the misnaming of Gypsies as Egyptians in medieval Europe), while they are "strangers and outcasts in the land which has given them a name and which has long been supposed to have given them birth." Burton also recounts that in Sindh, he personally met Newbold, whose studies had raised acute interest, particularly because he had noted "the manners and habit of a singular wandering tribe called the Jats, whose remarkable physical appearance reminded him strongly of the Gypsies of Egypt and Syria" (1898, 251). It was upon visiting more villages and tents belonging to some of those groups between Karachi and the Indus that Newbold, according to Burton, had become convinced that Egyptian Gypsies originated from India. Burton quotes Newbold's conclusions: "The dialects spoken by the numerous tribes which swarm upon the territories adjacent to the Indus, from the sea to the snowy mountains of Himalaya and Tatary, have, with those spoken by the Gypsies, a certain family resemblance, which, like their physical features, cannot be mistaken. I find it impossible at present to place my hand on any particular tribe, and say, 'This is the parent stock of the Gypsies'; but as far as my researches have gone, I am rather inclined to think that this singular race derives its origin, not from one alone, but from several tribes that constitute the family of mankind dwelling on, or adjacent to, the banks of the Indus" (1898, 251–52).

Alfred von Kremer was an Austrian Orientalist who was posted as a consul in Cairo in 1859. In 1864, he wrote "The Gipsies in Egypt," published in the *Anthropological Review* by the Royal Anthropological Institute of Great Britain and Ireland. The article opens with his remark that while "excepting the Jews there is no people so scattered over the earth as the gipsies," it appeared that "Egypt is the classical soil of the East, which shows them in their primitive form" (von Kremer 1864, 262). He then contends that Egyptian Gypsies insist on their Arabic roots and are proud of being of Arab descent.

> According to their own account they consist of different tribes; but all of them describe themselves as genuine Arabs, and are very proud of their pure Arabic descent. They pretend to have emigrated from West Africa, but are unable to determine the period. The following circumstance speaks in favour of their assertion, namely, that they all belong to the religious sect of the Malikites, which is in the whole of North-West Africa the chief of the four orthodox sects of Islamism. (von Kremer 1864, 263–64)

Another group he depicted was Gypsies from Upper Egypt (Sa'idis).

> The gipsies of Upper Egypt call themselves Saaideh, i. e., people of Said (Upper Egypt). They travel through the country as horse- and ass-dealers, pedlars, and fortune-tellers. Their features are altogether Asiatic; colour, tawny; eyes, black and piercing; hair, black and straight. (von Kremer 1864, 264)

Von Kremer used linguistics to draw additional conclusions as to where Gypsies might come from. He noticed the foreign roots of many words used in their language, which had probably "been imported from the West whence the gipsies pretend to have migrated to Egypt" (1864, 266). He considered the possibility of the words being loaned from the Berber language. Unlike Newbold, who collected and categorized words in the Halebi, Nawar, and Ghagar languages, von Kremer collected words from what he called "the Gipsi language," also identified as "Sim," from several "gipsies from Upper Egypt," but mostly from his "chief authority . . . Mohammed Merwan in Cairo who gave himself the pompous title of 'Sheikh of all the snake-catchers of Egypt'" (265). Here are some of the words from his glossary, contrasted to Newbold's.

Von Kremer (1864, 243):

English	Gypsy
Father	*Arub*
Mother	*Kodde*
Brother	*Sem* or *chawidsh*
Sister	*Semah* or *ucht*

Newbold (1856, 296):

English	Halebi	Ghagar	Nawar
Father	*Garubi*	*Balo*	*Bayabi*
Mother	*Ammamri*	*Kuddi*	
Brother	*Buwjji*	*Burdi*	
Sister	*Khawishti*	*Semah burdi*	

We can see that in Sim, 'father' *(arub)* is close to the Halebi *garubi*; 'mother' *(kodde)* is close to the Ghagar *kuddi*; 'brother' is not really close to any word in Newbold's glossary; and 'sister' is closest to the Ghagar *semah*. There is no consistency in the transliteration and the words may have been phonetically transcribed. *Ucht* is very close to the Arabic *okht*, possibly with a Germanic transliteration. The reproduction of Sim in von Kremer's glossary appears to be a combination of what Newbold had identified as three distinct dialects. The term 'Sim,' used by von Kremer to refer to what he construed as the Gypsy language in general, is often used nowadays to refer to the language spoken by contemporary Ghagar. Von Kremer describes it in disparaging terms.

> All these subdivisions of the Egyptian gipsies speak the same thiev-
> ish slang language, which they call Sim. Nothing certain is known
> concerning the origin of this word. According to the opinion of the
> natives Sim means something secret or mysterious. Sim is also called

a spurious gilt wire imported from Austria. The Bahlawan tribe alone are said to speak another language. I was, however, unable to procure any evidence to that effect, nor does it seem to be well founded. (1864, 264)

Von Kremer also attributed to Sim the characteristics of a secret language, a language that would serve to alienate non-speakers.

The preceding vocabulary throws some light on the character of this language. There can be no doubt we have here to do with a thievish slang dialect, made use of by the gipsies in order not to be understood by strangers. The circumstance that amongst themselves they speak Arabic, and Sim only in the presence of strangers, is decisive on this point. (1864, 266)

That perception continues to be held by modern Egyptian observers, who have constructed Sim as a secret and exclusionary language, whose sole purpose is to be indecipherable. Von Kremer continues:

All grammatical forms are, with exception of the suffixes, which seem not quite clear, perfectly Arabic. There occur, however, a number of words evidently of foreign origin, probably imported from the West, whence the gipsies pretend to have migrated to Egypt. Such words are: *zuwell*, the ass; *ashum*, spirit; *bitug*, silver or money; *atreshent*, sour milk, the last word having a Coptic sound; *sanno*, dog; *handawil*, Turkish maize, a word made also use of by the Egyptian fellahs. Also *hantif*, the camel; *baruah*, fat; *buhus*, beans; *damani*, thief, all these are foreign words, though they sound like Arabic words. (1864, 267)

While suggesting that these words may be derived from the Berber language, he ultimately recognizes his lack of sufficient material to draw any firm conclusions.

I confine myself to note these philological facts without drawing from them any hazardous inferences, for which the material at hand is scarcely sufficient. The old original words seem to become obsolete, and are replaced, according to a conventional scheme, by an Arabic slang. Thus the Egyptian gipsies have probably forgotten the ancient names for colours, sun, moon, earth, fire, etc, and know only their Arab denominations. (von Kremer 1864, 267)

Burton compares von Kremer's and Newbold's linguistic analyses, observing that Newbold's collected vocabulary presented more convincing signs of Eastern influence and displayed more words of Indian origin, as well as Persian influence in some cases, such as the Nawar numerals. Von Kremer, on the other hand, while calling the groups "Gypsies," appears less convinced about their origins, which he believes to be possibly Arab, or Western (Berber), or even possessing "Asiatic" features. Burton appears to second Newbold's conclusions.

Captain Newbold's studies in Egypt, where he was assisted by the Shaykhs of the Romá, complete those of Von Kremer, and prove that the latter had chiefly noticed the Ghawázi and Ghagar families. The former would divide the vagrants into two—the Helebis and their wives, the Fehemis (wise women), who practice palmistry and divination, and look down with supreme contempt upon their distant kinsmen the Ghagar or Ghajar, whose better halves are musicians and ropedancers. The Helebis, who evidently derive their name from H'abel (Aleppo), claim to be derived from El Yemen, and declare that in the early history of their race a great king persecuted and expelled them. The tribe then wandered over Syria, Egypt, Persia, and Europe under some brotherchiefs, whose tombs are still held holy to this day. The Helebis confined their wandering to the Rif or Nile Valley and the Delta. They rarely go deep into the desert, except when they sally forth to sell cattle medicines, or to buy jaded beasts from the returning pilgrim caravans, and a few perform the pilgrimage in order to win the title of Hagi. (Burton 1898, 252–53)

Charles Godfrey Leland (1824–1903) was a journalist, traveler, and folklorist who became the president of the English Gypsy Lore

Society in 1888. In his book *The Gypsies* (1882), he compiled information about Russian, English, and American Gypsies. One chapter of his book, displaying strong Orientalist features, focuses on the Gypsies in the East. Leland eloquently describes his first encounter with a mysterious woman in Cairo.

> Noon in Cairo . . . Beyond the door which, when opened, gave this sight was a dark ancient archway twenty yards long, which opened on the glaring, dusty street, where camels with their drivers and screaming *sais*, or carriage-runners and donkey-boys and crying venders, kept up the wonted Oriental din. But just within the archway, in its duskiest corner, there sat all day a living picture, a dark and handsome woman, apparently thirty years old, who was unveiled. She had before her a cloth and a few shells; sometimes an Egyptian of the lower class stopped, and there would be a grave consultation, and the shells would be thrown, and then further solemn conference and a payment of money and a departure. And it was world-old Egyptian, or Chaldean, as to custom, for the woman was a Rhagarin, or gypsy, and she was one of the diviners who sit by the wayside, casting shells for auspices, even as shells and arrows were cast of old, to be cursed by Israel. (Leland 1882, 288–89)

Leland admitted that he "saw many gypsies in Egypt, but learned little from them" (1882, 294). He nonetheless gathered from a discussion with Khedive Ismail that the Gypsies of the East (known as Rhagarin or Ghagarin) were "probably the same as the gypsies of Europe" (1882, 294), characterized as wanderers, living in tents, and regarded with contempt even by the peasantry. Women seemed to engage in fortune-telling and men in ironwork. In his quest for Egyptian Gypsies, or Rhagarin as he usually refers to them in his book, Leland eventually met a Rhagarin woman, whom he addressed in the Romani language, which she did not understand because, according to Leland, her "people in Egypt had lost the tongue" (1882, 296). However, when he later asked her if the Rhagarin had a particular name for themselves, she answered "Yes; we call ourselves Tatâren" (1882, 296), a comment that prompted Leland to draw a conclusive link between Rhagarins and the Gypsies of southern Germany and Norway, incidentally referred to as 'Tatâren,' which "means Tartars, and is misapplied, it indicates the race" (1882, 297).

In an earlier version of his account, *English Gipsies and Their Language* (1874), the tenth chapter is devoted to "Gipsies in Egypt." There, Leland recounts the same story of the Gypsy woman. In the first version, he describes his encounter in these terms: "I spoke to the woman in Romany, using such words as would have been intelligible to any of her race in any other country; but she did not understand me, and declared that she could speak nothing but Arabic" (Leland 1874, 296). In his second version, the woman is described slightly more carefully: "She was dressed like any Arab woman of the lower class, but was not veiled, and on her chin blue lines were tattooed. Her features and whole expression were, however, evidently Gypsy" (1882, 191). The rest of the story is the same and the woman calls herself Tatâren, which, as we have seen, Leland took as indisputable proof of the racial connection between Egyptian and Norwegian or German Gypsies.

In the rest of his chapter, however, absolute explanations are shattered by his encounters with a number of Rhagarins, who, while "they were certainly Gypsies, none of them would speak Rommany." He was then led to consider alternative origins, seeking help in the writing of other scholars, such as Bonaventura Vulcanius, who had believed that Gypsies were Nubians, or August Friedrich Pott, who in 1844 declared that Egyptian Gypsies were in reality "Cophtic Christians" (Leland 1874, 193). The last option seemed to strike a chord in Leland, as he recounted an encounter in Minya with a Coptic man.

> at Minieh in Egypt, I asked a Copht scribe if he were Muslim, and he replied, "La, anan Gipsti" (No, I am a Copht), pronouncing the word Gipti, or Copht, so that it might readily be taken for "Gipsy." And learning that romi is the Cophtic for a man, I was again startled; and when I found tema (tem, land) and other Rommany words in ancient Egyptian, it seemed as if there were still many mysteries to solve in this strange language. (Leland 1874, 193)

A later addition to his work also mentioned Captain Newbold's article that linked Egyptian Gypsies to India. This seemed a plausible explanation to Leland, who nonetheless pondered the question of why Romani had kept more Indian words than the language of the Eastern Gypsies, despite the large geographic distance.

Impact of Orientalists in the Construction of Eastern Gypsies

Linguistic analysis has often provided evidence of similarities between the Domari and Romani languages. This thesis is supported by the proponents of an ethnicized view of Gypsiness, who point out the existence of homogeneous cultural practices concomitant with the linguistic similarities. Linguistics has also shown that the languages are different in their structures, pointing to possibly different times of emigration and to groups that were also differentiated well before their displacement. Many of the previous studies on this group of people (Fraser 1992; Liégeois 1986) agree that the Gypsies originated in India, migrating westward between the fifth and the twelfth centuries. These questions seem to be among the main preoccupations of many scholars: When did the split between the different subgroups occur—pre- or post-migration? Was there one migration or successive migratory waves? Did the potentially distinct groups nonetheless display ethnic, linguistic, or occupational similarities? Were those populations already marginalized in medieval India? Did they constitute an outcaste similar to the untouchables? Why did they leave? Were they entertainers, were they soldiers? The exact period and the specific reasons that triggered that departure, as well as the boundaries of the group, if there were indeed specific ones, are still open to controversy. In 2001, Marushiakova and Popov wrote in favor of a post-migration split, which they dated around the tenth to eleventh century.

> Reaching the land of Northern Mesopotamia and the east boundary of the Byzantine Empire toward the end of the 10th and beginning of the 11th centuries, the Gypsies split into three major migration groups—the ben-speaking Dom, who took the southern route or stayed in the Middle East, and the then shen-speaking

groups of Lom, who took the northern route, and Rom, who took the western route. (Marushiakova and Popov 2001, 5)

Angus Fraser mentions the fifth century as the time of departure from India, alluding to the role of Shah Barham Gul, who is said to have invited Indian musicians to entertain his people. Adrian Marsh contends that the migrations have occurred at different times: initially the Dom around the eighth century, then the Roma between the ninth and tenth centuries, which would indicate strong differences between the different groups. That thesis has been supported by linguistic evidence, specifically in the fact that the Domari language preserves the neuter for nouns, while Romani only has two genders, feminine and masculine. This has led scholars to believe that the Dom left India before the neuter disappeared, and therefore well before the Roma (Kenrick 2004, 85). Acton and Gheorghe agree that "recent linguistic arguments suggest that the Romani language and identity derive from a relatively late 12th century emigration, distinct from the earlier 8th century migration which created the Dom or Nawar and similar groups in the Middle East" (2001, 59). Ian Hancock also abandoned the theory of initial unity of the migrants and their later separation into Dom, Lom, and Rom. He at first attributed warrior origins to the Romani people, arguing that the Roma first started to migrate when Gazneli Mahmut began to enslave Indian soldiers between AD 1001 and 1026.

Following the same line of thought, Donald Kenrick (2004) wrote a tentative chronology of the migrations between India and Persia. On this model, Indians would have first migrated to Persia during the period of AD 241–72. Persia had invaded the north of India (present-day Pakistan), which promoted economic migration between this area and the rest of the country. The migrants had different functions: farm workers, mercenary soldiers, palace guards, bookkeepers, or traders. Often, as is typical of migrants, they would offer their services for less than Persians, and were therefore in high demand. According to Kenrick, they formed an ethnic group simply because they stayed together and intermarried, since Persians were reluctant to marry the Indian migrants. They called themselves 'Dom,' which meant 'men' in the local language as constructed by European Orientalists.

The Dom and Rom currently have little contact and do not necessarily acknowledge each other's existence. Some commonality exists, nonetheless, particularly in the way both groups and their subgroups are marginalized and stigmatized in the various countries where they have settled (Williams 2005). The current situation in Turkey is compelling, as Dom and Roma groups actually coexist, and while suffering from homogenizing marginalization and stigmatization from the majority, the two groups also display many cultural and linguistic differences, as well as dissimilarities in their interactions with non-Gypsy Turks. While the Roma have been sedentarized for more than twenty years, the Dom have abandoned nomadism only in the past five years. Consequently, the Roma are typically more integrated and display a higher level of education, while the Dom still constitute an underclass with very little education and virtually no upward social mobility.

The study of the Romani language and its etymological and grammatical connections to Sanskrit certainly encouraged the racialization of Gypsies. Gypsies were already Orientalized in Europe, as the local others, not only because they were thought to have Oriental roots—initially Egyptian, and then Indian after the eighteenth century—but also because they were objectified as a passive other, crafted in terms of what the outsider expected within the ethnic boundaries created around the group. In the case of Egyptian Gypsies, it could then be argued that their Orientalization by Europeans affected the way Egyptians may have eventually perceived them, contributing somehow to an Orientalization of Gypsies by Egyptians themselves, not only as objects of study but also by constructing them as others, stranded in a limited set of preconceived characteristics.

European Orientalist scholars, travelers, and explorers struggled to come up with a definite answer as to where Egyptian Gypsies originated and how they should be classified: as different tribes, or as groups with heterogeneous origins and habitus? They did nonetheless symbolically, if not always scientifically, draw some connections between Egyptian Gypsies and the Gypsies of Europe, identifying similarities or contributing to constructing them: women were often sexualized and represented as independent, strong, and mysterious, while men were characterized by their supposed criminality and depravity, all of them living in marginalized communities and often engaged in trades that were deemed impure by others. All of these were characteristics of the European Gypsies. We can wonder whether Orientalists' perceptions influenced how Egyptian Gypsies' identities have been, and continue to be, constituted and negotiated, and whether Egyptian Gypsies, for instance, are now Orientalized, including by Egyptians, in imitation of the Europeans' projections of their own fantasies and fears. This question is hardly addressed by scholarly research on Middle Eastern Gypsies, which primarily focuses on the different theories explaining their ethnogenesis. It mostly questions whether one group left India and subsequently divided into subsegments of Roma, Lom, and Dom, each group heading in a different direction, or whether already distinct groups emigrated separately and successively, the only commonality being their westward migration and constant movement.

Critical race scholars have suggested that the concept of race has been constructed through projects of modernity, colonialism, and slavery. These writers observe that Europeans came to understand and articulate Europeanness, whiteness, culture, democracy, and citizenship by way of contrast to the Oriental or colonized subject they had come to know (see Said 1978; Goldberg 1993). They also brought their racialized constructs to the places they had colonized. The Ghagar could have become a racialized minority under the influence of the European gaze and production of knowledge, a process that happened in many other areas of the Middle East and Asia: in Algeria, for example, where the French made the Kabyles into a group different from other Arabs (Lorcin 2006; Cabanel 2007), or in India or Malaysia, where the British racialized various groups (Hirshman 1986). In this way, colonizers have created different ethnic or racial groups, often to assert their own superiority and to create divisions among the colonized; many of those groups have persisted and still affect the social structures of former colonies.

What may have 'saved' Egyptian Gypsies from being subjugated into a racial group, as happened to many other minorities in the region, is twofold. The first factor is Egypt's relationship to the concept of minority, which usually takes the form of rejection in favor of a homogenized identity, particularly starting during Nasser's era of modernization of the country which was anchored in anticolonialism. Secondly, and more prosaically,

Ghagar and other Gypsy groups have attracted very little interest in Egypt. Unlike the European Roma and other Middle Eastern Dom, they have not been turned into an object of study, with the danger of essentialization which that process comprises. The Roma have been extensively studied, the Dom far less; and when they have, it has usually been in contrast to the Roma in order to highlight their linguistic and historical similarities and distinctions. The Dom sometimes appear as mere Eastern mirrors of the Roma. As noted by Bernhard Streck in his speech commemorating the late Nabil Sobhi Hanna and his work on the Egyptian Dom, "the social scientific and anthropological study of the Gypsies of the Orient has hardly begun" (2006, 177). Indeed, Egypt is most likely the country with the least amount of research conducted on Gypsy groups. As a result, Gypsies are far less socially visible in Egypt, and they have not been constructed as a racial or an ethnic entity in accordance with what Europeans scholars and colonizers had hegemonically started to engineer.

Alternative Narratives and Myths of Origin

The embryonic racialization of Gypsies by European Orientalists, linguists, and travelers led to the creation of a 'foreign' group with rigid boundaries, scientifically linked to India among Europeans, and sometimes among Egyptians as well even if many Egyptians are oblivious to the existence of Gypsies in their country. In fact, Egyptian narratives, while they may have been influenced by Orientalists, have however often diverged from the linear production of pseudo-scientific racialized knowledge. Academic research on the topic has been scarce since Hanna's seminal ethnographic publication of "Ghagar of Sett Guiran'ha," in 1982, in which he mostly examines the cultural and social practices of the Ghagar and seldom questions their origins. Hanna nonetheless indicates the perceptions of outsiders about Ghagar: "Some people think that the Ghagar are nomadic people without roots, living in tents, settling for a brief period in any area" (1982, 101). Different Gypsy groups seem to have often been perceived as tribes, differing neither racially, ethnically, or in terms of origin from other tribal entities, but characterized chiefly by their extreme poverty, their nomadic practices, their spatial marginalization, and their dedication to specific occupations. Those occupations, such as entertainment, sorcery, dealings in animals, peddling, or begging, may have contributed to their marginalization, as some of them belong to impure or somehow sacred domains, but they have also fostered their identity, serving to situate them socially and culturally, particularly in rural environments. More recently, Kevin Holmes, in his article in the Dom Research Center's *Kuri Journal*, explains that the Dom are both virtually indistinguishable to the casual observer and constantly denying their heritage, claiming instead to be Egyptian or Arab. He adds that when someone, usually "local neighbors," know of the presence of a Dom family, they tend to speak of them in a derogatory manner and to feel deep differences, which are mostly based on cultural rather than ethnic or racial elements (Holmes 2004c). The Doms' 'foreignness' appears to be constructed on their different social practices, not on allegations of actual foreign origins. Hanna nonetheless reports a few legends on the 'origins' of the Ghagar, particularly one that associates them with Jews.

> No recorded history is available about the Ghagar of Sett Guiran'ha. The oral history told by Ghagar and non-Ghagar varies and contains different stories. A non-Ghagar informant was of the opinion that the Ghagar were originally Jews. The content of this hypothesis is that the biblical Joseph once lived in this area, after having been sold into slavery in Egypt. The narrative tells how his people lived on after him until the arrival of Moses. When going out of Egypt with the Israelites they were said to have crossed the area east of the Red Sea. But for a variety of reasons, a certain number of these Jews were unable to follow. Some had ties of work with Egyptians and so refused to leave; others were not persuaded to go with Moses; still others were assimilated into Egyptian society and preferred to stay. Some were said to have feared the unknown destiny, while others were impeded from joining Moses by physical weakness or old age. All of these, according to the tale, are remainder who continued to live in the area and whose descendents live here today and are known as Ghagar. Trying to appear as natives, they embraced the official religion and lived as the natives around them lived. But as Jews, they remained a category in respect to work, marriage and their general social situation. (Hanna 1982, 11)

Hanna remarks that while the hypothesis may find geographical support because of the proximity between the area of Sett Guiran'ha and the Red Sea, it lacks historical support. Later on he suggests: "Some may be mere legends that focus on the origins of the European Gypsies and suggest a link between them and the Jews or Egyptians or Bohemians" (1982, 12). Those 'legends' are, interestingly, still very present, particularly in the media, on the Internet, and through more conventional forms.

The relatively few articles that focus on the Dom, under the appellation 'Ghagar' or 'Hanagra' (Hanagra are sometimes presented as Ghagar who supposedly sojourned in Hungary, which may explain their name), tend to take a sensationalistic form. Many articles construct stereotypical representations of the group essentially associated with deviant behavior. News items about Hanagra specifically focus on the crimes they commit, mostly in urban environments. Their urban identity becomes anchored in criminal representations and deviance, or, as Stanley Cohen (1972) suggests, under the label of 'folk devils.' The reporting is largely in a singular narrative (all members of a group are identical and easily identifiable), resting on an exaggeration of the facts, and on the fatalistic prediction that further immoral actions from the 'folk devils' can inevitably be expected. The representations of the Hanagra in media discourse have generally incorporated these dimensions, portraying them as 'intrinsic criminals' (or as 'having crime in the blood'), whose membership in this suspicious group is both the cause and the consequence of their deviant acts.

Media discourse tends to utilize the group's 'roots' to explain its deviance in two complementary fashions. The first one consists in ascribing to the group foreign origins that have morphed into rigid boundaries embodied in the permanence of their exclusionary practices: they came from outside of the national sphere and have remained social and spatial outsiders, confined to their group, which is built on bizarre practices. The second approach builds upon their historical background, or more likely their myth of origin, to explain their current practices, which thus become historically and mythically anchored. One major rationale used to explain the quest for a group's origins is to explain their foreignness as the root of their ascribed deviance; it therefore becomes crucial to demonstrate the persistence of the group's exclusionary practices. The group is often said to have originated in India, although the dates of migration range from one thousand years ago to about three hundred years ago, and to have remained a closed group post-migration: "those tribes and families that came from India arrived as one tribe and then dispersed in Egypt, but many relationships remain between all of them" (al-Qalb al-hakim 2014). Their migration and segregated practices are typically presented conjointly: "[They arrived] three hundred years ago from India" and "[they are] concentrated at the edge of Cairo . . . and live like outcasts to engage in the work of theft and pick-pocketing." They are represented as outsiders originating from a foreign land, who remain marginalized by virtue of the fact that they settle on the edge of cities. The terms of marginalization shift from being a foreigner to being unintegrated into urban environments, both because of where they settle and because of the activities they engage in.

An article from the online publication *Rosa Magazine* explains the presence of Ghagar among Syrian refugees. It concludes with a small paragraph on their origins, remarking that they are uncertain, but definitely foreign, and that those origins seem to have "logically" generated a group stuck in its habits and prisoner of its irremediable "character": "According to some historical accounts of the multiple origins of these groups that reside in Syria, Iraq, and Jordan, some say they are of Indian origin and others from Pakistani origins, some books say that their origins are Arab, but their character and habits remain the same as what they are and that is to collect money by any means possible" (Mansur 2015).

The representation of the group as deviant is enfolded in questions about where they come from and how rigid their group is. Shifts in what is known and what is unknown, what is rigid and what is fluid, take place constantly. For example, one article contends that Gypsies are *clearly* criminals (or beggars, or specialists in robbing pilgrims during the Hajj), but their provenance is *unclear*, even confusing, since their deviant habits are un-Egyptian; still, "it is evident from their dialect that they are Egyptians." Suppositions and assertions alternate, creating a subversive and unsettling entity whose origins are unknown but potentially different and fluctuating, and whose practices are, contrastingly, very well known and unchangeable. As a result, the deviant rigid practices become the whole identity of the group: Ghagar or Hanagra are un-Egyptian *because* of their abnormal practices. And they engage in abnormal practices because they are outsiders.

The 2014 Ramadan television series *Women's Prison*, directed by Kamla Abu Zikry, involuntarily helped to reify the group as stuck in a series of deviant practices. The popular series portrayed jailed females in the setting of the Qanatir Women's Prison, an infamous real-life prison in Cairo. The series, based on a 1982 play written by the feminist Fatheyya al-Assal, received a lot of attention, particularly for its feminist and socialist undertones, as well as for its crude depictions of characters reminiscent of Emile Zola's nineteenth-century social realism. For the journalist Charlotte El Shabrawy, "The series combines the prison, an all-encompassing metaphor for the situation of many Egyptian women, with multiple, seemingly minor symbolic details" (El Shabrawy 2014). One of the female characters is a Hanagra; like the other characters, she is described in a supposedly brutally realistic manner. Concomitantly, all the members of the Hanagra community are depicted as deviant, with a particular light being shed on inverted gender roles, presented as intrinsic to the community. Women are depicted as ruthless thieves, smoking cigarettes and forbidding their husbands from working or leaving their homes. In contrast, men are quietly raising children and submissively obeying their wives' orders. The community overall is represented as closed to outsiders, with all its members behaving mechanically alike. Based on the various blogs and news articles published after the series was shown, many viewers and reviewers appear to have uncritically accepted the representation of the Hanagra, repeatedly using it as substructure for further reflection about an exciting group of "strangers among us" which had been freshly (re)discovered, since that group had been largely invisible within Egyptian society, particularly in the last decades. The sensationalistic dimension that the series brought to the group, again depicting them as matriarchal criminals breaking gender and social norms, positioned them as profitable consumable material. Many articles constructed stereotypical representations of the group, as the embodiment of a subculture associated with deviant behavior.

Another strategy to explain the current behaviors of Gypsies consists of attributing meaning to their historical or mythical origins. They are not simply outsiders, but their existence, or the journeys they have engaged in (and the reasons for those journeys), both produce and explain their identity. Some articles suggest that Gypsies may be "descendants of Cain," intrinsic sinners condemned to spend their lives migrating. Their misfortunes and current practices are embedded in historical sins, as suggested in an article from *al-Badil* (Mamduh 2015) that skillfully combines their role as entertainers in India, their relation to the biblical Cain, and the fact that the principal occupation of the group is theft, an activity "usually carried out by women." Older women prepare young females for their criminal mission from childhood, while "the work of men is considered a shame and a disgrace for the community." The group is also depicted as "a closed group that does not allow marriage to outsiders," and which has established itself in poor urban areas so as to be "deployed in places where theft is easy." The apparent innate thievishness of the Ghagar/Hanagra is also occasionally rooted in their role in stealing the "largest nails" to be used in the crucifixion of Jesus Christ, therefore alleviating his pain, a redeeming act that nonetheless metamorphosed Gypsies into eternal thieves. Another explanation is that the Ghagar were Egyptian soldiers who chased the Jews to the desert and have been wandering ever since—an interesting mirror to the story mentioned by Hanna, according to which the Ghagar were a lost group of exiled Jews.

Susan Drummond, in her book *Mapping Marriage Law in Spanish Gitano Communities*, looks at the different myths of origin for Gypsy communities and connects traditional Gypsy occupations with these legends: for instance, the image of the wandering blacksmith stems from the legend according to which Gypsies forged the nails of the Cross and were thereafter compelled to flee the curse of Christianity (Drummond 2011, 104). She also mentions persistent legends that exploit the common imagery shared by Jews and Gypsies, of diaspora and persecution, and that depict Gypsies as one of the lost tribes of Israel, perpetually wandering and unwelcome. The wandering element in Gypsiness, while marginalizing, is still less othering in Egypt than it is in a European context since nomadism does not have the strong anti-national connotation it holds in Europe; in Egypt, there still exist (a few) nomadic communities that do not (yet) fully embody a threat to the very essence of the nation-state. Although mobility and national belonging are acutely perceived as mutually exclusive categories in Europe, a certain mobility is still acceptable in Egypt; in the same vein, migrants in Egypt do not have (yet) a specific role in the national discourse on identity formation and do not represent the threat that they have come to represent in a European context. If Gypsy myths inform us about the placement of Gypsies in the national scene, then nomadism is not quintessentially Egyptian Gypsy; the myths of origin serve primarily to explain criminality, deviance, and marginality. The outcome is the crystallization of their whole identity into restricted features: the criminal and the member of a matriarchally structured group. Not only is their multiplicity reduced to a restricted and restrictive singularity, but there is no possibility of escape. The singular identity to which they are subjugated is presented as the natural result of a factitious historical creation, and individuality and change are automatically denied to any member of the group.

The other notable distinction between the production of knowledge on Gypsies in the European and Egyptian contexts is that, while generally in Europe the notions of myths of origins have tended to decrease, and are being replaced by linguistic evidence and more empirical analysis, the mythical creation is still preponderant in Egypt, perhaps specifically because of the lack of research on the Dom themselves and on the Domari language. That lack of information confines every member of the group within a set of stereotypical characteristics and limits their individuality, alienating them further. The following quotation from Judith Okely in *The Traveller-Gypsies* is still strikingly accurate:

> It has been claimed that literate people have history, while non-literate people have myth, but in the case of Gypsy-Gorgio history there is a fusion of the two. The literate tradition of the dominant society has assisted in myth making, especially with regard to the myths of Gypsies' origins. (1983, 20)

Myths are often instrumentalized to convey contemporary political or cultural messages. Gypsies and Copts have been associated on many occasions, an identification that has ancient roots (Marushiakova and Popov 2001). Not only have Gypsies and Copts shared a rather subaltern part in Egyptian history, but the terms 'Gypsy' and 'Copt' have also often been confused. In many documents from the Ottoman Empire between the fifteenth and the eighteenth centuries, for instance, Gypsies were referred to as "Kypts" (Marushiakova and Popov 2001; Marsh and Strand 2006, 173). In Turkey, the Romani language is identified as 'Kiptice' ('the language of the Copts'), which further suggests in the Ottoman period "the association between Romani people and Egypt, as elsewhere in Europe" (Oprisan 2006, 164). The reason the term 'Gypsy' is so conspicuously similar to 'Coptic' is rooted in the fact that the terms are effectively linked. The terms 'Coptic' and 'Egypt' are both derived from the Greek *Aigyptos*, which meant 'Egyptian,' eventually shortened to 'Gupitos' and transferred to Arabic as 'Qobt.' The term 'Gypsy' was created on the misconception of medieval Europeans who assumed the newcomers had indeed come from Egypt, which does not necessarily mean that there are any ethnic connections. This linguistic proximity has created confusions and amalgamation. In Ottoman documents, the name 'Gypsy' is used with the term 'Copt' *(kıptî)*, and the Ottoman state considered 'Gypsy' and 'Copt' as two words serving the same purpose and used synonymously.

On a more symbolic level, some narratives depict the Gypsies arriving in Egypt from Europe, with the Romans as their servants (Aly 2013). After most Egyptians converted to Islam, in the seventh century AD, the Gypsies remained Christians and their descendants are the current Copts. That narrative simultaneously marginalizes Copts and Gypsies: the implication that Copts are Gypsies attributes impurity and foreignness to the Copts, and denying an Islamic identity to the Gypsies (who are mostly Muslim in Egypt) distances them further from the mainstream Egyptian identity, which is built on the specific elements of having roots in the region and being a pure Arab and a Muslim. Anecdotally, a columnist recently lamented on *Youm* 7, one of the most popular online newspapers in Egypt, that the English word 'Egypt' had no connection to the Arabic 'Misr,' turning this lack of connection into a conscious insult from Westerners. Its supposed intent was not only to betray the real meaning of 'Misr,' but also to color Egypt with barbarism, making it an 'uncivilized' country because the word 'Egypt' was derived from the barbarian 'Gypsy' people. To counter that insult, the columnist demanded that the English name be changed to 'Misr,' so that Egypt would no longer be constructed as 'the country of Gypsies.'

Ethnogenesis by Outsiders

Romani scholars are increasingly looking beyond a myth of origins and a single origin, and tend to understand Gypsies as heterogeneous people, from a variety of origins and the product of complex social, economic, and political elements (Hancock 2002; Marushiakova and Popov 2001; Marsh 1999). Looking at the way in which Gypsies' origins have been constructed throughout history and by different analysts tells us more about the imagination of the observer (Marsh, 2007); it is precisely the psyche of the non-Gypsy that needs to be understood when examining the representation of the Gypsies, as well as the construction of their origins. The construction of Middle Eastern Gypsies as a rigid and foreign group seems to have been influenced by the gaze of European Orientalists, coupled with the development of philology and racialism as scientific fields of study. European observers in Egypt focused largely on the Dom language and drew comparisons with European Roma, their habitus, and their occupations as entertainers, peddlers, or thieves. The transfer of the imagination of European Orientalists needs to be understood at different levels. The first, as we have seen, encompasses the transfer of the European obsession with Gypsies, the development of linguistics and the study of language as a metaphor for race, and the development of racial ideology. The other aspect is the broader spread of racial ideology from Europe to its colonies and the development of a colonial political economy. The idea of the British 'divide and rule' theorem that engendered mistrust and fear among the colonized groups often led to tense racial politics in many colonies. Many of these antagonistic and ethnic divisions, formed during the colonial era, continue to affect the social and racial structures of formerly colonized nations (Hirshman 1986; Lieberson 1980). Often, European imperialism introduced the idea of 'race relations' and the racialization of minorities and groups who might formerly have been viewed simply in terms of temporary differences, tribal differences, social differences, or occupational differences that did not possess the rigidity of race.

However, the process of racialization has not been thoroughly appropriated by Egyptians (neither in academic production of knowledge, in the media, nor in popular imagination), and even now, many different narratives coexist. The Dom, when they are acknowledged, may be constructed as a foreign group, mirroring the European Roma, with attributed Indian ancestry; or they may constitute a group whose origins are unknown (and may be either foreign or indigenous); or they may be linked to a myth of origins that serves to explain thoroughly their practices and character. The otherness of Gypsies is therefore not built on a different specific ethnicity, or on specific origins (which may be invented, but at least somehow traceable), but is based only on different lifestyles and values. They are other but not coming from anywhere, the essence of otherness, archaic in a world seeking modernity, disturbing in a world seeking cohesion and stability, dangerous in a world looking for safety, amoral in a world craving moral values.

The one commonality among those narratives is that the ethnogenesis of Ghagar and Egyptian Gypsies does not come from these groups themselves, which accentuates their vulnerability. They are constructed by 'real' Egyptians as outsiders, occasionally as foreigners from nowhere, with, paraphrasing Ian Hancock, a "vague understanding of Romani origins" (2002, 62). In this sense, the Ghagar cannot even aspire to own their own history. Without a narrative of an ethnic or national identity, and in a context of strongly imagined homogeneous national identity, it is easy for the Ghagar to disappear.

2

FROM BELLY DANCERS TO THIEVES

Historically, Gypsies have been regarded as a strange and mysterious group that falls outside normal culture and normal society (Bercovici 1928; Bhopal and Myers 2008); in Europe and in Egypt, they have been romanticized as exotic and erotic by Orientalists. In the villages of Upper Egypt and in the rural Delta region, they were familiar figures with specific functions that were integrated into the villagers' lives. They provided villagers with entertainment as dancers or snake catchers, and they offered their expertise in animal care. As tinkers, they mended household utensils; as fortune-tellers, they offered folk psychology which often had therapeutic effects on villagers. All in all, despite legends of abducted children or Gypsy women casting spells, they were not perceived as a threat to public order. The social organization of rural Gypsies—usually based on kinship, endogamic practices, and tribal structures—was not vastly different from that of the villagers. Gypsies' nomadism was not as marginalizing and threatening as it may have been perceived in the case of the European Roma, largely because the concept of nation-state with its norms of stability and rejection of archaic (tribal) structures did not really arise until Gamal Abdel Nasser's time and the construction of a modern Egyptian national identity. Ronen Zeidel, in his study of Iraqi Gypsies, notes that "whereas the Gypsies entered a detribalized Europe with a social organization that was different, contributing to their estrangement, that was not the case in Iraq. Iraqi society has never been detribalized" (2014, 73). This statement can be applied equally to

Egyptian Gypsies, who, despite their cultural unconventionality, seemed to fit better in rural and tribal Egypt than in medieval Europe, or in modern urbanized Egypt.

The current representations of the Ghagar have lost much of their exotic romanticism, and revolve instead around a sordid condition of poverty and marginalization embodied in the images of the Ghagar beggar and the Ghagar thief. In this chapter, we will follow the shifts in the meanings associated with Egyptian Gypsies in their cinematic representations from the 1930s until now, but also in their roles and performances in dance, as Ghawazi, in music, and in other fragmented instances of Egyptian folklore such as the saints' festivals, the *mulid*s. All of these fragments—and I use the term 'fragments' because Gypsies are rarely represented integrally—contribute to illustrating and creating the popular imaginary around Egyptian Gypsies.

Ghawazi and Orientalists

Ghawazi, often viewed as belly dancers, are notorious characters in Egyptian popular culture. Many Egyptian proverbs use the term 'Ghawazi' as a symbol of free movement and ephemeral pleasures, such as "Life is like a Ghaziya—she dances just briefly for each." In fact, Ghawazi were more than just dancers. In Arabic, *ghawazi* (singular *ghaziya*) means 'conqueror,' because they were supposed to conquer the hearts of their audience. Edward Lane described their moves in these terms:

> Their dancing has little of elegance; its chief peculiarity being a very rapid vibrating motion of the hips, from side to side. They commence with a degree of decorum; but soon, by more animated looks, by a more rapid collision of their castanets of brass, and by increased energy in every motion, they exhibit a spectacle exactly agreeing with the descriptions which Martial and Juvenal have given of the performance of the female dances of Gades. The dress in which they generally thus exhibit in public is similar to that which is worn by women of the middle classes in Egypt in private, that is, in the hareem; consisting of a yelek, or an 'anteree, and the shintiyan, etc., of handsome materials. [A *yelek* is a tight-fitting, floor-length, long-sleeved

vest, worn over a *qamis*—a wide-sleeved, gauzy blouse—and *shinti-yan*, voluminous pantaloons tied around the hips.] They also wear various ornaments: their eyes are bordered with the kohl and the tips of their fingers, the palms of their hands, and their toes and other parts of their feet, are usually stained with the red dye of the henna, according to the general custom of the middle and higher classes of Egyptian women. (1871, 87)

Ghawazi performed for various occasions: weddings, engagements, circumcisions, and *mulid*s. They were often contrasted with another group of entertainers, the Awalim, who, unlike the Ghawazi who were primarily dancers, were singers and typically more educated in the arts, although the distinction is not always clearly established. Ghawazi may have passed for Awalim occasionally, and singing Awalim may have danced. However, and more importantly for us, the Ghawazi identity may have been ethnically anchored, or socially, as a group belonging to a lower and perhaps less reputable class, occasionally represented as mere prostitutes.

Unsurprisingly, those mysterious and sensual exotic female dancers were bound to arouse Orientalists' imaginations and senses. The Ghawazi embodied perfectly the imagined sensuality associated with Arab women, presenting both submissive and erotically teasing characteristics, a systematic dichotomy in the Orientalist discourse. The Ghawazi embodied a sense of freedom, because they danced unveiled, and they were often associated with a pseudo-matriarchal structure. Edward Lane portrayed Ghawazi as exceptionally beautiful but also "the most abandoned of the courtesans of Egypt" (1871, 88), a cogent paradox: while Ghawazi were deemed beautiful, impetuous, and free, they were also perceived as entangled in the lowest class of entertainers.

The links between Ghawazi and other Gypsy groups/tribes were and still are contested. While many nineteenth-century writers described them as Gypsies, others depicted them as being of a separate race, or at least clearly distinct from other Gypsy tribes. Alfred von Kremer mentioned the "tribe" of the Ghawazi in his writing on Egyptian Gypsies. The younger females are described as belly dancers and the older ones as fortune-tellers; they marry late, after having "made a little fortune," and

their husbands are nothing more than their servants, playing the flute
or the drum and "even [introducing] to her new acquaintances." When
Ghawazi marry sheikhs, however, their "fidelity is as strict as their former
life was loose" (von Kremer 1864, 264). Von Kremer reports that Ghawazi
claim to be descended from Persians but, contradictorily, are also proud
of their Bedouin origins.

> The tribe called Ghawazi is in Egypt the most numerous. This
> tribe has in all the larger towns and villages female representatives,
> well versed in all arts of seduction, who become dangerous by their
> beauty. They call themselves Beramikeh, i.e., Bermekides, and try
> to trace their origin back to the famous family of the Barmecides,
> which, after having filled the highest offices in the Chalifate was
> destroyed by Chalif Harun-al Rashid. They are proud at the same
> time of their Bedouin origin, and lead, in fact, a Bedouin life, sleep-
> ing in tents and attending fairs. All Ghazieh girls are professional
> dancers, and all women fortune-tellers. (1864, 264)

Edward Lane found Ghawazi to be very similar to female dancers
depicted in ancient Egyptian tombs, dancing at private entertainments
"to the sound of various instruments," which led him to suggest that
the Ghawazi may be the descendants of the class of female dancers
who amused Egyptians in pharaonic times. However, Ghawazi are
"even more licentious; one or more of these performers being generally depicted in a state of perfect nudity, though in the presence of men
and women in high stations" (Lane 1871, 89). Edward Lane's writings
betray the intense pleasure he took in describing entertainment among
"modern Egyptians" and show a vivid fascination for that group of beautiful temptresses. He identifies them as being of "a distinct race," while
their origin was "involved in much uncertainty" (1871, 89). Unlike von
Kremer, he seems to refute their connections with the Gypsy groups,
aside from their shared predisposition for entertainment. The female
Ghawazi described by Lane are the main authority, as dancers, while
their husbands accompany them, usually as musicians: "the husband is
subject to the wife" (1871, 90). Lane concludes:

Though some of them are possessed of considerable wealth, costly ornaments, many of their customs are similar to those of the people whom we call "gipsies" and who are supposed, by some, to be of Egyptian origin.... it is remarkable that some of the gipsies in Egypt pretend to be descended from a branch of the same family to whom the Ghawazee refer to their origin; but their claim is still less to be regarded than that of the latter because they do not unanimously agree on this point. (1871, 90)

The question of the 'race' of the Ghawazi, whether Gypsies or otherwise, seems to obsess nineteenth-century writers. For the traveler Frederick William Fairholt, "these girls are a peculiar race, not acknowledged by the Egyptians as their lineage; 'the Ghawazee are Gipsies,' was the explanation I got in English from our Egyptian dragoman. Of course, he used the latter term to convey an equivalent sense of the wandering hordes from which they are descended" (Fairholt 1862, 347). For the British travel writer Bayle Saint John:

It seems impossible to obtain a distinct idea of the origin and history of the so-called tribe of Ghawazee. Of course the nature of their occupation precludes the possibility of any unity of blood; but there are certainly traces of a distinct type, which reappears here and there in remarkable purity. Forms and faces cannot surpass in beauty those of the complete Ghawazee; and, wonderful to say, in spite of the life of debauchery these women lead, they keep far better than their more virtuous sisters. (Saint John 1853, 18)

It may have been the French novelist Gustave Flaubert who best epitomized the image of the Ghawazi in the account of his encounter with the striking young Kuchuk Hanem, a "tall, splendid creature, lighter in color than an Arab" whom he met in Esna. Kuchuk became a central character in the description of his sexual adventures in Egypt and very much a symbol of his 'romance' with the East—a melancholic passion, archetypally Orientalist, that Said discussed in the first pages of *Orientalism*:

[Flaubert] was foreign, comparatively wealthy, male, and there were historical facts of domination that allowed him not only to possess Kuchuk Hanem physically but to speak for her and tell his readers in what way she was "typically Oriental." My argument is that Flaubert's situation of strength in relation to Kuchuk Hanem was not an isolated instance. It fairly stands for the pattern of relative strength between East and West, and the discourse about the Orient that it enables. (Said 1978, 6)

Twenty-five years after Flaubert, Charles Dudley Warner, an American journalist, editor, essayist, and sometime collaborator with Mark Twain, left the record of his Egyptian experience of 1874–75 in *My Winter on the Nile*. He described the Ghawazi not only in Esna, but also in Asyut, Farshut, Aswan, and Luxor. He characterized the women as

bold looking jades who come out and stare at us with a more than masculine impudence. —They claim to be an unmixed race of ancient lineage; but I suspect their blood is no purer than their morals. There is not much in Egypt that is *not* hopelessly mixed. —Their profession is as old as history and their antiquity may entitle them to be considered an aristocracy of vice. —But whatever their origin, it is admitted that their dance is the same with which the dancing-women amused the Pharaohs, the same that the Phoenicians carried to Gades and which Juvenal describes, and, as Mr. Lane thinks, the same by which the daughter of Herodias danced off the head of John the Baptist. Modified here and there, it is the immemorial dance of the Orient. (Warner 1881)

We can observe a disturbing ambiguity in the concomitant fluidity and rigidity ascribed to Ghawazi. They can constitute a fixed ethnicized group when they need to be marginalized, or in order to explain some of their moral or physical traits (animal beauty, sensuality, lack of morality). Their identity is also rather fluid, positioned in an overall unknown; perhaps they are foreign, perhaps their difference is grounded in their 'vocation,' or in a specific ethnicity, or in tribal belonging, or class (underclass), or matriarchal structure, or a pharaonic continuity. They were said to have Persian roots (von Kremer), they were called Gypsies by outsiders (Fairholt), they have presented "traces of a certain type" (Saint John), and they have been deemed dangerous because of their constitutive beauty (von Kremer). Whatever its anchor, however, the process of differentiation is always present. Whether being described as pure or mixed (they are 'mixed' when they cannot represent purity, either of blood or of morality), their 'race' is also constructed as dedicated to pleasure, and in that sense it is commoditized. It is a commodity whose origins may be uncertain, but nonetheless displays very precise characteristics—a beauty that "keeps" despite a "life of debauchery" (Saint John 1853, 348), and extravagant sensual pleasure.

The commoditization/objectification of the Ghawazi dancers applies to the whole group. This subjectification acts on different levels. First, females are turned into objects of pleasure—more precisely, the pleasure of dominant and perhaps specifically male Westerners, as per their intoxicated descriptions. The ensuing identification of the whole tribe within the transformation of women into objects of pleasure erases, or emasculates, the males. The question of masculinity within the tribe is never clearly addressed. Obviously if Ghawaziness does not invoke simply an occupation but also a tribal (or ethnic) belonging, the assumption would be that this group should include males and females. The tribal/ethnic construct is, however, so completely feminized here that males disappear or are occasionally described as subjected to the women: for instance, Lane remarks that "the husband is subject to the wife" (1871, 90), and von Kremer depicts "the husband" as a mere servant who even "introduces to [his wife] new acquaintances" (1864, 264). The husband is subjected to a subjected wife, thus doubly subjected and reduced to being powerless and dehumanized.

Current Views

The question of whether the Ghawazi were a distinct tribe and whether they were somehow related to Gypsies continues to be debated among modern scholars. Ahmed Zaki, in his article on Egyptian theater, writes about their tribal affiliation: "Most of the public dancing girls and men came from a tribe called Ghawazee; they usually married within their own *tribe*, although some of the women doubled as prostitutes" (2004, 26; emphasis added). Noha Rouchdy mentions that "Ghawazee were and continue to be identified as the female members of one of the 'gypsy' tribes (*al ghagar*) that settled in Egypt in an unspecified 'past'; they are thus believed to be from a distinct cultural background and to have no original connection to the Egyptian peasant or townsman" (2010, 78). The Wikipedia article dedicated to the Ghawazi starts with this undiscerning statement: "The Ghawazi (also Ghawazee) dancers of Egypt were a group of female traveling dancers of the Dom people (also known as Nawar)" (Wikipedia 2017). The article does not explain why the Dom are also known as Nawar, nor why the Halebi, the Ghagar, and other groups are not mentioned.

The connection between the tribal affiliation and the occupation of the dancers has also been challenged. Karin van Nieuwkerk, in her ethnographic research *A Trade Like Any Other: Female Singers and Dancers in Egypt* (1995), links the marginalizing profession of a dancer to a marginalizing ethnicity, such as Gypsiness. She notes that in Muslim countries, entertainers have been outcasts and rejected by the clergy in the past, while in more recent times, itinerant entertainers such as Gypsies have ranked low on the social scale. She connects profession and group affiliation in a common social marginalization as well as in a shared mobility (1995, 3) and alludes to Hanna's remark that Ghagar in Sett Guiran'ha engaged in entertainment. She nonetheless argues that the exact relationship between Gypsies (or Ghagar, which is the term she uses) and Ghawazi is unclear. The artist and choreographer Leona Wood, quoted by Stavros Stavrou Karayanni in *Dancing Fear and Desire: Race, Sexuality, and Imperial Politics in Middle Eastern Dance*, "informs us that the term appears after the advent of Islam and 'its apparent etymology from the Arabic *ghawa:* to be enamored seems to make it an appropriate appellation rather than, as has been repeatedly asserted, the name of a special tribe'" (2006, 28).

Wendy Buenaventura, a belly-dance specialist and choreographer, insists that "the original Ghawazee were Gypsies, though the word has come to be used as a generic term for dancers rather than to denote a particular tribe, or tribes, as was once the case" (1994, 39). Buenaventura explains that their Gypsy origins specifically contributed to their marginalization. She compares them to the Awalim, who were also entertainers but more often singers and poets than public dancers, noting that unlike the Awalim, the Ghawazi were not invited to respectable harems. "Like many who live by their wits on the fringe of society, the Ghawazee knew several languages and had a secret code of their own, which was not understood by outsiders. The dancers could be found performing in public squares, in cafes and on the steps of hotels" (Buenaventura 1994, 61).

On the other hand, according to Kathleen Fraser, there are compelling reasons to reject the Gypsy origins of the Ghawazi. She builds on Lane's differentiation between Ghagar and Ghawazi and argues that "compared to the great number of entertainers there were few Roma [*sic*] in Egypt" (2014, 171). She unfortunately descends the slippery slopes of racial description:

> The Romas, having a north-Indian heritage, were racially different and distinctive from the Egyptians and the Arabs [. . .] Many writers, in contrast, spoke admiringly of the fair complexion of the public dancers, although they could indicate their complexions were darker in Southern Egypt, as was that of the Egyptian population in general. To equate the entire population of public dancers with the Roma, then, does not jibe with the word use, population numbers and physical appearance. (2014, 171)

She also mentions the "exclusiveness of the Roma," which does not match the very public life of the Ghawazi. Later, however, she contends:

> Some of the Ghawazi of the 19th century and earlier may have descended from peoples who had come from elsewhere as we know some did migrate to Egypt. It was not these particular ethnic origins, however, that provided them with any status. Prestige came from the mythical link to the medieval past when foreign women set standards in the arts that still, after hundreds of years, dominated the notion of what was most admirable. Perhaps it was the "Persian" trait of these foreign slave entertainers that tempted certain public dancers eventually to capture a piece of cherished exotic by means of their invented histories about the distinguished Persian Barmacides

family who worked for the great rulers of Baghdad. At the same time, ironically, the Roma [*sic*] were despised everywhere in Egypt, their more authentic Persian national connections providing them with no social currency whatsoever. (2014, 172)

The Ghawazi, as a group, are situated at the intersection of racialized and genderized identities, in line with what Judith Butler (1990) calls gender performativity. Belly dancers, being over-sexualized, are turned into objects of desire and debauchery. They embody pleasure and license and use their bodies to literally perform gender; additionally, they also seem to perform an ascribed ethnicity, as the Ghawazi as a construct represents not only an occupation, that of dancers, but also a tribe, occasionally depicted as Gypsy or rooted in a pharaonic 'class' of dancers, or 'Persian in origin.' Literature on the Ghawazi oscillated, and interestingly still oscillates, between representing them as a group of females, or as a tribe with both males and females but where the females take the lead, since the tribe's identity (or even essence) seems constructed around the very performativity of the females, via their expertise in dance and more. The ambiguity associated with the definition of the group identity continues to marginalize it. Its over-feminization emasculates the male members and reduces the females to their sexual performance. This feminization of the Gypsies is a constant marker of their identity; the relationship between the group and the majority society is filtered via the society's relation with women. This trend is continued in the movies, which usually involve a stereotyped, *Carmen*-like plot, based on the relationship between a female Ghagar and an Egyptian male.

Cinematic Depiction

One of the first movies depicting Gypsies is *Suad the Gypsy* (*Suad al-Ghagaria*, 1928), directed by Stelio Chiarini. It portrays a young Gypsy girl, played by the actress Amina Rizk, who is forced to perform in a circus by her tribe. She is eventually rescued from their clutches by the mayor of the city, who, after he 'saves' her, asks her to marry him.

The Gypsy Town (*Madinat al-Ghagar*, 1945) directed by Mohamed Abdel Gawad, with Anwar Wagdy and Fatmah Roshdy, depicts the story of Gamal, a wealthy young man who is also surprisingly humble and generous to the poor. His arrogant fiancée, Thoraya, considers his generosity toward others aggravating and presses him to find a more prestigious and better-paid job. One day, he loses his wallet, and a friendly young Gypsy girl named Qamar (which means 'moon' in Arabic) finds it and returns it to him. They instantly fall in love. He eventually meets her Gypsy family and displays more of his exceptional generosity. One of the community members, who is in love with Qamar, asks the community leader to expel the stranger who is invading their privacy. Meanwhile, the arrogant fiancée Thoraya publicly portrays Gamal as insanely spending all his fortune on Gypsies. She tries to sue him, but loses the case, and the movie ends with the happy marriage of Gamal and his beloved Qamar.

Niazi Mostafa's *Wahiba, Queen of the Gypsies* (*Wahiba Maliket al-Ghagar*, 1951), a less well-known movie, depicts Gypsies and belly dancers. It stars the actress–dancer Kouka and is based on a story by Mohammad Kamel Hassan. In the movie, a landowner expels a group of Gypsy farmers from his land. The Gypsies respond by kidnapping his young daughter. His son, Sherif, goes searching for the girl. Wahiba, the female leader of the Gypsies, played by Kouka, hides her Gypsiness, and offers to help him. The two of them fall in love and decide to get married, defying the usual endogamic practices of the Gypsies. Sherif finally realizes that the fierce woman he has fallen for is a Gypsy, which is unacceptable to his family. He decides to call off the marriage. Wahiba moves to Cairo in the hope of breaking into the entertainment industry as a singer and a dancer. She becomes famous, and one day she and Sherif cross paths again. They reconcile, forget about social and cultural incompatibilities, and get married.

One of the most famous Egyptian movies representing Gypsies is *Tamr Henna*, a 1957 film directed by Hussein Fawzi. The lead actress is Naima Akef, herself an acrobat and belly dancer. She was born in a circus, and while there is no definite indication that she was actually a Ghagar, her native town is Tanta in the Delta region, host to a sizable Ghagar community. The movie is a revealing cultural representation of Egyptian perceptions of the Ghagar/Ghawazi. Akef plays a young Ghaziya (belly dancer) who performs during *mulid*s. As she is dancing sensuously, she is noticed by the son of the landowner on whose land the *mulid* is taking place. He is young, handsome, and wealthy. He looks out of place in his European-style clothing in an environment where everyone else is wearing traditional clothing. He admires the beautiful Ghaziya as she dances, embodying tradition, sensuality, and danger. The rich young man is engaged to be married to his cousin, but he falls in love with Tamr Henna. In a dispute with his father, he provocatively argues that rich people and poor people are all essentially identical and only differ in the opportunities they have had throughout their lives, while his father argues that the poor are intrinsically unchangeable. Whether because of love or, more prosaically, to prove his argument against his father, the young man decides to engage in a makeover of Tamr Henna. His mission is to teach her to behave like a woman of his own social class, so he can demonstrate that the poor are victims of circumstances and not inferior in essence. He assumes that if he can demonstrate Tamr Henna's ability to fit in with the higher classes, he will be allowed to marry her and simultaneously prove his father wrong. With the help of one of his friends, he arranges the gentrification of his Ghaziya: her wild hair is tamed and she starts to dress in a 'civilized' way, which means she wears European clothes. She also manages to modify her mannerisms and her language, and finally she changes her name to Yasmina. She vanishes without telling her clan where she is going. Later, she comes back to the area driving a car, with her new look and her new name. Her suitor is delighted and tells his father that she is the daughter of a rich family. The father believes the story, but the young man's abandoned fiancée, upset by her newly arrived rival, manages to uncover where Tamr Henna truly comes from. She organizes a family party and hires Tamr Henna's clan to perform, with the help of Tamr Henna's estranged fiancé who is also seeking revenge. Tamr Henna/Yasmina is then exposed and forced into dancing during the party. Partway through her performance, her Ghagar fiancé comes out and starts dancing with her. At the end of the dance, she flees the scene and runs upstairs to a bedroom. She overhears her rich suitor settling his bet with his father, which upsets her because she had honestly believed he had transformed her solely out of love. Her Ghagar fiancé bursts into the room armed with a knife. He stabs her, and the movie ends, leaving the viewers to decide whether she will die or survive her attack.

The Gypsy Girl (al-Ghagaria), produced in 1960 with Hoda Sultan and Shoukry Sarhan, depicts a Ghagar, Abu Doma, who works in the 'kidnapping business.' During one of his criminal operations, he kidnaps the daughter of a wealthy man, Hassan, and asks for a ransom. Hassan pays the ransom but he is given back another young woman instead of his daughter, whom he ends up raising together with his adopted son, Fathy. His biological daughter, Salma, is raised by the Ghagar thief Abu Doma himself. Years pass and Salma finds employment in the house of her biological father, Hassan, as a maid. She falls in love with Fathy, who also declares his love. They decide to marry secretly. However, a jealous woman, Maha, also in love with Fathy, accuses Salma of theft and takes her to court, where the loving Fathy defends her. They eventually uncover the real thief, who turns out to be Abu Doma. He confesses all his crimes, including the kidnapping of Salma, who is in reality the wealthy Hassan's daughter. While Fathy fears that these revelations may prevent his wedding to his now-sister Salma, Hassan then reveals that Fathy is in fact his adopted son, and the two lovers can happily marry.

In 1996, another movie about Gypsies, *The Gypsy (al-Ghagar)*, with the famous belly dancer Fifi Abdou, came out. The story revolves mostly around a group of Ghagar who live under the rule of an enlightened leader who maintains peace and justice in the community. However, he is forced to step down, and another, less enlightened leader, Kadorah, ascends to power. He is mostly controlled by his wife Hasanat, a power-thirsty woman. She wants him to take control over a local gang headed by Mossad (who is in love with a beautiful girl named Badaraa, played by Fifi Abdou). The mean wife pushes her husband to report Mossad to the police. Mossad shoots a police officer who has come to arrest him and he is taken to jail. Badaraa takes the officer to the hospital in order to save his life. They become friends and the officer promises to help her. Meanwhile, Kadorah has been able to accumulate all the power in the Gypsy clan. Mossad gets out of jail but he kills a young Gypsy who had married a non-Gypsy, breaking the rules of endogamy, which seem to be very powerful in the group. At the end of the movie, the police officer arrests everyone and Badaraa becomes the leader of the Gypsies. She brings the whole community back to a peaceful and fair environment.

After the 2014 Ramadan television series *Women's Prison*, which depicts the life of women in an Egyptian jail and focused for a few episodes on Gypsy women, many Egyptians (re)discovered the group and took an interest in them. I will use the term 'Hanagra' here, as it is the one used in the series. In one episode, one Hanagra woman goes home after a day of crime and theft and her sister welcomes her with high-pitched screams for "having let her husband go to the streets and attempt to work." The sister is also yelling at her own husband, who is carrying and soothing a baby; he then lights a cigarette for her as she bosses everyone around her. Gender roles are satirically reversed: the women are not supposed to let their husbands go out into the streets, the men look after children and quietly tend to their wives, and the wives distribute the money they stole to other family members.

Toward the Impossible Union

According to Bhabha, "gender, race and class" are pivotal to any "articulation of cultural differences and identifications" (1994, 2). The representations of Gypsies in Egyptian cinema embody those articulations and help to make each area of differentiation more prevalent or rigid at times. The Gypsy represents a set of characteristics different from those of the majority, and potentially symbolizes how Egyptian society constructs its others.

In the movie *The Gypsy Town*, the main character, Gamal, is an idealist who wishes to help the poor and who falls in love with a Gypsy girl whose main characteristic is to be honest and candid: a stark contrast with the usual representations of Gypsies as thieves and deceiving creatures. Both Gamal and Qamar are breaking social and ethnic boundaries by their love, as well as cultural stereotypes by their generosity and honesty respectively. Antagonistic characters within each group, Gypsy and non-Gypsy, are set up as contrasts to the selfless heroes: both Gamal's fiancée and Qamar's suitor are driven by greed and blatant bigotry, and feel threatened by Gamal's disregard of ethnic and social conventions. They represent intolerance but they are defeated, as the movie ends with a marriage between a Gypsy and a non-Gypsy—a consecration of authentic ethnic and class transgression which will rarely be depicted in later movies.

A similar marriage takes place in *Suad the Gypsy*, but Suad is saved from her own people by the mayor of the city where she performs, in a very typical process of "saving the brown women from brown men" (Spivak 1999, 284). The act of saving is stronger than the personality of either the Gypsy or her group. The movie is not about Gypsies; it is about emancipating a beautiful, oppressed woman from her uncivilized community and bringing her to civilization, a popular plot in Western cinema and more broadly in colonialist ideology.

Wahiba, Queen of the Gypsies also ends with the marriage of an empowered Gypsy female who became a famous artist and her non-Gypsy suitor who, after having postponed the marriage because it would have broken conventions, decides that the union is conceivable. Wahiba, the main female character, is a deceptive and agile Gypsy. First, she passes for what she is not (a non-Gypsy); later, she leaves her poverty behind and becomes rich and famous. Perhaps because of her ability to cross social and ethnic boundaries, which each time brings her suitor closer to her, the marriage is possible. The marriageable (savable) Ghagar is one who can leave her traditional identity markers behind her.

The turning point in these still relatively fluid practices and conceivable cross-class and interethnic unions is the movie *Tamr Henna*. *Tamr Henna* ends with the fatalistic impossibility of transgression: Tamr Henna, the beautiful Ghaziya, returns to her tribe, where she is stabbed in the back by her estranged fiancé. Both social and cultural boundaries prove to be uncrossable. This position is defended by the father, who insists that there are intrinsic differences between rich and poor, and is reinforced by the fact that while Tamr Henna could, superficially, play her part as a modified agent entering upper-class spheres, her Gypsy roots prevent her from truly crossing social boundaries. Interestingly, the movie is not portraying a devastating failure of conventional upward mobility, nor the impossible rupture of a class taboo, but it illustrates a somehow comforting outcome where the characters remain within the social and cultural communities to which they belong. If the functionalist order of remaining within social boundaries is not constructed as tragic, this is probably because it is an embodiment of (desired) stability. Tamr Henna is, from beginning to end, a victim. She is coerced into playing the role of Yasmina and abandon her tribe; she is the victim of a conspiracy by her suitor's jealous fiancée and her own fiancé, who eventually stabs her in the back; but despite being a victim, she is not saved at any point. In contrast to *The Gypsy Town*, where the estranged fiancés are also plotting against the transgressive love of the heroes, in *Tamr Henna* the two abandoned fiancés who try to expose the potential miscegenation end up triumphing as Tamr Henna and her non-Gypsy lover are doomed. Tamr Henna is also deceived by that lover himself, who may have indeed desired her sexually, perhaps as a commodity, but is simultaneously attempting to convince his father of the inherent similarity between rich and poor—a task at which he unequivocally fails, as the boundaries remain brutally intact.

Three years later, in the movie *al-Ghagaria*, the marriage is possible only because, while the main character has been raised by Gypsies, she is not a 'true' Gypsy, since she has been abducted from a wealthy family. The movie plays upon deception and last-minute revelations about the identities of the lovers who, thankfully, are neither siblings nor Gypsy, which allows them to be married in all morality. The aberration of marrying a brother and the aberration of marrying a Gypsy are superposed and hence carry the same amoral connotations. The only 'true' Gypsy character of the movie, Abu Doma, is a deceiving criminal who kidnaps girls and who robs the home of Hassan, the man whose daughter had been kidnapped. The storyline bears a certain resemblance to western movies about white young women, abducted and raised by Native Americans, who eventually fall in love with a white man (who most likely believes they are Native American), but then reveal that they are truly white, reassuringly discarding the potential for miscegenation. The other Gypsy female character, the young girl who was raised by Hassan, is kept in a very subaltern role. Eventually, the non-Gypsy Egyptians marry non-Gypsy Egyptians, and Gypsies will stay with the Gypsies and be relegated to perform as either a community of irrational individuals who fight over power, as in *The Gypsy*, or as a community of matriarchal thieves, as in *Women's Prison*.

From the 1940s until recently, interethnic marriages have gradually become inconceivable, even within the context of saving (a brown woman from her own people) or of dissimulated origins (when the Gypsy girl is not truly a Gypsy, but has merely been raised by Gypsies). The groups are becoming irremediably segregated. This inevitable evolution can be interpreted at different levels: as an embodiment of the construction of the modern nation and its relations to traditions and the past that in turn could be embodied by rural Gypsies, or as an illustration of the continuous closure of Egyptian identity to heterogeneity and proof of the further entrenchment of Gypsies in marginalized spaces, combined with the limitation of their contact with non-Gypsies to purely economic interactions.

Muhammad Ali, the *Baladi*, and the Construction of Modernity

The urge to associate cultural change with decay and lost authenticity has been a powerful force in Western thought (Clifford 1988). These tensions have been represented in different dichotomies by Tönnies (community–society), Durkheim (mechanical–organic societies) or Weber (communalization–societal action). They have also affected Egypt's transition from a traditional society to a modern one, encompassing seemingly conflicting desires for modernity and intense fears of identity loss. Furthermore, in Egypt, this process was combined with nationalistic preoccupations, particularly in the postcolonial era, characterized by the fear that modernity could be nothing but a direct import from the West. To limit this representation, the transition had to be enhanced by the persistent presence of Egyptian traditions, or at least some of them, alongside modernization. The traditions were often characterized by the rural, the *baladi*, which carried both positive and negative connotations. It could signify the unsophisticated and crude, or invoke authenticity, the essence of Egyptianness, with obvious nationalistic undertones (Armbrust 1996). In that context Gypsies, in their cinematic representations, are situated at the intersection of the relationship between nation-states, modernity, and exclusion, as well as within the historical construction of the modern Egyptian nation-state and its negotiations with the concepts of national and Western values.

In other words, Gypsies embody the tensions that come with changing social and political environments as well as the traditional past. Not surprisingly, Gypsies have often been called upon to play the role of social buffer in other nations, mainly in Europe. In Egypt, the evolution of the representations of Gypsies mirrors social and political transformations. The rejection of Gypsies has happened at different times, taking different forms. I will focus on two of these: the eviction of the Ghawazi from Cairo by Muhammad Ali, and the slow dismissal of the *baladi*, embodied in Gypsiness during the Nasser and Sadat presidencies and visible in the cinematic representations of the Gypsies.

Muhammad Ali, Leila Ahmed suggests, wanted to make Egypt independent and modern. Modernization indicated a willingness to allow, even invite, Western influence, involvement, or dependence. Ahmed explains that "Muhammad Ali's policies adversely affected some women, particularly lower-class urban and rural women" (1992, 131, quoted in Karayanni 2006, 69). She does not mention the Ghawazi or their ban from Cairo. Morroe Berger suggests that Muhammad Ali may have been embarrassed not only by his economic backwardness, but also "of his popular art as well. Partly because of the bad impression they made on foreigners and partly because of pressure from religious leaders, Muhammad Ali barred the public dancing girls from the Cairo area in 1834" (1961, 30). According to Jennifer Fisher and Anthony Shay, in their book *When Men Dance: Choreographing Masculinities across Borders* (2009), in order to understand the motive for banning the Ghawazi we need to look mostly at the poor impression made on foreigners by the dancers, which also constitutes one of the early examples of imperial dismay over the production of kinesthetic art.

In that sense the ambiguous relationships, expectations, and representations built at the intersection of Eastern and Western perception are again embodied in the image of Gypsies, and in this specific case Ghawazi, whether they are 'true Gypsies' or not. The Ghawazi, as we saw with Flaubert specifically but also countless other Orientalists, represent the dominant fantasy of possession of the East, both in its savagery and in its sensuality. They are also constructed as archaic, as shown by some comments of travelers that lament the prostitution in Cairo: the dancers' art is morphed into vice. The relationship and the gaze of the Westerners helped to create that sentiment of cultural depravity and backwardness among Egyptians themselves, who associated modernity with economic development and cultural advancement, based on a sense of cultural dignity. In other words, "the Ghawazee were banned because, under the Western gaze, the quality of their art was questioned, thus turning their dancing into cultural embarrassment" (Fisher and Shay 2009, 320).

The expulsion of the Ghawazi from urban centers is therefore an initial symbolic rejection of what was perceived as immoral and, above all, archaic. If we look at this event in the light of our analysis of the rejection of Gypsies as embodiments of anachronism in the 1950s cinema, history seems to repeat its treatment of Gypsies on the national scene, as immoral and archaic, yet somehow embodying an essential part of the Orient that both seduces and repulses. This effect was felt not only by European Orientalists, but similarly by Egyptian modernists and (for different reasons) religious authorities.

Interestingly, the vice associated with artistic expression was constructed as a seductive and repulsive 'Eastern perversity' by Westerners, 'anachronism' by modernist Egyptians, and 'moral depravity' by religious authorities. With uncanny predictability, this view expresses the role of Gypsies as a buffer, as a scapegoat, or as the representation of any group's personal fantasy or fear—or, more probably, ambivalent sentiments between those two emotions. The actions derived from those emotions had concrete repercussions; Said has well documented how the artistic representations of the Orient made by Orientalists participated in the construction of a very tangible Orient. The simultaneous banishing from Cairo of the Ghawazi dancers and prostitutes by Muhammad Ali blurred the distinction between the two groups (Mostyn 2006, 144). Later on, all the Ghawazi and prostitutes were subjected to a homogenized treatment, and under the reigns of Said and Ismail prostitution returned openly to the streets of Cairo, while in 1866 a tax was imposed on all 'dancing girls.' There is a story that has been told by different travelers, and later by scholars, according to which Napoleon had four hundred Ghawazi beheaded and then thrown in sacks into the Nile. The explanation is that he wanted to put an end to the depravity of his soldiers in associating with these corrupting females. Whether the story is true or not, it reinforces the notion of depravity associated with Eastern women that the French wanted to control and sanitize, and it ascribes to the Ghawazi the role of corrupting prostitutes more than mere purveyors of entertainment.

The Ghawazi are at the intersection of the relation between Egypt and the West, by their objectification in Orientalist writings, but also in the meaning they acquire within the Egyptian context when interacting with

Western actors. As argued by Fisher and Shay, the Western gaze allows the Ghawazi to embody their "own tense dynamism and potency as well as that of the East. Therefore, they must be banished if order is to prevail over sexual anarchy in the emerging, modernized Egypt" (2009, 222).

About a century later, under Nasser, the promotion of a popular culture, as a manifestation of national pride as well as the representation of greater social equality, was translated into the embracing of traditional culture, while the subsequent neoliberal era associated with Sadat recreated social divides and relegated those traditions to marginalized social spheres (Rouchdy 2010). In the movies described earlier in this chapter, Gypsies first embodied traditions and nostalgia for a past that needed to be preserved in the name of nationalism. That past was not symbolic of backwardness, but of cultural authenticity with kin-based/tribal values that could be accepted, integrated, and even glorified. Gypsies represented characters that belong to the natural world, and they were contrasted with the new, modern national character that was societal and rational. The Gypsies' authenticity was illustrated by their sensual dances, their childish ability to deceive, and the animal beauty of the women, as if none of those characters were fully aware of their changing surroundings and still bore the heritage of a bucolic past. They lied easily, they passed for what they were not, they seemed to be naively trying to defeat rational social norms, even if they were less successful than they expected. Symbolically, in those early stages of national identity construction, the union between past and present was still conceivable, just as was marriage between a Gypsy and a non-Gypsy.

That situation, however, slowly became less acceptable and the connection to the past turned into a metaphor of regression and pollution. The contamination of archaic values became more and more threatening, to the point that it had to be abandoned. Perhaps Gypsies represent what Lou Charnon-Deutsch, in *The Spanish Gypsy: The History of a European Obsession*, called "a collective expression of national interest and anxieties" (2004, 242). They served as a buffer in the early stages of modernization and the eruption of a new imagined national identity, but once their characterization of a romantic, rural, magical past became unnecessary, the marriage could no longer happen, not even for authenticity purposes. We can then identify two concomitant phenomena: the shift in the character of the nation-state, with its tensions between modernity and tradition, and the transfer of Gypsies into other spheres of representation—not so much Egypt's past and traditions, but her new-found problems associated with modernity, a desire for greater homogeneity, and growing social inequalities.

Homogenization, the National, and the Foreigner

Timothy Mitchell reminds us that "the Nation is made out of projects in which the identity of the community as a modern national can be realized only by distinguishing what belongs to the nation from what does not, and by performing this distinction in particular encounters" (2002, 183). In opposition to the modern rational nation, what does not belong can be characterized not only as archaic, but also as foreign. The foreignness of Gypsies is both symbolic, because they are foreign to the new modern nation's norms and values, and literal, because they are perceived as not being true Egyptian nationals. We saw in earlier chapters that their foreignness has occasionally been reified, particularly under the influence of European Orientalists who transposed their own situating of European Roma to the Egyptian context. Perhaps one of the modernization projects was to inject 'otherness' into Gypsies and orientalize them, transferring the exhilarating power of othering the archaic weak from Europeans to modern Egyptians. Furthermore, illustrating the rather sorrowful process of disposing of the past can be less disturbing if those who embody that past are not only archaic but also alien. In that sense, Gypsies are perfect symbols of the unsalvageable past to be abandoned in the name of modernity, not only because they are linked to an older, more 'primitive' way of life, but also because they are constructed as eternal outsiders, which means that they are less intrinsically linked to the national psyche and they can be humiliated without the shame that would ensue if a 'true' member of community were rejected. They are sufficiently close and adequately far; they are sufficiently central to mean something significant, and appropriately marginal to be eliminated without triggering any internal wound to society. They perfectly embody the paradigmatic scapegoat, always (re)becoming foreign elements, despite their frequent centrality to the national construct, as described by the anthropologist Michael Jackson.

The scapegoat is an intimate stranger—someone who is simultaneously of us and not of us. When the scapegoat is, so to speak, sent
up in smoke, or sent packing to where we have decided he or she
properly belongs, we simply reverse the sequence of events whereby
he or she came to be among us in the first place. (2005, 46)

Lou Charnon-Deutsch shows how cinematic representations of Spanish Roma have changed, illustrating how they have come to be situated
intimately inside Spanish society. For instance, she explains, seeking solu-
tions to the problem of prejudice against the Roma was largely discouraged
under Franco, for it would have required an admission of entrenched class
inequities and racism. Therefore, in Franco's Spain, the 'Romantic Gypsy'
migrated to the entertainment industry, especially to cinema, where she
became the "darling of the post civil war Española films" (2004, 233). The
Gypsy icon eventually disappeared from Spanish art when art became
preoccupied with other social issues, such as AIDS, immigration, globalization, sexuality, drugs, youth culture, and urbanization. The last quarter
of the century returned to viewing Gypsies as a problem, especially for
educators, social services, and municipal governments.

Similarly, in Egypt, Gypsies first represented the exotic, as Dina Iordanova suggests in the introduction of the special issue of the journal
Framework, focused on "Romanies and Cinematic Representations."

The persistent cinematic interest in "Gypsies" has repeatedly raised
questions of authenticity versus stylization, and of patronization and
exoticization, in a context marked by overwhelming ignorance of the
true nature of Romani culture and heritage. (2003, 6)

The representations are constructed by outsiders who know nothing about Gypsies and may over-romanticize them, as we can see in the
beautiful naiveté of the Ghawazi Tamr Henna or other Ghagar female
characters, who are always beautiful and erotic. Eventually, when Gypsies stopped being the exotic and when society's problems led people
to focus more on other social issues, such as violence, urbanization, and
social inequalities, Gypsies reappeared under a different character, still

problematic, perhaps even more problematic: the socially marginalized. In contemporary movies, Gypsies represent Egypt's 'modern' problems: endemic poverty and exclusion, the uncontrollable growth of urban centers like Cairo or Alexandria, and crime. In other words, up until a certain point, social and sexual interaction between Gypsies and non-Gypsies was still possible—mostly via the females, who were savable and even *had* to be saved—but later on Gypsies became too impure even to be engaged in any kind of social relation that would not imply regression on the part of the non-Gypsy. They were relegated to the status of criminals, exaggerating their negative traits. They are reimagined, transferred from a bucolic vestige of the past to a social problem within the new, modern identity. This later image is certainly less erotically appealing and less consumable.

Female Representations

In discussing the representations of Gypsies in Egyptian cinema, a very crucial aspect is the appropriation of female Gypsies in particular. In the movies that depict a love story between Gypsies and non-Gypsies, and whether the marriage materializes or not, every single interethnic romantic encounter involves a Gypsy female and a non-Gypsy male. This relation is epitomized in the archetypical *Carmen* model:

> [A] melodrama, with a plotline usually evolving along inter-racial romance. The story usually revolves around a pure and spontaneous liaison between a Romani girl and a man from the main ("white") ethnic group whose relationship quickly gains mainstream disapproval and comes under attack, sometimes leading to tragic consequences. (Iordanova 2003, 8)

Why is it so rare for a story to depict a 'white' woman (or a woman belonging to the main ethnic group) falling in love with a Gypsy male? First, in all hegemonic/colonialist encounters, the dominant male *penetrates*, literally, the dominated society through their women. Second, males symbolically embody the future—modernity as well as individualism and rationalism—while women epitomize the past, a collectively organized world linked to traditions. Third, beautiful exotic women also concretize the fantasies of dominant males; they are mysterious, sensual, and animal. Finally, in subjugated groups women are the acceptable face of exoticism. While they are hyper-sexualized, the males tend to be emasculated.

According to Adriana Helbig, quoted by Ian Hancock:

> The alleged lack of morals among the Gypsies was vehemently applied to the critique of their sexual practices and their disregard for decency and respect toward the body, especially by Gypsy women. In much of the art, music, and literature of the 19th century, the female Gypsy in particular was characterized and stereotyped as free-spirited, strong, deviant, demanding, sexually arousing, alluring, and dismissive. This romantic construct of the Gypsy woman may be viewed in direct opposition to the proper, controlled, chaste, submissive woman held as the Victorian European ideal. This "oriental" fascination with the forbidden and taboo world of the *Gypsy* other in music is best characterized in the opera *Carmen*. (2004, 1)

In Egypt, the chaste Victorian European ideal for women is replaced by the social norms of modesty that prevail in conservative Egyptian society. Often, as noted by Okely, Gypsy women have been the object of the "dominant society's exotic and erotic projections and disorders" (1983, 201–202). In our case, we can replace Western, male-centered culture by 'dominant' or 'Egyptian.' The Egyptian male embodies the dominant role, a role of civilization, modernity, and focus on the future, but also focused on modesty and strong moral codes for women.

For the non-Gypsy, the Gypsy woman becomes a fantasized character and allows the imagining of the other, as Iulia Hasdeu (2008) suggests; the female Gypsy emblematizes sexual pleasure without legal liabilities or moral obligations, more specifically "unmarriageable but endowed with sexual attraction" (Okely 1983, 203). She also embodies the freedom in which the dominant male can indulge in his fantasy. Okely's read on that relationship of power is that it has to do with "the fatal combination of both gender and racial differences that, combined with the figure of the Gypsy woman, satisfy a lasting need for engaging the other that has been endemic to Western, male-centered culture" (1983, 241). Gypsy women may not have been considered to be fully Egyptian, and therefore the need for social protection of their chastity and morality is waived. Historically, they have been given more social freedom. For instance, as dancers the Ghawazi could be unveiled and provocative; they could show parts of their body, essentially because they were foreign bodies that could be exposed and did not need social and moral shelter.

The parallel with the relationship of nineteenth-century European men to non-white females is striking. For instance, erotic photography in the nineteenth century consisted largely of naked African or Asian women (Stenger 1931, cited in Hancock 2008). It is worth noting, as Ian Hancock does, that a tradition of double standards in terms of acceptable erotic representations continues in the practice of magazines such as *National Geographic*, which never include photos of unclothed white women (Hancock 2008). Hancock also reflects on how Gypsy females have come to represent sexuality and can be prized as such by white males, present in their "endless erotic fantasies," maybe because of their stereotypical freedom, boldness, and exoticism. Gypsy females become this 'exotic other' within Egypt, an embodiment of fantasies and an illustration of power relations between the 'other,' fixed and passive, and the Egyptian, modern and powerful. Similar power relations exist between males and females. The reason female Gypsies (or women from any other subordinated group) are more likely to be depicted as the acceptable partner in a cross-ethnic relation is because they represent the dominated and not the dominant member. The dominant member in the relation (male) also needs to belong to the dominant ethnic or cultural group (the Egyptian).

The male Gypsy is often nonexistent, depicted only as a fiancé who has been betrayed and who eventually, as in *Tamr Henna*, commits the vile act of stabbing his fiancée in the back. The Gypsy female, when she can, will often choose the (better) white/Egyptian male. In *Suad the Gypsy* she is 'saved' by a well-intentioned mayor who rescues her from her uncivilized and brutal clan, in the literary tradition of white men "saving the brown women from brown men" (Spivak 1999, 284). The female Gypsy marries the son of a rich landowner in *Wahiba, Queen of the Gypsies*; she is seduced in *Tamr Henna* by a wealthy Egyptian young man who convinces her to change her name to Yasmina, cut her hair, change her clothes, and literally abandon her old clan's ways. Again, Okely's analysis is useful in looking at the power relations at stake, from the perspectives of both gender and ethnicity: "Gypsy women are beautiful despite or in contrast to the projected inferiority of their Gypsy males, who are victims of more derogatory stereotypes and negative projections in a dominant patriarchal ideology" (1983, 202).

The emasculation of Gypsy males is acutely discernible in more recent movies. In *The Gypsy*, the main female character becomes the leader of her clan, which can be interpreted either as a very progressive illustration of gender equality or, more probably, as the demotion of the Gypsy male. In the patriarchal Egyptian society, female leadership may be more of a commentary on the weakness of the males, incapable of leading their peers, than on the strength of females. In *Women's Prison*, women are portrayed as dominant, having appropriated symbolically masculine roles: they smoke, they work outside of their home, and they delegate the child-rearing tasks to their devoted and weak husbands. In one of the scenes, the main character comes home from 'work' (stealing a bag in a women's bathroom) and reprimands her husband, who is carrying the child on his hip. She is angry for a variety of reasons, one of them being that he went outside without her permission. He tirelessly tries to calm her down, and finally lights her cigarette with care and reverence. The typical gender roles are inverted in such an extreme and caricatured manner that both males and females are ridiculed. The males come across as further emasculated, and the females are situated in the dark realm of deception; they have become natural thieves and have been stripped of their archetypical characteristics, such as animal feminity or mysterious beauty.

As always with Gypsy representations, each character is exaggerated, becoming symbolically dehumanized, a mere caricature. This process tends to serve a moral purpose: the caricature embodies the undesirable other against which the desirable self should be contrasted. In most movies female Gypsies are a metaphor or a symbol. They are never represented as real human beings. They are overly beautiful and sensual, or exceedingly old or bossy. They represent depravity or illuminate gender relations; they serve as a mirror to reflect the creation of a national identity or social change and poverty.

Gypsies are not only rarely represented as human beings, but they have also rarely had the chance to portray themselves. Typically they are left to the descriptions of Orientalists or explorers or scholars. Interest in Gypsies has raised the questions of "authenticity versus stylization, and of patronization and eroticization, in a context marked by overwhelming ignorance of the true nature of Romani culture and heritage" (Iordanova 2003, 6). 'Knowledge' of Gypsies is usually stereotypical, based on representations of Gypsies as irresponsible, unethical, disregarding conventions of law and morality. In many European countries, Roma have started to fight these stereotypical representations by engaging themselves in production of knowledge and in artistic representations of their group, but this has not been the case in Egypt, where Gypsies are not involved in any production of representation of their group. The difference with Europe, however, is that until recently most actors who have portrayed Gypsies were not Gypsies themselves. In Egypt, it may have happened that the belly dancers who portrayed Gypsies were themselves of Dom origins, possibly because they needed the dancing skills to engage in the role. It is, however, very difficult to know how many actresses or dancers were Gypsies, simply because, unlike in Europe, Gypsy roots are not acknowledged in Egypt, partly because ethnic affiliation is less important than nationality, and partly because the Dom are ignored. Naima Akef, for instance, was born in Tanta and her family owned a circus, the Akef Circus, but nowhere are her Gypsy origins even alluded to. Kouka is also an actress–dancer, but it is impossible to verify whether she is Ghagar. Amina Rizk, like Akef, was born in Tanta, and like Akef, her possible Gypsy connections are not known.

Depicting the Other
Gypsies in the popular imagination and in cinema have had the role of the other. They have also embodied a symbolic representation of social tensions between past and present, archaic and modern, sexual and intellectual—a complex national identity torn between the existence of cultural subgroups and the desire for homogeneity, a nostalgic memory of the past and the reality of the problems of urban poverty and social exclusion. This situation sadly mirrors the trajectory of Gypsies in the

European imagination, where in the eighteenth and nineteenth centuries, with the advance of bureaucratic rationalism, they started migrating from exoticized stereotypes to new ones borrowed from the culture of poverty and came to represent cultural decline, degeneracy, and criminality.

The seductiveness exercised by the figure of the other often becomes encapsulated into a special concern with women. And as postcolonialist theorists from Edward Said to Gayatri Spivak have emphasized, the other is always gendered (Hasdeu 2008, 347). In the cinema of the 1950s, female Gypsies were represented as sensual, promiscuous, dangerous seductresses. However, this assumed looseness of female Gypsies is inconsistent with some of the more recent research conducted on female Gypsies, particularly by Okely, who focused largely on the question of cleanliness. She does not talk about the Dom in the Egyptian context, but mostly about Western Gypsies; nonetheless, she points out some contradictions that can be applied equally well to the Dom. In particular, within the community, women have to be "cautious with other men. Yet nearly every day she is expected to go to 'enemy territory'" (Okely 1975, 58–59) as a peddler or fortune-teller.

Dom women are usually constructed as seductive, to be described and saved in relation to the non-Dom world, in their interactions with what Okely calls the "enemy," as if it is only in that interaction that the female Gypsy has an existence and a purpose. As a beautiful dancer or as a thief, the female is the most significant character in all the movies, and she is mostly represented in relation to the dominant society.

3

UNCROSSABLE BOUNDARIES?

Habiba is a middle-aged Egyptian woman who has worked with Ghagar for over twenty years. Her tiny office is situated in a poor area of downtown Cairo called Sayyida Zaynab. She offers Ghagar and other impoverished urban dwellers of the area micro-loans to finance their small business projects. During our first meeting, she introduced herself as someone with deep understanding of the Ghagar's ways, 'wise' in the Goffmanian sense of the term, an initiated intermediary who interacts with the stigmatized, a "person who [is] normal but whose specific situation has made them intimately privy to the secret life of the stigmatized individual and sympathetic with it, and who find themselves accorded a measure of acceptance, a measure of courtesy membership in the clan" (Goffman 2009, 28). While we were talking, she held a small bracelet made of white shells, the kind of bracelet that Ghagar fortune-tellers use to capture the spirit of their customers and foresee their destiny. It had been given to her by one of "her" Ghagar, she explained proudly, a symbol of the trust and respect that seemed to have been established between her and the outcast community. She explained that it had taken her a while to gain the Ghagar's trust but that she now felt respected.

> They will not harm me. I can go and see them and feel quite com-
> fortable now. I understand their ways, and I know what I can do or
> not around them. It takes a lot of time and a lot of practice because
> they don't like to open up to foreigners. They always feel like

they have to be careful. They fear the police, they fear the social workers . . . they are very suspicious of whoever wants to approach them. But with me, well, now, it is all right.

Once she established her position as an initiated intermediary, she engaged in a series of observations about the Ghagar's way of life. Despite the trust and the understanding, the Ghagar, in Habiba's eyes, were still very *other*. She slowly started to dissociate herself from her experience as an individual who had gradually been able to break some of the distrust of the group and instead focused on the collective differences between 'us' (Egyptians) and 'them' (Ghagar).

The Ghagar, they are always fighting, you can see it. They all have scars on their faces. The truth is, they are very violent . . . they have hot blood and always end up fighting. And their kids are like that too, even when they are very young. And the women, oh the women . . . they scream, oh, the women are so loud. We, Egyptians, usually, we don't like to deal with them, because they are scary. And they don't like us. In fact, they fear being known too well.

Shaima, another social worker who had worked for more than twenty years with Ghagar in Cairo, reflected on her relations with members of the group in similar terms.

Well, I know them well. I have dealt with them for many years. They respect me. They don't scare me any more, but still, I can't help but think that they are so different from us . . . . They would never marry someone who is not Ghagar. They like to stay together . . . like a tribe. They all have their leaders. They don't mix.

Both social workers position themselves as intermediaries. As individual professionals they have been able to establish enough trust to engage in basic business relations with the Ghagar; however, in their collective perceptions, they construct the Ghagar as a group which is impenetrable and alien.

Magdy, a middle-aged Egyptian man, has been dealing with the Ghagar in Alexandria for about thirty years. At one point, he owned a small Peugeot van and collected Coke bottles from Ghagar families that he then sold to factories for recycling. He explained that he would give the Ghagar a weekly 150 Egyptian pounds in return for Coke bottles that he would sell for five Egyptian pounds: "The way I had set up my business was based on trust. I gave them the money in advance, at the beginning of the week, and then they gave me the bottles. It was foolish; you cannot base anything on trust with those people." He eventually abandoned the business, after a few "problems" working with Ghagar, including non-fulfillment of responsibilities from some Ghagar families. On one occasion, I met someone from one of these families; Magdy was present, looking unhappy, while the elder daughter was staring at him. Finally she said, "Stop giving me that attitude, Magdy, I know you are still mad about your 150 pounds, but get over it. My mother did so much business with you, she made you rich, so we can keep this as a little commission!" She laughed and Magdy rolled his eyes. After we left her house, he told me: "You see, they cannot be trusted and they will always find excuses, and then on top of it, they make fun of you, too." Magdy presents himself as 'wise,' to the extent that he is occasionally thought to be a Ghagar by some of his non-Ghagar friends—which he denies vehemently. Because of his former business relations, he feels as if he knows their ways; however, the relationship appears to remain mostly economic. While interactions sometimes *almost* go beyond professional relations, they always stop before a threatening intimacy could be created. For instance, Magdy has been invited to a few Ghagar weddings and funerals, but he has always declined.

> I really don't want to go to their parties. But one day, one rich guy passed away, a very rich guy who, of course, used to be a thief. It is their only way to become rich . . . so with my van, I drove his son to all the relatives' homes to let them know and invite them to the funeral, and then they invited me, and of course, I did not go. But that day, I also had to go and visit my brother who lives near the place where the funeral took place, so I saw it. And what I saw . . . well . . . there was so much wealth, I swear, it was the most beautiful funeral ever. There

were many tables, and on each table, there were packs of tissues and a pack of cigarettes, and a lot of food, including meat, and people were there, like a big party. The Ghagar, you see, they like to show off. It can be a funeral, it can be a wedding. What they like is to show off, to impress everyone. That's the way they are.

Magdy did not physically attend the funeral but he managed to witness it from the safety of his brother's house, which allowed him to remain on the margins of the Ghagar's intimacy, while satisfying his curiosity. He was then able to pass judgment on the Ghagar, who "like to show off" and use an occasion such as a funeral to try and impress others, which he thought was "vulgar."

Similarly, Habiba provided an example of negotiation on the margins of the Ghagar's intimacy when she described how, although she had built enough trust to occasionally be invited into Ghagar homes, she was always kept at the entrance, symbolically on the periphery of their homes. She nonetheless was able to peek in and grasp a few images.

I could not see really well, but those rooms, they looked very poor and dirty. They didn't have real carpets, but some kind of plastic thing on the ground, and from what I could see they had very high beds, and under the bed some curtains. I understood that the children slept under the parents' bed.

It was not clear from her narrative whether the Ghagar did not invite her in, or whether she decided not to go inside after being invited in; most likely both parties felt more comfortable with this intermediary arrangement of managed proximity.

I have been welcomed into Ghagar homes. On many occasions, I received a phone call a few hours after leaving, and the person who had hosted me invariably expressed worries about the "bad things" that could be triggered by my visit. They were afraid that welcoming a foreigner, both non-Ghagar and non-Egyptian, into their homes would bring them unwanted visibility from their neighbors or the police. They may also have felt that they revealed too much of their intimacy, often very candidly, during our discussions, which, upon second thought, may have looked ill-considered. The fear was both practical (the authorities) and emotional (having opened up too much), as if the short encounter had put them in a position of vulnerability, as if the strong boundaries erected around their group had been temporarily softened.

Outsiders' depictions of Ghagar tend to illustrate the outsiders' manufacture of fragments of boundaries around the community. The idea of boundaries to explain both the positioning and the disengagement of Gypsies with respect to the wider society has been used extensively (Holloway 2005; Mayall 2004). The boundaries are often presented as constructed by both sides. The outsiders are willing to 'other' Gypsies; David Mayall reflects on how the group is shaped by "the fixing of boundaries; the use of labels and the meanings given to them; the nature of information and knowledge about the group, derived from stereotyping and experience, characteristics of the group itself, in terms of size, location and visibility; external factors such as the socio-economic and political environment" (2004, 12).

Gypsies themselves also use boundaries as a means of protection and survival. Okely (1983) identified the ethnic boundaries between Gypsies and non-Gypsies as a particular set of traditions or rites that were very specific to Gypsies and served to separate them from non-Gypsies. She emphasized the internal construction, contending that the most important means of identification of Gypsies is self-ascription, which allows Gypsies to be defined by themselves, instead of being subjugated to an imposed identity. Liégeois (1987) articulates the opposition to dominant culture as a building block to Gypsy identity, not so much in terms of the rites and traditions, but in showing how their otherness allows Gypsies to foster a sense of solidarity and cements their identity, in opposition to mainstream norms and the usual hostility of the majority. The tensions between the inside and outside architecture, between practices of social exclusion by society and of self-exclusion by Gypsies, seem somehow to create a balance of power between the different actors (Bhopal and Myers 2008, 106).

Where the power originated, however, is still arguable, and the self-preservation of the excluded group, by reinforcing mechanisms of rigidification of the boundaries, may be the response to an initial social rejection. Nonetheless, once the boundaries are created, the processes become interactive and the relative strength of the push or pull factors fluctuate on each side of the boundary. At times, self-exclusion may be stronger than the outside othering, and vice versa. Historically, the Roma in Europe have been either marginalized and excluded from society or forcibly assimilated through systematic destruction of their culture and identity. At times, they have leaned toward incorporation of the dominant society's norms and values, smoothly disappearing into the mainstream. Other times, they have forcefully rejected it, rigidifying their identity or instrumentalizing it. Often these practices alternate, with outsiders and insiders playing the role of dance partners, each gauging what practices are appropriate and when things go so far as to threaten each side's integrity or safety.

In many studies of European Roma, their difference from the mainstream is embodied in the use of the Romani language and the nomadic habitus. Language externalizes the Roma, and linguistics has linked Romani to Sanskrit. This anchors the Romas' origins in India, which, while alienating them, also made sense in a normative environment that promotes the nation-state as unit of analysis (Acton and Mundi 1997). Nomadism positioned them in an anti-national sphere, nomadic practices being seen as anti-national, since European nations have built their ideal norms of belonging on sacredness as well as uniqueness (Brubaker 1990) and fixity. Language and nomadism are often more situated in the area of perceptions of differences than in tangible reality, and therefore become components of the construction of difference. Liégeois (1987) points out that nomadism was absolutely not central to the Romani lifestyle. The use of language as a marker of identity has also been critiqued recently as not being a stable indicator of identity.

The contextualization of boundary construction in Egypt first decentralizes nomadism, as it is not represented as an alienating element; large portions of the national population have engaged in nomadism, so this practice is not intrinsically associated with foreignness or with anti-nationalism. Undoubtedly nomadism has come to be more and more associated with archaism, largely under the influence of Western colonial powers, as noted by Dawn Chatty: "Assumptions and suppositions drawn from ideas of backwardness of nomadic people were held by colonial powers and the emerging nation-states of the region in the mid-20th century. Later they also came to be integrated into the philosophy and guidance of major development aid agencies and other international organizations of the time" (2006, 2). It has not, however, served as an anchor to the creation of difference between Dom and non-Dom.

The Dom language, formally called Domari, or more often Sim in Egypt, also has not been formalized as a marker of foreign belonging, in part because it may not be used extensively by different Dom tribes, and also because no formal linguistic study of different forms of Domari spoken in Egypt has been undertaken to assess the Doms' origins.

Finally, the Dom are seldom identifiable in urban settings, where they do not customarily fulfill the stereotypical role of itinerant merchants, providers of folk medicine, or entertainers. They dress like the majority of Egyptians. Many women wear black *abaya*s and black headscarves. They speak Arabic, and they are usually Muslim (Holmes 2002; Marsh 2000; Thomas 2000). Nonetheless, the creation of boundaries takes place in a ubiquitous way by emphasizing the intrinsic inability of Ghagar to integrate Egyptian norms and values, or their slightly inaccurate practice of cultural or religious conventions. This chapter will focus on how different fragments of boundaries are erected and reinforced from the outside by non-Ghagar, in the religious, cultural, 'racial,' linguistic, spatial, and occupational spheres.

Religious Boundaries

The Doms' Muslim religious affiliation does not foster a sense of proximity with the predominantly Muslim Egyptian population. Non-Ghagar generally emphasize that Ghagar are Muslims "out of necessity," and not because they are truly embracing their faith, which discounts the possibility that there may be some truly religious Muslims among the Dom of Egypt. As Kevin Holmes notes: "One local man told us that he did not think they were very strong Muslims or that they cared about religion. It was our experience that his opinion is widely held by the local people" (2002). The tendency by non-Ghagar to downplay the religiousness of the Ghagar is tangible, both in different journalistic accounts of the culture and religion of the Dom and in the narrative of Egyptians with whom I have spoken. In Cairo and Alexandria, many interlocutors explained the Ghagar's lack of religiousness in a utilitarian manner: they are Muslims because they have to be, as Gypsies often adopt the dominant religion of the place where they have settled. Holmes (2002) notes:

> Many studies of both the Roma and the Dom report that in an effort to fit into a community, the Gypsy will outwardly accept the host country's religion. Considering the lengths at which the Dom in Egypt attempt to hide their ethnicity, one should not be surprised to discover that the Dom, at least outwardly, practice Islam.

In general, Gypsies have been perceived as having "no firm religious convictions or perhaps no religious belief at all" (Acton and Mundi 1997, 160). Occasionally, their lack of religiousness is presented as another illustration of their stubborn refusal to integrate norms, or even as a deliberate and provocative way to distort them. One interlocutor from Cairo remarked:

> They are not . . . how can I say . . . practicing Islam correctly. For instance, they would not wash themselves before praying. I doubt they would even pray five times every day—they just sort of pretend they are Muslim.

When first presented with this question, a social worker who works with young Ghagar laughed that "all Egyptians are Muslim but not religious," almost creating a space of shared identity between Ghagar and non-Ghagar in that admitted lack of sincere religiosity. However, after giving it more thought, he quickly added: "Well, not really. The Ghagar, they are really not religious, you know they are not educated, they are not cultured, they would not even know how to pray!" Magdy noted that he had never seen a Ghagar going to a mosque because "they love life and not religion." He added that if Ghagar ever went on the Hajj, it would be with the exclusive intent of robbing pilgrims. Many interlocutors related scandalous stories of Ghagar women going to Mecca in Saudi Arabia and engaging in blasphemous practices, such as "robbing pilgrims" or "being naked under their *abayas*" and finally "dancing naked in Mecca." When asked how they had obtained that information, the answers would be along the lines of: "Everyone knows about it. The only reason Ghagar go to Mecca is to behave badly. There cannot be another reason!" Robbing pilgrims, very much like kidnapping children in European narratives of Gypsies' misbehavior, embodies abnormal and blasphemous practices, as well as the ultimate disrespect for the most sacred behavior that a Muslim can engage in, the Hajj. Some interlocutors suggested that Ghagar women covered their heads to hide their blond hair or their facial tattoos, or to look pious to arouse sympathy while begging, but not out respect for the Muslim custom. It would seem almost impossible for any Ghagar to be considered a genuine Muslim; they are automatically denied the chance to be sincere, and are depicted as ignoring their religious duty or using religion for criminal ends.

In the area of Cairo by the Sayyida Zaynab Mosque, many beggars are often grouped, waiting for the charity of worshippers. Among them, female Ghagar have established their territory; however, local residents often identify them and question their motives, noting that they beg by the mosque despite being themselves "fake Muslims," or that they mostly "conduct business" around the mosque. One of the beggars was singled out by a Sayyida Zaynab resident, who described her as "one of the most dangerous women in the neighborhood." According to him, the woman would confront other beggars, Ghagar and non-Ghagar alike, and ask for a percentage of their earnings; she would threaten other beggars and forbid them from begging by the mosque. "She heads a gang of thugs and everyone is scared of them. They are all Ghagar thugs, of course."

Other narratives illustrate the perception of the Ghagars' essential inappropriateness, which automatically prevents them from being accepted as true Muslims. One interlocutor from Sayyida Zaynab declared:

They are all dirty thieves. How can they even pray? It is not in their nature to pray. It is not in their blood. They have dance and crime in the blood, and that is all.

Another said:

> I have never seen a Ghagar pray, not even on a Friday. I know they
> don't go to the mosque on Friday. They have other things to do.
> Even us, even if we don't pray every day, we still make the effort to
> go to the mosque on Friday, but they don't, they don't even care
> to do that!

A third interlocutor asserted that Ghagar did not fast during Ramadan because "they don't have the will to do it . . . and also they cannot stop
smoking, cigarettes or their drugs. So just they cannot do Ramadan."

The practice of palmistry, attributed to female Gypsies, also marks
them as reprehensible in terms of religious norms. Predicting the future
is against conventional versions of Islam. The practice also situates them
in a threatening zone of interaction with mythical creatures such as the
djinn, which many Muslims denounce as a pagan intrusion into Islam.
When I first talked to Salima, a middle-aged woman from the Delta
region, she said that she knew of Ghagar, mostly the fortune-tellers, but
she had never been interested because she did not believe in "all that
magic." In another meeting, she admitted that a "very long time ago"
she had used the services of a Ghagar fortune-teller because she was
engaged to a man she did not like.

> I did not know what to do . . . the only thing left was to go and see
> one of them. I went to her house, and then she asked me to speak
> into a shell, but I had to speak without making any noise. I had to
> say the name of my mother, the name of that man, and his mother's
> name. I said it very quietly, but then, that woman, she repeated the
> names, she had guessed them! Then, I had to cut my nails and put
> them in a small bag in my bra. I had to go and leave the bag behind
> a mosque, that is all she said. She also said I should not go to the
> bathroom with the nails in my bra. But I forgot and I went there.
> Then the bag disappeared. I was so scared. I went back to the lady
> and she had the bag, it had come back to her! She gave it to me
> and said not to go to the bathroom again, so I did not, but in the

evening, I left the bag behind the mosque, like she told me. And then, well . . . it worked. We did not get married. Only Ghagar can do that. It is because of the djinn. That is how the Ghagar do it.

Later, she added:

The Ghagar, they can do a lot of things, like magic, because they can get in touch with the djinn. They call the djinn and then the djinn work with them. That is how they can know things. But if we Egyptians call the djinn, it can be very dangerous. They never leave.

Salima then explained that she suspected that her own father had called the djinn one time, and that they had not left him—"They stayed in him, in his legs"—explaining that he had become paralyzed and died shortly after. While initially Salima had rejected any encounter with fortune-tellers on the basis of her disbelief in magic, which is a very common narrative, she eventually admitted having appealed to them because of the desperateness of her situation. The episode occurred many years before she told me the story, and yet she did not share it very easily, perhaps because of the shame associated with having to resort to such a strategy and the fear of what she believed had happened. She tried to explain the event in semi-rational terms, stating clearly her motive for turning to the power of djinn, which are known creatures in Islamic mythology, and then reflecting on the dangers that they can bring to someone. The Ghagar, in her narrative, fulfill the role of the option of last resort. The Ghagar had also, in this narrative, transgressed norms by fraternizing with the djinn, a practice that would kill any other 'normal' individual, like her father.

Ghagar are described as situated on the margins of the acceptable, which is unacceptable in terms of morality but becomes pragmatically tolerable when a situation demands it. In that sense, they embody the concept of 'useful pariahs,' fulfilling a role rooted in impure power acquired by breaking conventions and placing themselves in marginalized, unprotected zones, or as described by Barth: "The [pariah groups] are groups actively rejected by the host population because of behaviours or characteristics positively condemned though often useful in some specific, practical way" (1998, 31). Gypsies correspond to the Simmelian notion of the stranger, simultaneously far away and close: the stranger is among us and may appear as one of us, but the stranger is also slightly absent and never completely one of us. In an environment where religious affiliation is crucial, not being accepted as a truly religious person is marginalizing. While Gypsies are Muslim, cluster around mosques, and participate in *mulid*s—the very central, albeit occasionally frowned-upon, religious festivals—in all these activities they are nonetheless perceived to be slightly foreign to the normative environment, or to distort the social norms from within, by utilizing religion and sacredness for antithetical objectives.

Although Nabil Sobhi Hanna provides an in-depth study of many aspects of Ghagar social life, their economic, cultural, and marital practices, and their means of social control, he puts little emphasis on the religious aspects of their community. He presents their approach to religion mostly as a means of integration. "Trying to appear as natives, they embraced the official religion and lived as the natives around them lived" (1982, 11). He also believes that religion helps to explain the underdevelopment of the Ghagars' own language: "As Moslems, the Ghagar must recite their prayers in Arabic. Thus in religion as in economic and social life there is little opportunity for this group to further develop their own language" (1982, 96). Their true spiritual beliefs, he writes, are mostly linked to supernatural phenomena: "The Ghagar share with other villagers around them many folk beliefs, and related fears concerning demons and fairies, envy, the evil eye and birth marks" (1982, 88).

Unsurprisingly, other Middle Eastern Gypsies are also represented as 'flawed' Muslims. A study of Turkish Roma shows that "the nomadic Romanalar assert that they are Muslim. Despite this, they frequently manifest different syncretic forms of religion, which have nothing to do with Islam" (Oprisan 2006, 165). Elin Strand notes that the contempt for Gypsies' syncretism is based upon a series of "value judgments that place monotheism in a superior position to that of religious syncretism" (2006, 45). Gül Özatesler, in his study of Turkish Gypsies, summarizes: "Gypsies have always been suspected of not being true Muslims. Although they followed Islamic religious traditions, some Turks did not accept them as sincere" (2012, 86). While most Middle Eastern Gypsies are Muslim, their religion is discarded as insincere, either because it is syncretized, or because it still contains aspects of unholy practices, or because it is used for other motives (Mecca pilgrim robberies, charity from mosques). Whether or not those contain some portion of truth, what is striking is that the perception of the outsiders automatically denies any individual spirituality to the members of the group, thus constructing the group as homogeneously impious and amoral.

The implication of religious exclusion in Egypt is particularly severe because of the central role that religion plays in Egyptian national identity. The fact that religion is of such little importance to the Ghagar, according to the outsiders' perceptions, further alienates them in the Egyptian environment, where religion has been historically constructed as the reference point for determining minorities. Exclusion on the basis of religion not only marginalizes Gypsies morally, as religion is a gauge of normative social morality, but also politically, since religion is the building block of group creation and differentiation within the Egyptian national community.

Cultural Boundaries

The knowledge and practice of normative cultural practices are generally denied to Gypsies. The ethnomusicologist Kevin Holmes, in an account of his encounters with the Ghagar, mentions the concept of shame.

> An Egyptian will say that the Gypsy does not understand 'eeb. Habits or mannerisms that do not reflect this worldview distinguish the Dom from the Egyptian population. This was illustrated while driving through an integrated Dom and Egyptian community. We observed a woman riding down a road on a donkey loaded with green plants. Our knowledgeable guide confirmed her identity as a Gypsy given that she was unveiled and unescorted. This worldview difference helps to explain why Dom and Egyptian families, although living next to each other, will not formally visit each other. (Holmes 2002)

The boundaries are erected by formulating negative judgments on behaviors and stressing the incompatibility of 'their' values and 'ours.' For instance, Habiba suggested that the Ghagar did not treat their children properly—yet another breaking of an implicit norm, parental love.

> Children in Ghagar families, they go or don't go to school depend-
> ing on their parents' occupation. If the parents have a trade, they
> learn the trade, metalworking, craft . . . if they are thieves, well, they
> learn that trade, too. If they are beggars, then they go to school, and
> beg after school.

Going to school does not, however, lead to upward mobility, as she
quickly added that "often parents cut their [children's] ears off to have
them beg better." She expressed her concerns for the well-being of children, because Ghagar "do not really care for their children. In fact, I don't
know if they live with their own children, or if children are exchanged
between families." When asked for the basis of that assumption, she
replied matter-of-factly: "They are like that . . . . They have their own
ways that we can't understand." The same narrative is found among other
Egyptian interlocutors who have engaged in relationships with Ghagar.
A young Alexandrian coffeeshop waiter whose family lives near a Ghagar
neighborhood declared that "Gypsies exchange their children between
families." This is also Shaima's perception: "If someone does not have a
girl, they can get her from their cousins."

The abnormal relationship to children is often utilized to marginalize the Ghagar, embodied in accusations of not raising their own properly
or stealing other people's. The belief that Gypsies are child thieves has
been and still can be found in Egypt. According to the Orientalist Captain Newbold, "The Arabs and Copts charge [Ghagar] with kidnapping
children, but this they strenuously deny, as well as the common accusa-
tion of eating their cats and dogs, and other animals held in abhorrence
by Moslems" (Newbold 1856, 293). Tales of child swapping and kidnapping reflect both the myth of the group homogeneity (children belong to
the group in general as a homogeneous entity), and the belief in absolute
distinction that the dominant group tends to hold with respect to the
pariah minority (Nord 2006). Furthermore, the myth of kidnapped children is representative of the apprehension about intermingling, which is
more reassuring than the specter of intimacy and closeness to the group.
The only conceivable interactions are contrived: children are bought,
exchanged, or snatched. The boundary is drawn based on the impossibility

of consenting interactions between Ghagar and non-Ghagar. Those tales contribute to alienating them by forging them as scary and threatening silhouettes, and provide a basis for socializing non-Ghagar children in the fear of the Gypsy. One interviewee reflected on the fact that since his childhood he had felt "this lingering fear about Gypsies, I mean, we all heard the stories of kidnapping . . . that was very scary." A small shop owner from Alexandria recalled:

> When I was a child [in the village], the Ghagar would come in small carts pulled by donkeys. In the back of the cart, they had puppets and they would do shows near our school. Many children would skip school to go and see the puppets, but people said that sometimes, the Ghagar would tell you to go in the back of their cart to see how the puppets worked, and then they would go away with their cart, taking away the child. One day, I went to see them after school. When my mother found out she hit me. It was the first time she hit me so hard, she was so scared. I never went to see them again.

The way the other is constructed outside the boundaries is sometimes contradictory, as the outsider, exclusively constructing from the external side of the boundary, is not grasping the intrinsic mechanisms motivating the practices he observes and objectifies. The intimate nature of that other is established in a paradoxical desire to go deep inside its essence, while using superficial judgments based on the objectifier's perspective. Egyptians who come into close contact with Ghagar tend to say that they "stick to themselves" and refrain from social interaction. Consequently, belonging to the group becomes their main identity, the root of their nature. At the same time, many of my interlocutors noted that "every single Ghagar" dreamed about leaving the group, and once they had managed to do so, they would never turn back. I was provided with profuse examples illustrating that "some Ghagar" had gotten rich and managed to leave the ghetto; he or she had then ignored his/her former Ghagar peers, and changed name. Occasionally, a Ghagar belly dancer married up and forgot her past and her people. However, the wealth and position obtained by this change of status were described as polluted by the fact

that Ghagar could only "become rich dishonestly" (for males) or "amor-
ally" (for females, usually associated with entertainment and prostitution).
The perception is that they would still remain dishonest or amoral in
essence. A student who had interacted with Ghagar communities as part
of a research project on impoverished Coptic communities in downtown
Cairo explained:

> The Ghagar's dream is to get out of that community. . . . I mean
> they are not proud to be Ghagar . . . they hate it! And as soon as
> they get out, of course they never go back; you know it is like the
> nouveaux riches, they forget their roots. I heard of a guy who had
> changed his name to sound less Ghagar, he pretends he doesn't
> even recognize his brothers, he pretends he doesn't even know
> what a Ghagar is . . . Like they play the rich and so on, they want to
> forget where they come from.

I was also provided with some contrasting accounts. Magdy, for
instance, mentioned that affluent Ghagar always kept in touch with their
community, and when they held weddings and funerals, they made sure
to invite "all the other Ghagar"—mostly, he added, "to show off and to
show they became successful and also because non-Ghagar really don't
want to go to their weddings anyway." These contradictory interpretations mainly reflect how outsiders perceive the group, from their own
point of view: belonging is ascribed and one can never leave the group,
one can never stop being a Ghagar. However, simultaneously the group
symbolizes a polluted place where no one would wish to remain deliberately, hence the claims about the Ghagars' willingness to leave and never
go back. Outsiders construct a group that represents how they position
themselves vis-à-vis its members: both excluded and disgusted. Those
contradictions, within the same narrative, demonstrate that outsiders
do not seek consistency in their descriptions of Ghagar, who seem situated beyond the need for logical explanations. At the same time, these
blatant contradictions embody the extent to which Gypsies are seen as
representations of a rejected behavior, or parcels of rejected behaviors,
which may be contradictory.

The perceived lack of origins is another dimension that serves to alienate, particularly in a society where roots, like religious affiliation, are such an essential part of collective and individual identities. There are striking paradoxes in the narratives of interlocutors. While the student quoted above noted that "[Ghagar are] like the nouveaux riches, they forget their roots," the roots he alludes to are mostly socially defined and used in the specific essentialization of their poverty. Ghagar are often described as having no history and not belonging anywhere. Even if they have supposedly been living in Egypt for more than a thousand years, they are still ahistorical outsiders. One interlocutor reflected on the lack of history of the Ghagar, perceived as a chip on their shoulders.

They have no history, they don't know who they are, they don't know their roots, they are like the Kurds . . . they know they are not Arabs. They make all these secrets because, in fact, they are embarrassed not to know where they come from.

For some interlocutors, Ghagar come from 'elsewhere,' which may be outside of Egypt or an elsewhere situated within Egypt; for instance, some suggest that they may come from the desert, or from somewhere in Upper Egypt. The idea of desert origins injects some essential differences into their identity: they cannot produce because "they are not farmers like people from the Nile Valley;" they resort to violence because those are the ways in hostile environment such as deserts.

'Racial' Boundaries

While Egyptian Ghagar are usually hard to identify in term of physical differences, since they wear typical Egyptian clothing and speak Arabic, interlocutors were often convinced of their ability to identify Ghagar based on their physical characteristics. Their descriptions typically highlighted a variety of 'Gypsy traits,' ranging from "they look mean and scary," "they have many scars," and "their eyes are threatening" to the supposed sensuality and animal charisma of young Ghagar women. For Habiba, "All Ghagar have big scars on their faces, they always fight with knives." The scarred faces are often used as the quintessential description of male Ghagars, proof of their innate desire for fights.

Racial and class descriptions are intersected, as Habiba reveals. "They also have lower-class people's habits," she explains. "It is the way they behave, they are very disgusting, they are dirty and they use their children to steal and beg. They do not wash their homes or their hands before or after eating." This enduring perception, or at least the naming of Gypsies as 'dirty,' seems in some part directed at disrupting the confusing visual marker of the Gypsy's potential invisibility. Bhopal and Myers (2008) show that while Gypsies in Europe are somehow white (particularly in comparison with other racialized groups), this whiteness, which is the majority color, needs to be modified by a layer of dirt, which provides Gypsies with an additional coloring and constructs a visible physiological differentiation from the majority population. Creating physical or biological differences serves to reassure by ensuring that the pariah is indeed different from 'us' and cannot be visually confused with a normal member of society. The stigma has to be recognizable in order to be real.

Any part of the Gypsy's body can be used to achieve the reification of difference. The social worker Shaima explains that the Gypsy eye is recognizable because it is "dark and scary, with a certain something in it." Not only are the eyes themselves, as organs, singled out, but also, metaphorically, the Gypsy eye seems to be linked to the sacred and over-utilized concept of 'evil eye,' a folk belief (widespread but by no means universal) according to which the gaze of one individual at another may cause problems to a second individual or to an object belonging to that individual (Dundes 1981). Men and women alike are capable of casting spells, which they can then also break, usually in exchange for a financial contribution. Many fortune-tellers, knowing their audience, mention the 'evil eye' or some kind of 'jealous eye' in their predictions, which they usually offer to cure. The 'Gypsy eye' goes back a long way, as this 1841 description of the Spanish Gypsy by George Henry Borrow illustrates.

> There is something remarkable in the eye of the Romany . . . but the eye of the Gitano is neither large nor small, and exhibits no marked difference in its shape from the eye of the common caste.

Its peculiarity consists chiefly in a strange staring expression, which to be understood must be seen, and in a thin glaze, which steals over it when in repose, and seems to emit phosphoric light. (1846, 307)

Another Cairo interlocutor explained that he knew instinctively who was a Gypsy. When asked to elaborate, he explained: "Well . . . first, their skin is red, like Indian skin . . . and their hair is different from ours, it is also often blond, they dye it." It is remarkable that the artificial dye itself becomes a racial attribution, and the skin of the Gypsy as differentiated from the 'normal' Egyptian skin should become 'red,' which may also denote confusion between 'Indian' and 'Red Indians,' a term used in English by some Egyptians when referring to Native Americans. The most offensive accounts compare Gypsies to 'monkeys,' in the length of their arms and their general look, particularly the males or the older females. In typical Orientalist fashion, while men are described as threatening, ugly, or scary, women, and particularly the younger ones, are described as sensual and mysterious, with that 'animal sensuality' evoked by European novelists and painters (Cocteau compared the Gypsies to 'jungle tigers' and Mérimée compared Carmen to a cat), and whose dangerous, uncontrollable beauty could lead to the downfall of non-Gypsy men.

Racialization is often a process that translates the moral characteristics ascribed to Ghagar into physical features. The males are represented as thieves, therefore their bodies need to be scarred by knives, their faces need to appear threatening and deceptive, and their eyes need to be mad and violent. The women who are fortune-tellers need to possess the capacity to cast spells through their eyes, and those who are entertainers or prostitutes need to be beautiful in a dangerous and savage or animal way. As Okely noted, everything about Gypsies needs to be exaggerated, in order to create a creature that barely possesses humanity and individuality and simply embodies the fantasies of the outsider. The fact that their bodies seem to translate their character or occupation makes that identification easier.

Linguistic Boundaries

While most of the research on Roma in Europe has been conducted in the linguistic field, very little has been done in Egypt aside from the attempts of the Orientalists mentioned in earlier chapters: Captain Newbold, Consul von Kremer, Sir Richard Burton, and Edward Lane, among others. Although their languages tend to be lost when nomadic Gypsies become sedentary, 'secret languages' emerge as a result of syncretism, with combinations of words and linguistic principles borrowed from a variety of languages (Incirlioglu 2006). The secret language is mentioned by the nineteenth-century analysts, who often construct it as a way for the Ghagar to create boundaries between themselves and outsiders, or to plot something in front of people in their unintelligible "thievish tongue" (von Kremer 1864). The 'secret language' is still mentioned today, and most interlocutors spoke of it. Some call it 'Sim,' which means 'code' in Arabic; others refer to it simply as the 'secret language.' The concept of secrecy and social advantage is explained by Hanna: "As the language is connected with the idea of secrecy, they feel they own something which others do not. This feeling increases understanding between them as other people cannot know what they are saying" (1982, 35); "they have their private language that nobody understands" (1982, 92). He adds that the use of the secret language is not necessarily malicious and that their language fulfills specific aims.

> On social occasions when they have non-Ghagar guests and they want to converse about what food should be given to the guests. In this situation, members of a family may feel shy to speak openly in Arabic, especially if they are short of food or drinks. (1982, 94)

The idea of an excluding secret language is prevalent among Egyptians; according to some of my non-Ghagar interlocutors, Ghagar recognize each other primarily because of their secret language, like a code. The secrecy associated with the Ghagar language can be interpreted from both sides of the cultural boundaries. From the Ghagar's point of view, as suggested by Hanna, it fosters a sense of proximity because they share a language unknown to outsiders. It creates a sense of superiority, as outsiders are not able to grasp what is being said. More pragmatically, it can help them deal with delicate situations, such as lack of food or what decision needs to be taken, in the presence of non-Ghagar. Symbolically, the separation from outsiders by means of secret codes is prevalent in groups that want to remain exclusive and also need to recreate a sense of dignity for themselves, particularly among negatively privileged groups (Weber 2011), who do not enjoy a natural sense of dignity because of their inferior social status.

On the other hand, accused of using a secret language, Gypsies may appear as the ones willingly excluding the non-initiated, and the secret language becomes not only the ethnic marker, or a way to create proximity for the insiders, but it also embodies a desire of exclusion and the formation of an esoteric identity that is both closed and threatening. It makes Gypsies linguistically and culturally incomprehensible. Von Kremer has little doubt about their intentions: "We have here to do with a thievish slang dialect, made use of by the gipsies in order not to be understood by strangers" (1864, 266). Nor does Captain Newbold: "Their own [language] is used . . . for purpose of concealment" (1856, 291). An incomprehensible language also conveniently constructs a group that cannot be understood, which is 'untranslatable,' not only linguistically but also socially and culturally, which is in line with the stereotype of the eternal outsider associated with Gypsies. Hanna compares the two perspectives, noting that the use of the Ghagar language "constitutes a major factor in the division of these two social groups and stops interaction between them. The secret language sets up barriers and closes channels of communication, making the non-Ghagar feel like strangers," while on the Ghagar's side, "it is generally true that a person who speaks Ghagar is 'one of us' and a person who does not is 'one of them,' but it must be realized that knowing this language is not enough to classify any person as a member of the Ghagar; there are other social considerations" (Hanna 1982, 95). He adds that given the fact that "society often views the Ghagar language as a secret one used to fulfill secret aims, some Ghagar insist they do not know the language and most of them insist they do not use it" (1982, 95).

Still, many non-Ghagar interlocutors had an opinion about the secret language. Some explained that the language was mostly used in criminal contexts when Ghagar wanted to steal something, saying "take her bag, her watch, the policeman is coming" in Sim. Others noted, in contrast, that Ghagar spoke both their language merely in order not to be understood by non-Ghagar, and only when they were "among themselves," not wanting outsiders to grasp fragments of the mysterious language: "They only speak the Sim when they are among themselves because it is something very special and they don't want foreigners to hear it," stated one interlocutor. The use of the language is constructed like a secret ritual and its mysterious practice makes it alien and threatening.

Spatial Boundaries

Initially, the Ghagar lived as nomads, which contributed to the construction of their marginal identities. Even now, however, while becoming increasingly sedentary, they somehow still live on the outskirts of villages or cities. Hanna noted that

> In Sett Guiran'ha, the Sawafa (wool dealers) families have settled on the outskirts of town, in the desert area behind the main cluster of houses. The reason for this is their strong desire to close in upon themselves and preserve a certain degree of freedom away from the rest of the village. (1982, 19)

When Ghagar moved to Cairo, they stayed in poor neighborhoods, often marginalized, like downtown Sayyida Zaynab or the City of the Dead. Some of my Ghagar interlocutors live in Helwan, which is situated at the end of Cairo, at the last metro stop. The location carries metaphorical meaning because this neighborhood used to be where Europeans living in Cairo would go and spend their weekends, but it was turned into the most undesirable area in Cairo after Nasser declared it fit for a cement factory. The air is unhealthy, with a high rate of respiratory diseases among Helwan inhabitants. In Sayyida Zaynab there is a large concentration of Ghagar who live in clusters of six or seven families, usually relatives.

The City of the Dead (al-Araafa) is Cairo's famous cemetery where about three hundred thousand individuals live, unable to find affordable homes in Cairo. The social organization within the City is structured, and some neighborhoods are more bourgeois than others. Many homes have running water and electricity. Sobhi is a retired governmental clerk who has spent the thirty years since his retirement in a beautiful gravesite where one of King Faruq's relatives is buried. As he was approaching retirement, he heard from a colleague that a grave in the City had become available. He "applied for it" and obtained permission from the family to become the guardian of the tomb. He moved in with his wife and three teenage children, grateful to have secured a highly covetable place for his retirement: a home with a large garden, no rent to pay, and a salary. The deceased's family gives him a comfortable amount of money to wash the grave, which is a sumptuous tomb made of shiny white marble that dominates a vast yard planted with palm trees. In exchange for his salary, he trims the trees and ensures that no one enters the marble tomb, which is furnished with delicate inlaid chairs and coffee tables, old paintings, and alabaster vases. His wife makes sure that a bunch of fresh flowers is displayed on the small table by the marble coffin. Sobhi and his family live in a small house by the tomb. Two of his children have left and live in downtown Cairo. One is a driver and the other a government worker. His daughter, a nurse, still lives with her parents.

We were sipping sweet tea under the palm trees and he was reflecting on how fortunate he was to have gotten the deal, "when so many people in Cairo struggle to get a house." Sobhi explained that the more fortunate City residents lived in the tombs of wealthy people whose families were willing to pay well, while other less fortunate dwellers had had to move into the tombs of the forgotten, with no family to pay for the care of the tomb. I asked him if he knew of any Ghagar, or Hanagra, in the City. "No," he said. "And anyway, those people barely exist anymore, and they are all in the villages in the Delta or Upper Egypt. Not a single one in our City, and believe me, I know everyone here."

In fact, down the dusty alley from his home, two Ghagar families had moved into forgotten tombs fifteen years earlier. One woman had left her village in Upper Egypt to get married in Cairo to another Ghagar, who had also left Upper Egypt a few years earlier in search of work. Since the couple had not been able to find either jobs or an affordable home in Cairo, they had moved into a dilapidated tomb in the necropolis, where they built a small shack from materials found in the streets. Everything they owned they had found in the garbage that the husband occasionally collected. Fifteen years later they were still in the City, with their two children: one boy, who had left school because he had to work at small jobs and bring money home (the woman never elaborated on the nature of the small jobs), and a thirteen-year-old girl, who was to be married the following month. The second Ghagar family had a similar story: husband and wife had left their village in Upper Egypt, and after wandering in Cairo for a few months, they had finally settled in the City of the Dead next to the first Ghagar family, unable to find a job or affordable lodging outside of the City. The two families knew of each other's existence and socialized at the most basic level, sharing information and gossip, but they did not interact with the other dwellers of the City, somehow insulating themselves from any type of interaction. Even within the environment of the City of the Dead, there exist boundaries between Ghagar and non-Ghagar. In a place where the harsh conditions could be expected to create some sense of community, as they indeed do for some of the residents, who have created a community and rely on its solidarity to get organized, the Ghagar are outsiders, the forgotten neighbors living in the forgotten tombs.

Another marginalized, yet central, neighborhood of Cairo is Garbage City, a neighborhood built by the Coptic Zabbalin, nestled against the rocky area of Muqattam, where trash from Cairo is divided up among families, sorted, and recycled. Every morning, Cairenes see the small trucks or the wobbly wooden carts pulled by skinny donkeys go around the streets of Cairo to collect garbage and bring it back to the streets of Garbage City. The Zabbalin and Dom communities would seem to have a lot in common, sharing a marginalized position as ethnic or religious minorities, and pariah-like characteristics that associate them with impure practices, such as collecting garbage. Indeed, Gypsies in many areas of the world do engage in trash collection. Adrian Marsh reflects on the process of creation of collective identities and compares the Coptic Zabbalin to the Ghagar of Egypt. He shows how the Zabbalin have been able, as an act of resistance, to establish themselves as a community, defined both "by their occupation and their marginalized status, who also experience dislocation on a generational basis. The Zabbalin are very similar to the Ghagar and other Gypsy groups" (Marsh 2005). However, the Zabbalin have been able to produce a new meaning for their marginalized status in order to be integrated into Egyptian society; they have been able, despite many obstacles (such as the slaughter of their pigs in 2009 during the swine flu epidemic) to secure their monopoly over garbage collection and creative recycling. They also have been able to establish themselves as a powerful community.

The Gypsies are more on the periphery of Egyptian society than the Zabbalin have ever been, and the comparison with the Zabbalin accentuates the challenges they encounter in the process of identity formation. Unlike the rootless Ghagar, the Zabbalin, being Coptic Egyptians, perceive themselves as 'true' Egyptians, and they have internalized that notion. Furthermore, they have been able to concretely embody their existence as a specific group in a creation myth that involves the moving of the Muqattam Mountain in the tenth century and the recent construction of the Cave Church, an imposing structure that can accommodate up to thirty thousand people and serves as an anchor for their community, both physically and spiritually. The Zabbalin successfully managed to inject the prestige of 'chosen people' into their condition of outcasts. They have also been able to construct themselves as a political group that has secured its monopoly over garbage collection and recycling. All in all, the Zabbalin have been successful in formalizing their identity, which has created group cohesion, through forging a sense of dignity anchored in their marginalized social status and occupation. They have thus been able to brand themselves socially, politically, and economically, both domestically and internationally.

In contrast, the Egyptian Dom are far from any process of communalization and creation of an identity that they would control and drive. Their identity is an object-construction (that is, a construction by outsiders), while the Zabbalin have been able to appropriate their identity and construct it in their own terms. Symbolically, the Dom are marginalized in terms of identity construction and even in terms of garbage collection, compared to the Zabbalin. Indeed, occasionally the Ghagar engage in trash collection, but they do so on the margins of the group that has the real monopoly on collection. The Ghagar collect only the trash that the Zabbalin do not wish to collect.

Occupational Boundaries

Exclusion from the mainstream comes with a constant association with criminal activities. After the exotic magical nomad, the criminal seems to be the main contemporary category of identification for Ghagar. The 'culture of crime' stereotype is reproduced in the discourse constructed by the media, as well as in popular assumptions, both from people who are not familiar with Ghagar and, perhaps more surprisingly, from people who interact with them routinely. As a matter of fact, one of the most interesting aspects of this research has been the negative perceptions of individuals working with Ghagar. According to researchers in crime statistics at the Institute for Criminological and Sociological Research in Cairo, there are no specific data about Ghagar. When my research assistant met with one person responsible for criminological data, he explained that they had recently conducted a large study involving more than four thousand individuals engaged in criminal activities, and that "surely" their sample included Ghagar, but this kind of group identification was never indicated. As a result, we are left mostly with suppositions and sensationalist stories reported orally or in newspapers.

During most of our conversations, one social worker insisted that the Ghagar, whom she also admitted "liking," were nonetheless irremediable criminals, and that the criminal 'genes' were transmitted from one generation to the next. She categorized the Ghagar into four distinct groups, each of them viewed as thoroughly inescapable. These groups were the metalworkers, the entertainers, the beggars, and finally the thieves. In her narrative, each of these occupationally based groups appeared to be very rigid and essentialized in its systematic generational transmission, partly because of the biological heritage (such as having "crime in the blood"), but also because the members of each subgroup were depicted as raising their offspring according to what was expected by their profession; each dimension of the children's education seems anchored in what their occupation is predestined to be.

The children go or don't go to school depending on their parents' occupation. If the parents have a trade, then the kids learn the trade, metalworking, craft, mostly that . . . . If the parents are thieves, well, the children will learn that too, and from the earliest age, really . . . they can master all their tricks. If the parents are beggars, then the children go to school, and they beg after school.

Attending school seems to be an option for beggars' children only because learning the begging trade does not require extensive training. It does not, however, promote upward mobility, as she quickly clarified: "Often beggar parents cut their children's ears off to have them beg better, you know, so we have pity, the Ghagar always do things like that." The heritage is an occupational one, which does not contain space for variation.

Other 'wise' who engaged with Ghagar communities and offered education to young working Ghagar had a more limited scope of Ghagar occupations; they depicted them primarily as criminals and drug dealers. However, they too explained that Ghagar children automatically entered the trade of their parents, and that the attempts of their own organization to extract Ghagar children from the criminal circle were usually unsuccessful. One of them related a story of Ghagar children with whom the organization had worked.

> Well, at one point, there were seven of them and only one stayed . . . the others went back to their families after one year. They don't want a better life, they think the life of violence and criminality is exciting and prestigious, they like to be feared, they feel like it gives them power.

The 'they' he used seemed to refer to both the parents and the children, suddenly merged into one single category. He later explained that parents pressured their children to join their criminal activities, but also that the children perceived criminal occupations as "prestigious" or as "a display of power." The dream of a "better life" is abandoned because it seems impossible for the children to escape what their families seem to have constructed for them, and because of their own internalization of what their life ought to be like.

The irremediability of a Ghagar's future is illustrated by a number of stories different 'wise' matter-of-factly related. A recurrent one is the

Mecca story, according to which Hanagra/Ghagar females go to the holy site in order to rob pilgrims. I have heard the story from most of my non-Ghagar interlocutors who had some knowledge about the Ghagar, but also from different Ghagar who would accuse "other groups" of committing the crimes. Since I mostly talked with people who presented themselves as Ghagar, they usually claimed that the Hanagra were the ones going to Mecca to rob pilgrims. On one occasion, the Mecca story was also related to me as follows:

> They pretend that they sell incense, but when they get there, they have someone who helps them stay in Saudi on their tourist visa, and then they work as thieves and give a share of what they get to that person. And when they come back, they usually buy a whole building for their family.

When I asked him how he knew of that story, he first replied, a little defensively: "Well, everyone knows about that story!" We then talked about something else, but after a while he said he had more to say about the Mecca story; he had visibly thought about the question. He articulated his argument around three crucial points: first, how could Ghagar buy a "whole building" merely from selling incense; second, why would they work in Saudi Arabia when they seldom work in Egypt; and finally, what he seemed to consider the most compelling argument—not based on speculations but on facts, the disclosure of the story by other Ghagar: "When Ghagar families fight between themselves, which happens a lot, they start telling secrets about each other, and I have heard a family saying the people in the other family had gone to Mecca as thieves."

Those arguments seemed to illustrate some of the mechanisms in the construction of the discourse on Ghagar. A story is first presented, which is then corroborated by a series of seemingly logical arguments, selected to support the story and make it appear real. It becomes difficult to assess if the reality precedes the discourse, or if the discourse is created first and becomes a reality that is then proved by a series of arguments that come to justify the now accepted story instead of leading to it. Another recurrent argument is that the Mecca story has to be true simply because "there is no smoke without fire," an overused adage to prove that any story must contain some truth whenever it contains details that appear vaguely factual and so, instead of questioning its validity, one need only find fragments of explanation to support that truth. "Common sense" seems to be enough to justify a claim, which reminds us of the Gramscian definition of common sense: "a reservoir of historically discontinuous and disjointed ideas that functions as the philosophy of non philosophers," a folklore whose fundamental distinction is its "fragmentary, incoherent and inconsequential character" (Gramsci 1971, 419). Others have demonstrated how unquestioned truths which we accept as common sense are, in fact, culturally derived mythologies specific not just to individual cultures but also to particular points in time (Barthes 1970; Foucault 1977; Geertz 1973).

Many other 'truths' about the Ghagar circulate, usually supported by common-sense explanations, which often explicitly leave a lot of space for interpretation, based on the assumption that the recipient of the comment will interpret it with the same 'common sense' as the one who formulates it, because of a certain discursive connivance that may exist between them. For instance, during Muhammad Morsi's presidency, gasoline became very scarce, causing devastating problems, particularly for taxi and truck drivers whose livelihoods depended on it. Magdy, the Alexandrian 'wise,' explained that Ghagar would steal gas from stations and sell it to truck and taxi drivers at an exorbitant price. When asked how they managed to do it, since there were very long lines in front of the stations and often armed soldiers guarding them to avoid fights, he said, "They could enter the gas stations because of their reputation." He did not elaborate as to what that "reputation" was, leaving me to imagine what it could be: whether the Ghagar would be cunning enough to outsmart the armed guards, or whether they would be dishonest enough to bribe them, or whether the guards were simply scared of the Ghagar.

The Ghagar's relations with the authorities and the police are often depicted as conflicted: on the one hand, Ghagar are portrayed as fearing the police, but occasionally they are depicted as being unfairly targeted by the police. According to one interlocutor:

At the end of the year, the police have to arrest people, you know. . . . If they don't know who to arrest, they will arrest a few Ghagar. Everyone will be convinced that they really are criminal, so it is an easy way to get enough people arrested.

On the other hand, Ghagar are depicted as not fearing 'even the police,' particularly since the 2011 Revolution and the weakening of the police institution. Abdelrahman explained that in the area of Umraniya the police would not dare to chase Ghagar: "The roads are bad and small, the Ghagar can disappear when they want, the police cannot go after them . . . and they are no match for gangs of Ghagar." He explained that in one notorious "Ghagar street" one Ghagar family had locked the doors of their building and climbed onto their roof, armed with guns; when the police arrived, the Ghagar showered them with bullets and stones, forcing the police to leave.

However, while the antagonism between Ghagar and the police is often explicitly described, there are also stories of Ghagar working *for* the police, "doing dirty jobs" such as breaking up protests and strikes, as well as being informants. Many interlocutors, both 'wise' and less knowing about the Ghagar, have claimed that during the 2011 Revolution, Ghagar were recruited by the police to infiltrate protesters, or to break up their protests and commit violent acts against them. Earlier, I mentioned how Ghagar were depicted paradoxically as both unable and unwilling to escape the group and simultaneously dreaming about deserting it—and then never looking back when they did. This contradictory representation can be seen in their relation to the police, who simultaneously represent social order, authority, and repression. When the police embody social order and go after criminals, they antagonize the Ghagar, who are represented as a threat to social order. On the other hand, when the police symbolize repression by breaking up democratic protests, they supposedly utilize Ghagar.

The duality seen here is represented in the question of whether Ghagar possess identity cards. The little existing literature on Egyptian Dom has suggested that they may not own identity cards, which would practically and symbolically exclude them from national belonging. The lack of registration is generally attributed to their nomadism, or occasion-ally to the marginalization and poverty that exclude them from the formal social system. Some interlocutors have argued that Ghagar intentionally decide against being registered, in order to gain additional freedom and to self-marginalize. Shaima explained: "Many Gypsies are not registered: they do not enter the army, they do not go to school, and it gives them a lot of flexibility to travel. They can disappear as they wish." Their ghostly figures navigate society without ever taking root or wanting to. Inter-estingly, however, I was also told later in my interview with Shaima and Abdelrahman that the Ghagar were politically "meaningful" in the neigh-borhoods where they lived because they voted for the people who would be corrupt enough to support their trade, or to turn a blind eye to their drug trafficking and other criminal activities. Ghagar are supposedly also used by politicians to intimidate voters, perhaps in exchange for money. It was not really clear in the discussion with Shaima and Abdelrahman whether Ghagar actually participated as voters, or were simply used as intimidators. When I pointed out that perhaps Ghagar would not be able to vote because they were not registered, Shaima said that some were registered now. In this case again, their registration may serve either to exclude them from the political system or to include them as a negative, but influential, political power. They are both deeply disempowered and disproportionately powerful.

The criminal category tends to erase any alternative discourse. When an interlocutor was asked if Ghagar participated in *mulid*s, by dancing or playing music, the response was often, "There is nothing artistic about them. They come from a largely uncivilized area." The closure of the cat-egory creates a negative inevitability, represented by the impossibility of entering the work force or doing anything other than commit crimes. This exclusion from productivity is highlighted in studies of European Gypsies (Okely 1983; Salo and Salo 1986), in which Gypsies are depicted as refusing to engage in production-related activities, or refusing to work for non-Ghagar, which contributes to the creation of an alienat-ing image in opposition to the modern national narrative of productivity and active engagement in capitalist production. The self-exclusion of the Ghagar from productive channels is recurrent in the narrative of different interviewees, particularly the 'wise,' whose stronger engagement with Ghagar communities allows them to engage in deeper analysis. If Ghagar work, it is usually with an ulterior motive. Abdelrahman, considering the jobs that male Ghagar might pursue, finally said that they were occasionally tuk-tuk drivers; however, he quickly added "but they usually use their tuk-tuk to distribute drugs." When women are housecleaners, they also "engage in prostitution with the men in the families they work for." Shaima added that Ghagar sometimes sold used clothes that "they have stolen from drying racks." Magdy thought that wealthy Ghagar could only have become rich by "stealing more efficiently" than others.

Other events described by the 'wise' likewise suggest that it is impossible for the Ghagar to engage in socially normative and integrative practices, such as working in 'normal' channels with 'normal' goals. One 'wise' in charge of an organization that gives loans to Ghagar for various projects (business, education, or enlarging their homes), explained that they refuse the loan in order not to be indebted to anyone and therefore creating any type of social relation. In the office of Abdelrahman and Shaima's organization, I was told that Ghagar families initially agreed to have their children enrolled in the program in order to "teach them something for free," but eventually sought to remove them from the program "when they see their children may change."

There are clear traces of positivism in the discourse of the 'wise,' who tend to identify specific "natural" characteristics in the Ghagar, reminiscent of the work of the early twentieth-century Italian criminologist Cesare Lombroso, who crudely argued that criminals were physically different from non-offenders. The allusions to the dark, dangerous eyes, or the inevitable scars on the Ghagar's faces, are still commonplace in the discursive practices of individuals who have dealt with Ghagar.

Building Rigid Boundaries

Despite the apparent religious, cultural, linguistic, and even physical similarities with the Egyptian majority, boundaries are routinely erected around the Ghagar. These boundaries often take the form of fragments, as the group is not clearly defined as an entity, but the fragments accumulate into a clear differentiation. Often, the boundaries serve to reassure non-Ghagar that despite the apparent proximity, the group is indeed different. They are Muslims, but not true Muslims, as they engage in the most blasphemous behavior possible by robbing pilgrims in Mecca or dancing naked in a sacred place. They speak Arabic but also have a code, the incomprehensible language called Sim, that sets them apart from regular Egyptians—apparently voluntarily, as they appear not to wish to be understood. They have unacceptable cultural practices, such as kidnapping children and not knowing their own origins.

Despite the interactiveness of the practices around the construction of boundaries, more often than not the blame is put upon the Gypsies, who are depicted as practicing self-exclusion by their use of an incomprehensible language and their morally unacceptable practices. This reading of the situation ignores the hostility, racism, and oppression faced by the Gypsies at the hands of the majority population over many years by insisting on their intrinsic inability to integrate, or the essentially exclusory mechanisms of their culture: on this view, the Gypsies themselves are to blame for reinforcing the social boundaries between them and other Egyptians.

4

IDENTITY NEGOTIATION: IGNORING, PASSING, CHANGING, AND EXCHANGING

'Passing' means to cross a color line, to transcend racial barriers, or the ability of a person to be completely accepted as a member of a sociological group other than their own (Wehnert 2010). Individuals may borrow characteristics from various cultural tool kits, switch cultural codes (Bains and Johal 1998), or play with different "cultural styles" or "cultural masks" and develop some kind of ethnic hybridity, implying that identities are not fixed (Back 1996). Passing is an interactional activity: both passers and witnesses are involved in the phenomenon, with varying degrees of awareness and acceptance. When groups negotiate their visibility and presence in the mainstream, passing is often an option, as it is a strategy of self-preservation for groups confronted by a hostile environment. The phenomenon of passing needs to be explored at different levels, from the elements that trigger its emergence to its limitations and obstacles, and the meanings different actors associate with it, whether they are themselves transgressors or not. The common justification for passing is that those who pass are looking to gain something only obtainable by the members of the group they wish to belong to; they are trying to access social, economic, or political advantages. For instance, passing would allow Gypsies to be integrated into the dominant identity, or into a group perceived as more privileged. Romani groups in Europe have resorted to passing strategies in order to disappear into the mainstream, to appear non-Roma, or to be associated with a group socially less stigmatized; in Berlin, Bulgarian Roma pass for Turks, who, while not the dominant group, are perceived as a less stigmatized group and easier to melt into (Kyuchukov 2010).

One of the mechanisms of passing for Dom is to be perceived as genuine Egyptians or to highlight their Arab roots. The nineteenth-century Austrian consul von Kremer (1864) noticed that Egyptian Gypsies insisted with pride on their Arab roots and typically presented themselves as belonging to "different Egyptian tribes." More recently, the ethnomusicologist Kevin Holmes (2002) contends that most Dom will persistently deny their heritage and "claim to be Egyptian or Arab." Are the Dom using the concepts of "pragmatic flexibility" and "altered externalization" (Mahmoud 2009, 284, 290) and displaying a public figure that fits certain expectations while maintaining a different identity internally, and therefore experiencing what DuBois called a "double consciousness" (Reed 1997, 93–126)? In that case, their desire to emphasize their Arab heritage would be rooted in their consciousness of ethnic difference coupled with the knowledge of the implications of lacking the right roots, equivalent to a denial of belonging. On the other hand, it is possible that Ghagar and other 'Gypsy tribes' indeed perceive their roots as being genuinely Arab. In that case, they would have internalized the belief that their differences are merely tribal; they are not deliberately passing. Furthermore, the construction of an identity is also affected by the perceptions and expectations of those outside the ethnic boundaries. For instance, while early Orientalist observers such as Newbold and von Kremer reported that Gypsies insisted on the purity of their roots, claiming "Arab origins," they were identifying the Egyptian Gypsies through European eyes. They drew links with European Gypsies and automatically attributed to the Dom some kind of otherness/foreignness, which is why they intensely disbelieved in what they understood as mere pretense of Arab roots. Their surprise tells us as much about their expectations and the connections they drew between European and Egyptian Gypsies as they inform us about Doms' self-perceptions.

Gypsies and Their 'Origins'

Usually, Middle Eastern Dom are deeply embedded in the host society. The Dom in Palestinian–Arab society, according to the linguist Yaron Matras,

have lived among the Arabs for many centuries, they share customs, family organisation structures, and religious beliefs with
mainstream Muslim Arabs . . . . Arabic now serves as the principal
language of the community and is the only language spoken by the
younger generation of Dom. (2000, 54)

On the other hand, they may face intense divisions that they have not
been able to overcome to create a unifying identity. According to Allen
Williams, who studies Jordanian Dom,

as with many Arab governments, Jordanian leaders are resistant to the
demands of minority groups for recognition of their issues. . . . Ethnic
commonality will not be sufficient to unite them, especially since their
shared ethnicity is perceived to be dividing them. (2006, 209)

Nonetheless, we can assume that the absence of an official defined identity is concomitantly the result and the source of their social and political
invisibility. Many Ghagar do have a 'sense of difference,' but they do not
anchor it in specific origins. Up until recently, their self-perception was
rooted in tribal differences. Historically each 'tribe' had a different name—
Halebi, Nawar, Ghawazi, Ghagar—linked to a specific region or occupation.
Nabil Sobhi Hanna reported a story told by an old Ghagar man who

tried to connect their history with Muhammad Ali. He said that the
severity of tax collectors was such that peasants quit their land to
escape. It is said that the Ghagar were peasants who owned pieces
of land. When they fled, every one of them learned a new profession. (1982, 12)

Hanna remarks that linking the Ghagar to peasants is probably incorrect.
If they had indeed been peasants, he suggests, their primary occupation
would have been farming, in which they seldom engage.

A more contemporary sense of difference is associated with social differences; urban Ghagar particularly are perceived as a group situated at the
bottom of Egyptian society and stuck in marginalizing occupations. Some

Ghagar may internalize the representations of their groups that are consti-tuted by outsiders—not only characteristics of pariah-ness and violence, but also a cultural and social proximity with European Roma. While most of my interlocutors were unable and uninterested in asserting specific roots— "We belong to a different Egyptian group and people look down on us" was the most common answer—some established tenuous links with European Roma. One Ghagar woman in Alexandria explained that she had heard how European Roma (she called them "European Ghagar") were mistreated by Europeans, who thought of them as "dirty." She nonetheless marveled at their culture, "their beautiful dances . . . and the way women are dressed in those nice red dresses," which was very much a transposition of the Carmen-like stereotypes that have been built around the Roma. She mentioned that she has seen them in "a cartoon," which her elder daughter identified as Dis-ney's *Hunchback of Notre Dame*. When I asked her if she believed there was a link between European and Egyptian Ghagar, she said she did not know. Her daughter added that the European Ghagar seemed "more famous" in Europe and elsewhere than the Egyptian Ghagar, and that "people every-where" knew about their culture, their dances, and what they looked like. Another interlocutor from Cairo, Ramy, answered very assuredly that he knew the Ghagar came from India. He explained that his grandfather had told him their story. He then added that there was a "Book of Secrets" about Ghagar: "The book tells the story of Ghagar. My cousin has read it. I can't read but he read it. I can bring it next time," which he did not do, as he later claimed that his family would "kill him" if they ever found out he had brought the book to a foreigner (a non-Ghagar). When I asked him more about the content of the "Book of Secrets," he said, nervously biting his nails:

> There are secrets, but I have not read them personally . . . but I know
> that the secrets are about how we stand together, no one can under-
> stand who we are. We also need to protect each other because of the
> police. We need to be careful. We cannot say too much.

The uncertainty and the secrecy regarding the roots of the groups are seemingly both unsettling and reassuring. The creation of difference is based on mysteries that the Ghagar can utilize as they wish, as the absence of any specific construction of their identity rigidified in outsiders' hands provides them with a space empty of preconceived ideas. Often this space is filled with stories and with the notion of 'secrets' that cannot be revealed, even to other members of the group. Never revealing too much is another Ghagar technique for the creation of boundaries. Ramy came to our meeting in a coffeeshop in Sayyida Zaynab accompanied by two of his cousins, who he explained were there to "protect him." However, the cousins' presence was perhaps as much motivated by surveillance as it was by protection; they sat at a table far enough away to give us an illusion of privacy and close enough that they could hear everything that was being said. When Ramy talked about the "Book of Secrets," his eyes shifted nervously between my translator and his cousins. On another occasion, while I was asking a Cairene Ghagar female what she knew about Ghagar history, her daughter, seated next to her, whispered in Arabic, "Be careful, don't talk too much," perhaps hoping this would escape my translator's attention. The woman became evasive about Ghagar origins and mentioned the secrets that surround Ghagar history.

Secrecy is often associated with "part of what it means to be a Gypsy" (Okely 1983, 43). The secrecy enveloping the origins, as well as some cultural and social practices, not only serves as a protection obtained by divulging as little as possible about their identity and often hiding it, but it also offers additional prestige to the group, which becomes deliberately impenetrable. Unknown origins can be surrounded by more dignity when embedded in an apparently controlled secrecy, which confers power on this group who do not necessarily know their past. The game of secrecy is played on both sides of the cultural boundary. While outsiders indulge in trying to penetrate the secrets of Gypsies and fantasize about their mysterious ways, or, inversely, construct them as incomprehensible in an alienating manner, the Gypsies use secrecy to erect boundaries and cement the group around a mysterious sacred knowledge, or the belief in it. The belief in knowing something that no one else does brings some prestige to the negatively perceived group as well as an impenetrable identity.

Another strategy for passing is evasiveness in providing others with in-group information and offering alternatives to the person they interact with, from simple denial to partial admission. The decision is made by weighing the benefits of being a Ghagar. I met fortune-tellers at the Giza Zoo on multiple occasions. During one of the first encounters, I bluntly asked two women if they were Ghagar. The first woman, startled by my question, initially denied it and said she was "just an Egyptian" and that she had learned her craft from a Ghagar woman, defined as an "acquaintance." When I suggested that I would rather have my fortune read by a "true Ghagar," she told me she was in fact a Ghagar. Her friend, who had remained silent during the first part of our conversation, decided to intervene and explained that they were not Ghagar, but from the Halebi tribe, the "real fortune-tellers." Within a few minutes, my interlocutors had modified their identities three times, gradually gauging what would be the best stance to follow from our interaction, from denial to acceptance and even, when they understood that I indeed wanted to be assisted by a Gypsy, the adoption of the most revered identity in divination, the Halebi, a community whose female members are deemed experts not only by the nineteenth-century Newbold, but also by many other Ghagar interlocutors. When asked what it meant to be Ghagar or Halebi, the second fortune-teller explained that the main difference between the two groups was that the Halebi were the ones naturally gifted with the ability to predict the future and to control the evil eye. As often happens in these discussions, distinctions are based on the perceived essential differences between groups—the Halebi and Ghagar in their divination skills, the Hanagra and Ghagar in their aptitudes for crime—more than on the origins of the subgroups. The flexible readjustment of identity, depending on the context, or what Goffman (1959) called "impression management" from a symbolic interaction perspective, allows members of a group to fluidly modify the way they present themselves. The technique is based on how actors want to influence others' perceptions and how they want to direct the different interactions they engage in. The ability to shift and renegotiate their identities is another tactic useful for members of groups who need to survive in hostile environments.

Denial of Identity

Many encounters with Ghagar involve a phase of denial, followed occasionally by an assertion of their Ghagar identity. One neighborhood in

Cairo is supposedly the refuge of Ghagar. It is called Hosh al-Ghagar and was mentioned by Newbold, von Kremer, and Lane as a "squalid quarter" (Newbold 1856, 292) where Ghagar had settled, a dark place where police never went and a lot of scary events were going on. A few years ago, an Egyptian journalist wrote a sensationalist article, "The Secret World of Gypsies" (Nur, 2011), in which she related her adventures in that dark corner of Cairo. The whole article played on the mystery and strangeness associated with the place, and the journalist depicted herself as a brave adventurer in search of the Gypsy's soul. She described them in these terms (my translation):

> They adore freedom, and they don't hide their dream of destructing the walls of isolation between them and the rest of the society. They have a feeling of bitterness and anger towards their place that others see it as a representation of crime.

She explained that she had initially met a Ghagar fortune-teller in Heliopolis who had approached her, saying, "Do you want me to read your future by whispering to these sea shells, beautiful lady?," which aroused her curiosity. She then talked with the fortune-teller and asked her where she was from. She learned that the old lady was from Hosh al-Ghagar, that she was a Ghagar, and that she had inherited her skills from her grandmother. The journalist decided to explore Hosh al-Ghagar and was introduced to a certain Badr Farag, the neighborhood sheikh, who agreed to meet her in a café near the Hosh to talk about the Ghagars' ways.

I went to Hosh al-Ghagar with a translator. When we arrived near the Hosh, which is hidden behind a wall, we first met with a street seller pushing a small cart of roasted sweet potatoes who introduced himself as a Ghagar, and advised us against going inside. He explained that he had left the Hosh when his children were born in order to raise them "in a better way, not the Ghagar way." However, when his wife had died a few years ago, he had gone back to the Hosh, somehow resigned to his fate, but without his children, who were now grown up. He concluded, subdued, "But it does not matter for me to be back here . . . at least my children have escaped."

We continued toward the quarter, a few narrow streets opening into the back of the wall, adorned by mountains of trash. A young man came to us, and he too advised us against going to the Hosh: "They sell drugs there, especially since 2011, and no one does anything about it. It is very dangerous, people don't like outsiders there . . . . You need to be real careful."

We finally entered one of the narrow streets, where many women and children were sitting on small plastic chairs by their open doors. Most of the children were blond and the women whose heads were not covered were mostly displaying blond locks. Many women were wearing large gold earrings and a few had small blue tattoos on their faces. Everything seemed very much to embody the stereotypical representations of the Ghagar: blond hair, even in children, large earrings, tattooed faces. A middle-aged lady approached us and in a soft voice suggested that if we wanted to talk we would be better off in her house than in the street. Her home consisted of one room, with a high bed adorned with piles of clothes, two chairs, and three small benches. She offered us the chairs while she and her daughter sat on the wooden benches. She then offered us some of her cold *koshari*, the traditional Egyptian dish made of rice, macaroni, and lentils, from a plate she pulled out from under the bed. Another woman, whom she introduced as her daughter Fatima, was pouring Coke into a plastic bag for her children to drink. She then put two large spoons of *koshari* into two additional plastic bags that she gave the children; they started to suck on the bags, alternating between the Coke and the *koshari* bags. They all had dyed blond hair.

We explained that we were interested in Ghagar culture and had been told that there were Ghagar in the Hosh. The elder woman explained that she definitely was not a Ghagar. "The Ghagar are thieves, they are bad people. Everyone thinks that in the Hosh we are all Ghagar. But we are not. We are kind and honest people." She went on lamenting that the outsiders thought badly of them because of the Ghagar, but that the Ghagar had left the Hosh many years ago, and those who had not left had forgotten about their old Ghagar ways. She suggested that a better name for the place should be 'Hosh al-Nakhl' ('palm tree'), in order to get rid of any connotation of Ghagar: "Palm trees are beautiful . . . Ghagar are ugly!" she concluded. Fatima agreed vehemently with everything her mother said. Finally, they talked about the female journalist who had come to the Hosh and written "bad stories" about them being thieves, drug dealers, dangerous, bringing too much unwanted attention to the neighborhood: "All we want is to have peace, we are honest people, we are not those horrible Ghagar." When we asked if she wanted to leave the place or if she liked it, she smiled.

> No, I like it, it is all my family, we all know each other. And if I wanted to leave, I would be able to leave, despite what people say . . . you see, there are so many lies, like you cannot leave the Hosh, but if you want to go, you can, you can marry outside too, of course you can. And we are not thieves; our men are mechanics and painters.

She then called out to one woman strolling by her window and invited her in. The woman immediately spoke angrily, demanding that we leave, because "government people are not welcome." When we denied having been sent by the government, she repeated that whoever we were, we were not welcome. She reprimanded our host, blaming her for our presence, and eventually continued her stroll. Our host looked upset. "This is what people say about Ghagar women, that they are loud and crazy. She now looks like one of them when she screams like that, like a crazy person . . . now, yes, of course, she looks like a Ghagar." She went on to explain that the woman was in fact the sister of Badr Farag, who had been featured in the article "The Secret World of Gypsies" as a Ghagar sheikh and who had since died. The article, she said, was full of lies; although she admitted that she had not read it herself because she could not read, some of her relatives had told her about it. She said that she had heard that the article mentioned a secret language: "Another lie, we don't have a secret language, only the Ghagar and the Hanagra do. We are normal people."

It was an interesting case of denial and possible insider–outsider imposed identity. After all, the district is called Hosh al-Ghagar, and was mostly described a "Ghagar place" by Orientalists in the nineteenth century. It was revived as such by a journalist a few years ago, who, like the nineteenth-century Orientalists, enjoyed describing the fascinating, secret world of Gypsies, combining mystery, a sense of freedom, and illicit practices. The identity is negotiated differently by different actors. For instance, the late Badr Farag may have found it prestigious to present himself as a sheikh to Rania Nur (2011; my translation):

> I discovered that it is impossible to enter into that world without the permission of their leader "Am Badr Farag," as one of the youth whom I met earlier had advised me. I also knew that he sits in a café beside the bridge beneath "soor magra al oyon," and hence it was not difficult to find him. He was a man in his fifties, and before we spoke a word he asked us, "Who are you and what do you want?" I explained to him the nature of our mission, and that we want to get closer to the Gypsies' world that we always hear about, but never knew. At that point he agreed and said: "Okay, but not today, come after two days." We went after the two days, and when I asked him for the reason, he told me that on that day he had a problem with some of his wife's relatives, and if we had entered without him we would have been badly treated, because he is the only one whose word is respected and obeyed by all.

In that narrative, Badr seems to have constructed himself as a gatekeeper. The topic of respect and order is also touched upon in this narrative, as is Badr's position as intermediary. The group is recreated in the eyes of the individuals describing it, and I am at risk of doing the same thing. I could not help but note all the stereotypical Ghagar features of the people I met in the Hosh: blond hair, earrings, tattoos, and even, in the words of our host's visitor, the "loud women."

It is not uncommon for Gypsies to be reluctant to identify themselves as such, because of the stigma associated with their identity, and because they may have internalized that stigma themselves and want, as individuals, to distance themselves from it. The denial itself may almost seem part of the secret Ghagar identity. The distinction between the stigma and self-definition results in non-identification, or the inclination to distance themselves from the Gypsy label (Özatesler 2012, 26). However, on the other hand, the imposition of the identity counteracts its definition, in a sense: as soon as it becomes imposed, it serves as a tool for the outsider and becomes instrumentalized. At some point, the self-identification (subject definition) does not match the definition by others (object identification). When someone does not identify themselves as belonging to a certain group, is the object identification acceptable? Expectations were obviously present on both sides: I was looking for Ghagar "attitudes and practices," while the women I talked to were expecting that outsiders could only bring adversity to their group, and held preconceived ideas based on uncontested stereotypes that they themselves were aware of (being a thief, being loud and irrational). The self-denial of Gypsy identity may be rooted in the fact that members of the group are facing cultural imperialism, one of the five faces of oppression according to Iris Marion Young (1992), and find themselves defined by an externally imposed network of meanings, against which they occasionally resist, mostly by distancing themselves thoroughly from that outsider-constructed identity.

Group Divisions and Occupations

Carol Silverman (1982), in her seminal study of American Gypsies, noted that Gypsies in general did not rely on the natural environment to provide their needs; rather, they make their living from their social environment, specifically from the non-Gypsy population among whom they live. While Gypsies are marginalized and often do not mix socially (because of endogamic practices, constant movement, or neighborhood segregation), they constantly interact economically with non-Gypsies. Therefore, to ensure their economic survival and independence, they must "initiate regular friendly contacts with Gorgios and develop a multiplicity of roles and disguises: those who sell carpets will conceal their Gypsy origins, while fortune tellers will exploit them" (Okely 1983, 167). Overall, acts of passing can be analyzed at different levels. Gypsies pass in order to become integrated when necessary (which accounts for the Doms' claims of 'Arabic roots,' for instance), or they pass from one role to another, based on what they can gain from that role in the society they live in and from which they gain their means of subsistence.

More specifically, the Dom have had to adjust their occupations within certain constraints, namely the needs of the customer population, the profitability associated with the role they play, and their traditions. For instance, certain tribes or subgroups are assigned specific roles, and there exist taboos as to who can engage in certain occupations or not; even if those taboos may change over time, they are taken into account. The nineteenth-century Orientalists noted that each tribe had its own specific occupation. Their analysis and the delimitation of the occupational categories, however, did not quite match; for instance, while Newbold argued that fortune-telling belonged to the Halebi and that Ghagar women, being looked down upon by Halebi, could not practice palmistry, von Kremer associated palm reading with Ghagar in general. Belly dancing was also frequently connected to Ghawazi tribes (by Edward Lane, for instance, who does not recognize them as a real Gypsy group, and by Captain Newbold, as well as more recent literature on belly dancing as explained in chapter 3), or occasionally to all female Ghagar, regardless of their tribal affiliation.

Among contemporary narratives of Dom and non-Dom, this kind of division of labor is still prevalent (albeit not fixed), be it along tribal boundaries or within tribes. According to Habiba, a social service representative who works with Ghagar in Sayyida Zaynab, Ghagar can be divided into four distinct groups: the metalworkers, the entertainers, the beggars, and the thieves. Each segment possesses a specific habitus, and occupational boundaries are usually not easily crossed. Children are socialized as beggars, thieves, metalworkers, or entertainers, and they are expected to carry on the trade. Habiba depicts an environment where occupational divisions are mostly related to families' specialization; these families all belong to the larger Ghagar designation and live in the same neighborhood. Hanna noticed that in many instances—but not always—among Sett Guiran'ha Ghagar, trades were transmitted to the offspring.

> On the whole, those Ghagar who continue in their trades do so largely because of tradition, which is of great value to them. Having an occupation which is passed from father to son provides a security in their lives and a unity within the family and the clan. (1982, 23)

Other interlocutors marked a distinction between subgroups' occupations. For instance, some writers principally associated Ghagar with providing entertainment during *mulid*s and Halebi with fortune-telling.

Other accounts linked Hanagra to crime and located them mostly in specific neighborhoods, such as impoverished Dar al-Salaam on the outskirts of Cairo. Many newspapers that report on crimes committed by Gypsies specifically allude to the "Hanagra tribe."

Interestingly, the Dom themselves have constructed different occupational subgroups. Some of the Alexandrian Ghagar differentiated between Ghagar and Hanagra: the latter group was associated with robbing Mecca pilgrims and general crime, while Ghagar were described as occasionally engaging in theft, practicing palmistry, and mostly begging and working. Interlocutors in Hosh al-Ghagar identified the Hanagra as the thieves and the Ghagar as the beggars; however, they also distinguished between the knowledge that initiated people, such as the Hosh residents (self-identified as non-Ghagar, as we saw earlier), and outsiders would have concerning the different groups. It was explained to me that while outsiders usually tend to designate "everyone as Ghagar" and associate them indiscriminately with begging or crime, the Hosh residents knew that the "true criminals" were unquestionably the Hanagra, who would engage in trips to Mecca or rob commuters in buses or in the streets of Cairo or Alexandria. Many of the fortune-tellers identified Halebi females as the ones possessing the gift of predicting the future; however, in their narrative they would often switch between terms, using 'Ghagar' particularly when generalizing and speaking not only about the 'gift,' but about life situations and the endemic poverty of the group. For instance, in the same discourse, within a few minutes, a fortune-teller explained: "I am Halebi, we have the gift" and "People don't like us, Ghagar, they don't trust us." The first "we" referred to Halebi as fortune-tellers and the second "us" to Ghagar as a marginalized population.

Within these fluctuating categorizations, the occupational boundaries are in reality flexible and can be crossed when needed. This is an interesting paradox associated with Dom/Gypsy identity, which is very rigid and essentialized on the one hand, and incredibly flexible on the other. The feature is particularly salient in Egypt where the Dom can, at any given time, alter themselves to the point of becoming invisible. The urbanization of the Ghagar has affected their occupations, since they have mostly given up their nomadic lifestyle; they also have given up some entertainment activities and engaged in more sedentary ones. As noted before, nomadism and sedentarism are alternate strategies for negotiation in the economic and social realms (Silverman 1988; Salo and Salo 1977). Among the Alexandrian Ghagar, there are taxi drivers, waiters in coffeeshops, carpenters, street vendors, metalworkers. While they may still live in tight, ghetto-like communities where they are identified as Ghagar by their neighbors, outside of these specific environments, they are most likely not perceived as such. Ghagar and other Dom translate their Gypsiness differently in accordance with their varying occupations. In some instances it is a necessary attribute to their activity, as it is for fortune-tellers; in other instances, their Gypsiness can become an impediment to their employment.

Overemphasis and Underemphasis of Identity

Since Gypsies supposedly have 'the gift' of foreseeing the future, they overemphasize their identity when engaged in fortune-telling activities; in this context it is important for their credibility to look and act Gypsy. In Cairo, many fortune-tellers practice their art in places of high visibility, such as the Giza zoo. Customarily, small groups of fortune-tellers enter the zoo around 11:00 a.m. and either walk around the alleys of the zoo between the lethargic animals, or wait in small clusters near the mosque area. Workers at the zoo seem to know precisely when and where to find them. The fortune-tellers usually wear black *abaya*s and black headscarves and parade with small white shell bracelets that they hold in front of their dresses, quite visibly. Although they no longer cry "I perform divination! What is present I manifest! What is absent I manifest!" as Lane (1871, 98) described more than a century ago, they ensure that they are recognized and do not hesitate to approach passers-by to offer their talents, usually jingling their white shell bracelets in front of the potential customers. The fortune-tellers also practice their art in the downtown Cairo market of Khan al-Khalili, another place of high visibility. They approach their target, promising divination and neutralization of the effects of the evil eye. In Alexandria, Ghagar meet near the Corniche. According to one Alexandrian interlocutor, "Everyone knows that they are Ghagar and they can predict the future, but no one knows where they come from." They seem to appear from nowhere, like supernatural creatures, at a specific time, in a specific place, and they fulfill their prophetic duties before disappearing into a darkness that does not seem to matter. They are present at the time of the exchange and the rest seems of little importance for any party; customers are happy not to know where the Ghagar go and the fortune-tellers gladly become invisible once their task is accomplished. The passage between visibility and invisibility is motivated by the function the fortune-teller plans to fulfill: she is visible when she engages in a predefined economic relation, trading her divinatory skills for money, and she disappears when her performance is accomplished. More intimate details, such as where she comes from or how she travels, ought not to be disclosed. In this interaction all actors are at ease with the preset rules, involving a temporary and overemphasized visibility, followed by invisibility.

Fortune-telling is simultaneously perceived as an innate gift and an acquired skill that Ghagar obtain from their mothers and grandmothers. It is a uniquely feminine function. Fortune-telling is also a highly psychological and cultural skill. The reader needs to present herself in a manufactured way, in order to convey the message that she is an authentic psychic. She also needs to understand intimately the expectations, desires, and fears of her clientele. According to Carol Silverman, who analyzed impression management among American Roma fortune-tellers, "impression management is a technique of persuasion used by Gypsies when crossing the boundary into the non-Gypsy world. Close proximity of non-Gypsies, economic dependence on them and divergent cultural values all point to the need for Gypsy manipulation of the impression non-Gypsies receive" (1982, 395). First, the fortune-teller needs to construct a persona that exaggerates Gypsy attributes, mysticism, mysteriousness, and a certain ruthlessness that will fulfill the stereotypical expectation of Gypsy brutality and also instill sufficient fear in the customers to drive the distribution of power to her advantage. Usually, the fortune-teller attracts her clients by calling them or approaching them, displaying an uncanny confidence. She starts by promising them access to unknown truths, and protection from evil. She often overemphasizes her Gypsiness, usually with her screams, since many Ghagar have internalized the perception, supposedly held by outsiders, that female Ghagar are loud. She also relies on her looks: large gold earrings, necklaces, and the well-recognized white shell bracelet. She ostentatiously displays what she expects others to expect of a Gypsy. The simple fact of being a Gypsy, as a general identification since most customers are oblivious to the differences between Halebi and Ghagar, triggers respect and fear, both mandatory reactions to be able to initiate the economic relation that is to follow, as it is only when the fortune-teller has managed to establish herself as powerful, and concomitantly increased her customer's vulnerability, that the sacredness of her action can be appreciated. It is the interaction that she has crafted between her and the customer that will give her the prestige she needs to make her actions meaningful: the sacred is rooted in momentarily inverted, unequal power relations. The fortune-teller then needs to legitimize her position as a real expert, which is eased by the fact that traditionally Gypsy identity has been constructed around the myth of fortune-telling, so the identity becomes sacred in that context. She may say, and would say it only at that crucial moment, that she has the gift. Most Ghagar fortune-tellers I have met managed rather gracefully to create the spiritually powerful persona they needed to establish, and simultaneously to remain very businesslike in order to keep the necessary distance with their client. It is still, after all, a fundamentally economic type of interaction, even if it is tinged with spirituality. The next part of the game revolves around successfully instilling curiosity and fear in the client, who will want to know more, will be afraid to leave, and will most likely want to keep the relationship alive by paying the fortune-teller.

Many reading rituals follow precisely codified proceedings. The fortune-teller first asks a few questions of her clients: whether they have children, are married, and have known enemies—knowledge which will make her more informed and her clients more vulnerable. She then usually asks her client to hold a small white shell in his or her hand, a shell that will allow her to "enter the soul" of the client, and which will come to represent the client. She examines the shell carefully, holding it in her hands, as if she were symbolically holding the client in her hands, knowing that the least hint of a smile or a frown will not go unnoticed. Usually, she detects that someone is jealous or has negative feelings toward the client, or the client's family, and that thankfully this can be cured with a specific procedure. She asks the client to pick up some dirt from the ground and she puts it in a paper tissue; she explains that if the dirt disappears from the tissue, the evil eye will be removed. She carries out her magical process and usually exhibits a clean tissue to the client, symbolizing victory over evil. The encounter may stop there, or it may continue, as she may discern another problem that needs to be addressed.

To play on her client's most intimate fears, the fortune-teller needs to have understood what is culturally constructed as terrifying, and where the traditional roots of evil are usually situated. If most fortune-tellers mention the existence of a 'jealous person' in the client's environment, who will bring them misfortune, it is to comply with the Egyptian's internalized fear of the evil eye, which is at its core a belief that the gaze or praise of one individual directed toward another may cause illness or even death to the second individual or to an object belonging to that individual, such as a fruit tree or a cow (Dundes 1981, 7). Many Egyptians are afraid of prompting jealousy in others and misfortunes are often interpreted unquestionably as outcomes of the evil eye. People go to extremes to ensure protection to their loved ones. Parents do not hesitate to give their child an ugly name or pierce their baby boys' ears in order to pass them off as girls so as to avoid the jealousy of their neighbors and relatives. People get very suspicious of excessive praise of their children or of themselves. In this context, it is crucial for fortune-tellers to mention the evil eye and most fortune-tellers do, because of the intense fear it triggers and because it is an uncritically accepted explanation for misfortunes. The Ghagar fortune-tellers master very craftily the art of scaring and reassuring, playing on the customer's deepest cultural fears as well as the soundly entrenched representation of Gypsies as intermediaries between the sacred and the profane.

Other occupations require more constant invisibility, and in these cases Gypsiness needs to be understated. Since thievery is largely associated with Gypsies in popular perception, many Gypsies, whether they engage in this trade or not, try to hide their identity. Ghagar also often engage in begging and, as beggars, decide to hide their Ghagar identity, assuming that they can arouse more sympathy and that there will be more willingness to help an Egyptian female than a Ghagar. A taxi driver in

Alexandria explained that he once took as passengers two females who he assumed were beggars. As soon as they got into his cab, they removed their headscarves and he could see their blond hair, and he immediately identified them as Gypsies. When he initially stopped to pick up the two ladies, he explained, he was afraid they would not have enough money to pay and would try to negotiate a low price with him. When he saw they were Ghagar, he was sure he would not be paid at all, "not because they were poor, but because they were dishonest and thieves." Their ethnic affiliation was seen as a much stronger element to predict their behavior than their social class was.

Badr is an Alexandrian Ghagar who used to work as a private driver for "an important person in the police." He explained that his employer was not aware that he was a Ghagar, and probably would not have offered him the job "had he known." Badr reflected on the fact that he never told him: "Sometimes I thought I could tell him, he knew I was honest . . . but then, if I told him, he would not trust me anymore, so why bother? It was easier like that." Later on, he lost that job and found a new job working with a rich Ghagar. This time, he explained, he used the fact that he too was a Ghagar to get the job, counting on ethnic solidarity. The game of identity disclosure or dissimulation involves many players who often think they outsmart the other party. While Badr's sister quietly laughed at the fact that he had worked for a police officer who did not know who he truly was, an Egyptian man who accompanied me during my visit later explained that the officer was certainly aware of Badr's identity, and had most likely chosen him *because* of his identity: "The police use Ghagar to work for them, they know the Ghagar want to be on good terms with them . . . so they have them do all kinds of dirty jobs." The fact that Gypsies have worked as police thugs is explicitly mentioned by some early Orientalists observers, and is still found in the narratives of many Egyptians, who told me stories of Ghagar being recruited by the police to break up demonstrations or terrorize strikers, in exchange for immunity for their crimes.

Interlocutors from the Ghagar of Sayyida Zaynab pointed out that people usually were not aware that they were Ghagar, but that if their identity was uncovered, they would not want to have anything to do with them. They would not employ them or rent them an apartment. "When I looked for a flat, people refused to rent to us because we were Ghagar," explained one of them. As a result, many stay in the same apartments even when they would prefer to move. When asked why they thought landlords were usually so reluctant to rent, they mostly responded that it was because people thought all Ghagar were "thieves," or "[non-Ghagar have] a bad opinion of us." Upon further reflection, one of the young men observed that it would be easier for him to "completely change neighborhood" if he wanted to move to a new house, where people would not know he was a Ghagar, but that

> if I want to stay in Sayyida Zaynab, for instance, well, I can't really move to a new flat, like . . . people know me, I mean the neighbors know who we are, and they talk to each other, they always find out. Even if one does not know at first, then they will, things are always known in Sayyida Zaynab.

One of their friends, who lives in the very poor area of Dar al-Salaam in Cairo, objected that it would be difficult to go somewhere else and pretend he was not Ghagar because usually Ghagar lived close to each other: "We are always like three or four families in homes very close, you know, we are very close, always." They agreed that it was important for them to be in the proximity of other Ghagar, mostly because they belonged to the same families, so they could support each other. Support includes both moral and financial support, and many interlocutors indicated that at some point they had to borrow money from a relative, often an uncle or an aunt. They pointed out that money could *never* be borrowed from anyone other than a relative, and the thought of ever borrowing from an institution seemed preposterous. One young man who had recently gotten married explained:

> I had to pay a high dowry for my wife . . . so I had to ask for money. I asked my aunt, she gave me a lot of money, she understands that she needs to give me a large sum, because my wife, you know, she is good, I needed a high sum. No one else but another Ghagar would

understand what we do in terms of dowry and how important it is to be able to pay for a good wife.

He was referring to the implicit understanding among Ghagar regarding the elements that determine a 'good wife' and the calculation of the dowry, usually based on her beauty and her 'skills' (generally regarded as skills in begging or stealing).

Concealing Ghagar identity might allow families to find housing in a new neighborhood, provided it was far from the neighborhood where they have already been identified as Ghagar and would probably encounter reluctance from landlords. However, this rupture would also mean abandoning the community, which is perceived as problematic because of the deep ties of solidarity that exist within and between families. Passing may be more desirable and easier to achieve in the short-term relations linked to employment than in long-term and more intimate practices, such as finding housing. One Ghagar group in Alexandria has established itself within a cluster of habitations in a small alley, in the area of Muharram Bek. There are about five houses, each containing one or two rooms where the families eat and sleep. Everyone in the neighborhood knows they are Ghagar. Not a single Ghagar mentioned leaving the neighborhood, or having to dissimulate their identity for the purpose of obtaining housing. However, to find employment they may occasionally do so, as Badr described earlier.

Identity Management in Social Interactions

Scholarly literature on Roma and Gypsies emphasizes that interactions between Gypsies and non-Gypsies are mostly economically based. As we have seen earlier in this chapter, a variety of strategies are used in these interactions. Gypsy identities may be downplayed for fear that acknowledged Gypsiness will negatively affect the relationship and prevent Gypsies from obtaining a job or housing. On the contrary, there are situations when overplaying their Gypsy identity and paradoxically exploiting the prevailing stereotypes works to the Gypsy's advantage, as is the case with fortune-tellers and belly dancers. There is a danger of essentializing Gypsies as *only* capable of interacting economically with non-Gypsies and therefore reducing them to being providers of a specific economic function. Okely cautions: "Common misrepresentations of Gypsies have tended to include the assumption that the 'real' Gypsies were formally or ideally in a state of isolation, with unique, self-contained traditions. The isolation model presently ignores the Gypsies' dependence, as always, on the larger economy and the necessity for continuous relations with out-siders" (1983, 28). Certainly the isolation cannot be sustained indefinitely, because Gypsies have to engage in economic relations, and as a matter of fact, they are often in a state of economic dependency. But the economic relations still create distance because they are necessary and cold, not based on warmth, friendship, or exogamy. What about social relations? Can there be an organic bond, a bond that is not purely rational and pragmatic, between Gypsies and non-Gypsies? Or can the non-Gypsy's relationship with Gypsies only be economic? And how do Gypsies them-selves manage their identity in social interactions?

I have observed different types of social or semi-social encounters between Ghagar and non-Ghagar. One type of social encounter involves individuals I have identified as 'wise' in the Goffmanian sense of the term in earlier chapters—people who, because of their occupations as social workers or their business interactions with Gypsies, may potentially be able to engage in relations that also contain social components. The four 'wise' individuals who have discussed their experience extensively are Shaima, Habiba, Abdelrahman, and Magdy. Shaima, Abdelrahman, and Habiba are social workers whose objective is to engage in outreach projects with marginalized communities, and specifically with Ghagar communi-ties, where they offer small loans or education for working children. At one point, Magdy collected Coke bottles from Ghagar in order to sell them to a factory for recycling. He engaged in that business specifically with Ghagar because, like other poorer communities in Egypt, they were often associated with trash-collecting activities, but also because, unlike other communities (such as the Coptic Zabbalin, for instance), they had not developed an organizational net that supported their operations.

All four interlocutors had engaged in activities whose nature required dealing specifically with Ghagar. In earlier chapters, I have described how the 'wise' who manage to penetrate a space of social proximity with

Ghagar are nonetheless kept outside of the social boundary, often because they themselves choose to. For instance, Magdy declined invitations to Ghagar funerals or weddings, and Habiba never completely entered Ghagar homes. In those cases of semi-social encounters, Habiba, Shaima, and Magdy nonetheless all displayed empathy and knowledge about the community that seemed to go beyond what is needed in their work-based relations. During our first encounter, Habiba showed me a small shell bracelet, a gift from a Ghagar woman whom she described with warmth, as if she were talking about a true friend. Magdy related many social encounters with Ghagar; they would have a coffee together at a local coffeeshop, and he would go to their homes for coffee as well. When there was a wedding or a funeral, he would occasionally drive around to Ghagar houses in his van with the groom or someone related to the deceased in order to notify Ghagar about the ceremony.

Those interlocutors displayed empathy toward Ghagar, as well as a distinct sense of pride in being able to approach them and to "understand their ways." The Ghagar ways they generally described are archetypical of Ghagar/Gypsy stereotypes, which would appear to be the outcome both of their own observation and interpretation of Ghagar practices, based on prior expectations, and of the meanings provided by the Ghagar in their descriptions of these practices. Habiba, for instance, reported frequent fights in the neighborhood of Sayyida Zaynab. On one occasion, I was supposed to meet her in her office downtown. The evening before the scheduled meeting, she phoned me to warn me that, "Hopefully there won't be a fight tomorrow . . . however, it probably will happen." The next morning, she called to cancel our meeting because the fight that she had anticipated had indeed happened, someone had been killed, and the area was not safe. I could not help but notice a certain satisfaction in her voice when she told me that her predictions had come true, as well as her assessment that the Ghagar were intrinsically violent. She offered to explain why it was difficult to provide Ghagar with loans: since loans must be repaid, the debt would create a bond between Ghagar families and herself, which would take away some of their freedom, and "Ghagar like to be free," to the extent that they would prefer either to be given the money outright or not to receive anything at all. Her conclusion was that while this was impractical, it was nonetheless the Ghagar's way. She also reported discussions she had had with Ghagar about their own violence and exclusionary practices: "They tell me they like to be among themselves, they tell me they don't like strangers who don't know about their Ghagar ways, like, women tell me they would never marry a non-Ghagar." The 'wise' position themselves in a very limited available space: while they appear to display emotional closeness toward Ghagar, they still keep an outsider perception. Furthermore, their lack of personal experience of being stigmatized, marginalized, or racialized, despite their empathy, maintains a social distance from the Ghagar. Simultaneously, that awareness may also contribute to an exaggeration of their role as 'wise' and perhaps an exaggeration of the perceived closeness.

Ghagar themselves may not experience the same closeness, since they perceive the 'wise' as engaging in a relationship with them specifically because they are Ghagar, which may trigger an overemphasis of their Gypsiness as a means of justifying the relationship. In the case of the professed attitude toward the micro-loans, it is possible that Ghagar evoke their customs specifically to maneuver the loan process in their interest. A cultural explanation justifies the refusal of the loan as a debt which would obstruct their freedom, and a social explanation, based on the endemic poverty among Ghagar communities, justifies their demands to be *given* and not lent the money.

I was not able to directly witness interactions between Habiba and members of the Ghagar communities she engages with; so many of these assumptions are based on Habiba's narrative. I have, however, been present during interactions between Magdy and a group of Alexandrian Ghagar, and the interactions I witnessed seemed to support the hypothesis of an exaggeration of their expected role by each party, the 'wise' and the Ghagar. Before the meeting, Magdy offered many predictions, explaining that it was important to know that they were Ghagar and had "different ways," and I should not be scared: "That is the way they are, you know . . . not like us" (the "us" potentially consisting of him, an Egyptian male, and myself, a non-Egyptian female, grouped against the othered Gypsy). During the encounter, many games were performed between Magdy and his Ghagar 'friends.' Magdy was constantly rolling his eyes while his Ghagar 'friends' overemphasized some traits that they deemed archetypical of their group. For example, most Ghagar have Muslim names. I had been told that Ghagar had two names, a Muslim name and a Ghagar name in Sim, and would use their Muslim Egyptian name in public and the Sim name with peers. However, all the Ghagar I have spoken with told me they only had one Muslim name and the Sim name was rare now, maybe still done "in the countryside" or by the "Sa'idi Ghagar of Upper Egypt" where the traditions were stronger. Many Ghagar women also follow the Egyptian tradition of being called Umm ('mother') of their child's name: typically, it is the name of the first-born, but in practice, among Egyptians, it is most likely the name of the first boy. A woman may be called Umm Ahmed, for instance, so that her own name remains private, a sign of modesty. Nowadays, this tradition is mostly followed in more conservative environments. Some Ghagar use this traditional naming but use their first daughter's name, a sign of their love for girls and a subtle transgression of the Egyptian patriarchal tradition. One of the Alexandrian female Ghagar pompously presented herself as "Umm Zaynab," using the name of her eldest daughter. When she did so, she looked directly at Magdy and announced: "See, we Ghagar, we like females, not like you. We are proud of our girls. I am proud to have my daughter's name." During the rest of our encounter, she would regularly look at Magdy to declare a practice or a belief to be Ghagar, most of them related to women's role in the household, and occasionally criminal activities in which Ghagar or Hanagra are supposed to engage: women are the most skilled thieves, women are in charge. They also asked me a few times whether I was scared of being among Ghagar, and looked at Magdy, implying that he seemed to be scared of them, and then laughed. That playfulness created intimacy between the different actors and a certain level of sophistication in the interactions. Peculiarly, an illusion of friendship was more evident in this type of encounter than in any other circumstance of practical interactions, such as fortune-telling at the zoo, belly dancing, and limited, short-term commercial relations.

I wondered whether Ghagar could engage in genuine friendship with non-Ghagar. I was often told it was "impossible," which led many Ghagar to downplay their identity because they knew that Gypsiness would be received negatively. One of the zoo fortune-tellers explained that when she was not practicing palmistry, she never mentioned her Ghagar identity.

> Yes, I am Ghagar, that is OK, but at the same time, people don't really like us, they have a bad idea about us. Sometimes, we forget who we are, it depends. I think Ghagar are changing, they live more like Egyptians and less like before, in tents. When I was a child, we lived differently and women carried children on their belly, in a scarf. We don't do this anymore.

The "forgetting" of who they are perhaps refers to losing Ghagar traditions, or, in the context of her discourse, possibly not putting forward her identity because "people have a bad idea" about them. Remarkably, while many Ghagar, both in Alexandria and in Cairo, have mentioned that non-Ghagar had negative representations of them ("We are like second-class citizens . . . people are afraid, they think we are thieves"; "Egyptians don't respect us"; "They are afraid to deal with us, it is like we will always be different for them"), they also often admit to having non-Ghagar Egyptian friends. However, the admission of the very possibility of friendship seems to go alongside a statement that Egyptians are scared of Ghagar or treat them as second-class citizens.

The next level of immediacy beyond ordinary friendship is exogamy. Marriages between Ghagar and non-Ghagar are initially described as "impossible" or "very rare," but there are instances of mixed marriage. Alexandrian Ghagar talked about a marriage between a Ghagar male and a non-Ghagar female that was going to take place, and characterized it as unprecedented in their community. They were very excited and were planning to put on a beautiful feast, "to show them what a Ghagar wedding is like."

Ghagar also interact socially with non-Ghagar because of social proximity. Ahmed is a young man who lives in the City of the Dead. He befriended a young Ghagar, Karim. Karim presents himself as a tough guy. A large scar crosses his face that he described, with a certain pride, as "something from [his] past." He explained that he was now working in a marble factory and trying to get away from the stereotype that follows

Ghagar, but he had problems gaining people's trust both at work and in friendship. However, with Ahmed they "can be friends." They appear to be good friends, sharing frustrations about 'the system' and their interest in women, football, and drugs. They both met with my translator, an Egyptian male, to discuss relationships and marriage. It was decided that, as a female and a foreigner, my presence would inhibit them. They were nonetheless aware that the discussion would be reported to me. The three of them met in a coffeeshop in the area of Sayyida Zaynab. The meeting place had been chosen by Karim because it was owned by a friend, also Ghagar. As it was reported to me, the conversation began formally, but after a few coffees and shishas, Karim and Ahmed started to talk very freely about their relationship; they told jokes and engaged in raucous talk. When asked if they were friends, they both agreed. After they had been talking for a while, Karim ran after my translator to ask for his phone number, which we gave him on a piece of paper. Ahmed saw the transaction and ran after us to ask if he had given money to Karim. He later called my translator and explained that Karim was *certainly* going to ask us for money—which he did not—because the Ghagar always try to "get an angle on things." In later encounters, they separately made small comments about the distance that existed between them, often in a light and facetious manner. On one occasion, Ahmed mentioned that Karim could not be trusted and was always trying to make situations remunerative. Karim noted that Ahmed did not fully respect him and his group and thought they were "less good than regular Egyptians."

Fluidity

Passing for non-Gypsies is relatively easy most of time, when Gypsies wish to do so. They can dress like Egyptians, speak like Egyptians, worship like Egyptians, and follow most of the cultural practices. Many Egyptians would say that they can easily recognize Gypsies, however. When asked how, the responses vary from "blond hair and gold earrings" for women to even more racialist descriptions for men, such as a "mean dark look," "cruel black eyes," or even "monkey face." The truth seems to be that most of the time, Ghagar can easily be recognized when they want to, and pass for non-Ghagar when they wish to do so. Exaggeration of Gypsiness usually comes with a specific objective, which in the modern urban environment is usually to practice palmistry, or to engage in some form of specifically Gypsy entertainment. The denial of identity by Gypsies is well documented, the result of an internalized feeling of inferiority, or in order to protect themselves from discrimination, particularly in the areas of employment and housing. It is mostly in areas that imply short-term relations that Gypsies pass the most; it is a temporary passing that happens for the purpose of the interaction.

Passing is a strategy for protecting the group identity, using a subtle combination of interaction with outsiders and preservation of certain traditions in secret. The inside conservation of culture and tradition and the outside interactions are carefully balanced and necessary to ensure the survival of the group. Their ability to pass and to somehow fool the outsider, be it for a malicious reason or simply as a survival mechanism, also gives the group a sense of dignity. Weber and his definition of a caste come to mind: groups that are deemed impure and have internalized this inferiorization tend to build a system rooted in the spiritual, the divine, the secret, to regain some 'sense of dignity.' For Weber, "only with the negatively privileged status groups does the 'sense of dignity' take a specific deviation" (2011, 63). For the positively privileged, their sense of dignity is naturally related to their being; for the negatively privileged, that sense of dignity, less evident, can be embodied in the belief in a great past, or a brighter future lying beyond the present, whether in this life or another. It creates a sense of honor for the pariah people. The Ghagar do not believe in a glorious past, nor are they representing themselves as a chosen people with messianic aspirations; their sense of dignity is constructed in the secrecy of their practices and even of their identity. This secrecy is often used by the Ghagar to regain a sense of dignity.

5

UNDERGROUND WORLD:
CRIME IN THE BLOOD AND
SECRET LANGUAGE

According to David Mayall, Gypsies are not seen as a separate race, but "simply as outcasts from society, a people living on the margins of criminality and at the bottom of the class hierarchy. The sense of threat, nuisance, danger, conflict and confrontation runs throughout each element of this portrait" (2004, 2). Criminality in Gypsies is a fundamental topic. Much literature has pointed out how in Europe, the Roma have morphed from being eroticized and romanticized to becoming a dangerous underclass. Studies have also pointed out the role that media discourse as well as 'common sense' have played in creating the criminalized identities, with the result that these essentialized Roma embody societal fears and social dysfunctions. These representations are also present in Egypt, where we witness the genesis of a criminalized Ghagar identity. We saw in chapter 4, in the creation of 'uncrossable' boundaries, that many non-Ghagar, 'wise' and non-'wise' alike, tend to perceive Ghagar solely as criminals, and upon being asked if they know of other representations (artists, fortune-tellers), they often answer negatively: "No, there is nothing artistic about them," "They are just criminals." In Egypt, criminalized representations have not yet triggered public policies, as has happened in Europe, where the role of Roma, Gypsies, and Travelers as 'folk devils' is perceptible in public policy and reinforced by the media. This demonization demonstrates how governments react to media representation by introducing populist policies (Richardson and Ryder 2012). The Institute for Criminological and

Sociological Research in Cairo does not have specific data about Ghagar, although they recently conducted a large study involving more than four thousand individuals engaged in criminal activities and they assure us that "surely" their sample included Ghagar. However, in this research, group affiliation was never indicated. As a result, we are left mostly with suppositions and sensationalist stories reported orally or in newspapers.

Many empirical studies have demonstrated that the ubiquitous nature of media (of the majority population) plays an important role in articulating knowledge, meanings, and attitudes, as well as in communicating ethnic opinions and stereotypes (Schneeweis 2012; Sedláková 2006; Van Dijk 1989a, 1993, 2012). Van Dijk in particular has conducted extensive analyses on the roles and strategies of newspapers and other media in reporting and (re)producing prejudices and stereotypes associated with ethnic minorities. He argues that a kind of underlying racism in the news presentation, "a sort of ethnic hegemony . . . often tactically accepted by most members of the dominant majority group" (Van Dijk 2000, 34), has emerged. As Schneeweis puts it: "The 'Gypsies' are caught between different competing stereotypes." Common images of the Roma are based on understandings of their 'Gypsiness,' such as "poor, dirty, unhealthy, genetically inclined to commit crime, irresponsible, promiscuous and, above all, the racially inferior and unwanted other" (Schneeweis 2012, 675). On the other hand, Roma are constructed as bohemian, romantic nomads, artists, and singers. Both stereotypes are widespread in the media. The ambivalence between the exotic and the criminal may be less visible in Egypt because the exotic phase was primarily a creation of the Orientalist gaze, which, while fragmentarily internalized in popular imagination or reproduced in movies, had not fully penetrated the collective national psyche. This gap in representation leaves space for introducing a newly generated criminalized and socially marginalized identity that is normalized and unchallenged.

This chapter will focus on the discourse emanating from the media, a powerful discourse that is critical in "contributing to a fabric of knowledge that shapes the concept of Roma and interethnic interactions" (Schneeweis 2012, 676), and will evaluate how media discourse generates and articulates the category of the Ghagar criminal. It will also reflect on the implications that this construct has for the ensuing representations of the Ghagar, as well as on their own identity negotiation and contestation.

Media Discourse

Media discourses have a remarkable influence in constructing social images and linguistic choices. In this respect they must not be seen as accidental, but informed and meaningful (Fairclough 2003). There is a very popular story that many Egyptian interlocutors repeated on several occasions, which is also related in Egyptian newspapers and blogs. The story is about female Ghagar traveling to the holy city of Mecca pretending to sell incense, but with the goal of robbing pilgrims. *Al-Watan*, a widely read Egyptian daily newspaper, told the story of a young girl called Annaba, portrayed as a skilled pickpocket. She had married for a dowry of 150,000 Egyptian pounds, where the amount of the dowry is supposedly correlated to the skills of the bride, mostly in terms of stealing abilities. In the article, Annaba is quoted explaining that she went to Saudi Arabia to rob *'umra* pilgrims: "I stood among them wearing the same clothes, I stole and hid the stolen things." Annaba eventually repented and abandoned her criminal life after she felt guilty during one of her Mecca expeditions, and concludes with her ultimate rejection of the "ways of her tribe," embodied in frequent visits to the local mosque. While the article shows the potential for repentance among members of the community, which contrasts with the usual representation of them as criminal in essence, it also implies that switching to a principled life involves repudiating Gypsy ways, a laborious process hindered by the community's dominance over its members. Many of the fundamental paradigms of the media discourse on Hanagra can be identified in this article: criminality, amorality embodied in the ultimate disrespect of a sacred place, the crucial role of female Ghagars in crime, and the near-impossibility of leaving a rigidified group.

The articles focusing on Ghagar/Hanagra often address the 'Mecca story,' a story that illustrates not only crime, but more offensively the violation of the sacredness of a holy place. It embodies the intrinsic vice of the Ghagar, their disdain for the sacred and the religious, and their lack of a 'code of honor' which may be present among 'normal' thieves. The image of Gypsies as pilgrim robbers is not new. It was also present in the European discourse, whether they actually were depicted as robbing pilgrims and travelers or whether they utilized the justification of pilgrimage to travel safely through Europe, using religion and pilgrimage as an excuse to abuse others: "The allegedly religious motivation for their journey enabled them to be received in a friendly and hospitable way. In this respect, the obligation to supply pilgrims with food, lodging and money, an obligation which was taken very seriously by medieval society, suited them very well. Entries in various books of expenses show that this Christian duty was fulfilled everywhere, at least on the Roma's first appearance" ("Arrival in Europe," n.d.).

The Mecca story is continuously present in the narratives of Egyptians. In the different narratives I collected the story was validated by common sense, expressed in fatalistic adages such as, "There is no smoke without fire," or by 'logical' explanations, questioning the origin of the wealth Ghagar brought back from their expeditions into Saudi Arabia, their natural tendencies toward crime (so why would they decide to *work* in Saudi?), and the fact that Ghagar families would denounce other families' criminal practices in the course of feuds. Newspapers, however, use different argumentative strategies to support their claims. One of them is the quoting of "credible witnesses" (Van Dijk 1993) embodying order and authority: the police, customs officers, or airport security. An article from the Egyptian daily newspaper *Youm7*, a popular news website, describes how two Hanagra women tried to "travel to Yemen with forged passports, in order to cross over to Saudi Arabia and to carry out theft, looting, and robbing of pilgrims" (Sa'id 2011). The article supports the claim by explaining that airport authorities are aware that members of the Hanagra community, specifically females and children, typically travel to Saudi Arabia with the sole intent of "theft and pickpocketing," and that they have increased airport security to address that issue. The factual increase of security targeting children and women from the Hanagra community discursively morphed the Mecca story into an indisputable reality. The news representations of Ghagar serve to justify and reinforce the prejudice against them, presenting 'facts' that are more in the realm of representation and imagination, as well as a political message, recalling what Walter Benjamin said about newspapers: "The newspaper is an instrument of power. It can derive its value only from the character of the power it serves; not only in what it represents, but also in what it does, it is the expression of this power" (2008, 369).

Another strategy is to present specific details about the crimes, which endow them with materiality. An article from the O News Agency (2012) depicts a Hanagra family arriving from Medina with one quarter of a million Egyptian pounds in various currencies plus large numbers of mobile phones, iPhones, and iPads stolen during the pilgrimage; another family was found in possession of 5,000 dollars. The article in *al-Watan* mentioned earlier also gave specific data, in the amount of Annaba's dowry, which added substance to the story. One article published in *Shafaqna* in 2013 relates the story of a Hanagra woman who had in her possession a "bag full of 20,000 Egyptian pounds" that she had stolen. According to the article, that woman had long been engaged in pickpocketing and been previously accused in more than six cases in the area of Giza. The specific details of "20,000 Egyptian pounds," "six cases," and "Giza" give authority to the story. Other articles list precisely what was stolen by female Hanagra: golden necklaces (as "they love gold"), cell phones, iPads, specific amounts of money. These details have a function, which is "not only on contextual relevance, but also on whether or not this will contribute to (de)emphasizing our good practices and their bad one[s]" (Van Dijk 2000, 41). Beyond merely informing the reader about what was stolen, the details serve to make the crimes palpable. Furthermore, the amount of detail concerning their crimes contrasts with all the other uncertainties surrounding the Ghagar, such as who they are and where they live. Sometimes they are believed to live in the outskirts of Cairo, or they are "from the group that is linked to India" and have arrived "in the last century" or "two or three hundred years ago," or that "they come from South Sinai," or from the desert more generally. Their crimes (what they steal, where, how much) are certain; who they are is less certain. As a result, the substance that serves to create them is the one embedded in certainties and factual details: their crimes.

The crimes committed by the Ghagar thus become the basis for their identity, reinforced by the essentialization of their behavior. This essentialization is expressed in the article about the difficulty that Annaba had in leaving her tribe, which she could accomplish only by rejecting it and engaging in a pious life. The media discourse highlights that essential impossibility by noting that Ghagar do not value school, which is deemed 'useless,' but prefer to steal and, for girls, engage in prostitution; or that they "love to steal" and have an "irresistible attraction for gold" (*Rosa Magazine*), or that they "take pride in theft," and that the girl who refuses to continue in the trade would be a pariah—an ironic term, since it is usually used to refer to the Roma as a group. Thus a girl refusing to engage in crime would be a pariah within a pariah group, as described on Masress (Mahmud 2010). The article then explains that pickpocketing is "in their nature" and they may not be aware that "what they are doing is bad for society," a voice that Van Dijk calls "apparent empathy" (2000, 41). The journalist pretends to understand the Gypsies' reprehensible practices; the Ghagar are treated as irresponsible children, incapable of internalizing basic morals and societal norms.

Another story depicts the Ghagar as innately devoid of scruples and incapable of compassion. It starts by explaining that Ghagar do not steal from the blind. However, this is "not because of principle or ethics, of course, but because the blind and dumb are more sensitive to body touches and would feel them when they steal" ("Qabilat al-hangraniya" 2011). This sentence echoes the narratives of the 'wise' in chapter 4 that play on the audience's expectations. The journalist or interviewer initially describes an event or a practice unexpected from Ghagar—that they engage in paid work, or that they show respect for the blind—and then immediately challenges it: the Ghagar utilize the cover of their work to deal drugs or engage in prostitution; or they avoid robbing the blind because of their extra tactile sensitivity. This strategy results in the amplification of what was initially expected, as it proves that hints of any behavior counter to 'common sense' can be dismissed easily. Instead, apparent fragments of honesty or humanity appear to further prove the wickedness of the Ghagar and their inability to internalize social values, such as a desire to work or respect for the weak.

The inability to internalize basic norms of religious sacredness and morality not only creates boundaries but also serves to inject prestige into the outsiders. While the desire to engage in honest work, consideration for the blind, and respect for sacredness are by no means found in every aspect of Egyptian society (or any society for that matter), they become normative of that society when they are shown to be specifically not Gypsy; in that sense Gypsies and non-Gypsies are discursively constructed into "conflictual opposites" (Fowler 1991, 6, cited in Richardson and Ryder 2012, 170). The categories of 'normal' and 'deviant' are concomitantly erected, each displaying exaggerated dichotomic traits of honesty or dishonesty.

Conflictual Opposites, Sensationalism, and Blaming the Victim

The construction of conflictual opposites, which serves to hegemonically deprave the minority/Gypsy and assert, or reassert, the superiority of the majority, can happen smoothly and with little space for challenge, for a variety of reasons. First, the media discourse originates among the elite and not the Gypsy community. Egyptian Ghagar do not write about themselves, so the discourse originates from outsiders, who can decide to attribute certain characteristics of their choice to the Ghagar. The Ghagar are unable to defend themselves using the same discursive tools. When I visited Hosh al-Ghagar, some residents were visibly upset by the article "The Secret World of Gypsies," in which a journalist describes her adventures in the Hosh. However, whether they were Ghagar or not, the only defense they could engage in was to flatly deny their identity. The imbalance of power is striking. The Ghagar cannot defend themselves, and no outsider comes to their defense, mostly because they are so unknown, and thus the discourse that is being generated about them remains unchallenged. (In Western Europe, by contrast, the Roma have created organizations that not only defend their rights but also challenge stereotyped representations and offer alternatives.) There is very little contextualization in the Egyptian case. The Ghagar are simply presented in their full mystery and horror, and one discourse becomes their whole identity. Not only are boundaries created, not only are they othered, but they are also the product of a story that meets very little objection. It is a relatively unknown group, so we can witness the story's genesis: the group is given birth within the lines of those articles, which makes a discourse into a reality, and creates for the audience the powerful illusion of acquiring new knowledge, which is both exciting and scary. That genesis is reinforced by the fact that the representations in most newspapers present uncanny similarities, mostly because few journalists have actually ventured into Ghagar/Hanagra territories. Most news items are either short and superficial, or copied and pasted, in part or fully, from one article to the next, and then to countless forums and blogs. The articles carry identical themes: criminality, matriarchy, foreignness. The lack of variety implicitly gives credibility to what is being said: there is only one possible story.

Another aspect of the hegemonic construction of the Ghagar reality and its acceptance lies in the notion of a discursive bond between journalists and their audiences. The journalists can feed their audience what they want because they are on the same side, possessing a shared identity, which allows the journalist to construct similarity and sympathy with the readers. Journalistic discourse is not necessarily imposed upon society, but is rather the outcome of a steady interaction between the journalist and the audience. In other words, "journalism and society are bound by a two-way relationship in which society influences journalism and vice versa" (Desiderio and Desiderio 2012). Van Dijk thus argues that "there exists a body of generally shared beliefs on which such discriminatory actions are based, and which provides the tacit legitimation of the power exercised by the dominant in-group" (1989a, 202). Who would not be afraid of strangers who display characteristics so alien? They are criminals, they are foreign in their origins, they lack morality, and their cultural practices challenge traditionally respected gender roles. This too facilitates the acceptance of the story being told, like a story being shared in the intimacy of friends, or between individuals of sameness, against otherness. Foucault provides a similar analysis: he views discourse as a form of social interaction; a deep connivance is being created that includes the sender and receiver and excludes the one being talked about.

To seduce the audience, a discursive bond is created, a sort of connivance of us versus them. The pleasure of discussing the other also feeds on well-commercialized sensationalism, which is provided in the description of the bizarre aspects of the group. The Ghagar are depicted as criminals (threatening and scary), but they also display exotic characteristics (exciting). The news to be consumed by the reader needs to look attractive. Both writer and reader seek sensationalism, so the Ghagar/Hanagra are presented as different, not only to be differentiated from mainstream, but also, in Orientalist fashion, to be weird others, built on fragments of strangeness.

In an interview with *el-Mogaz*, the actress Shaima Saif, who played the main Hanagra character in the television series *Women's Prison*, reflected nostalgically on her role, explaining that she was given "a great opportunity" to depict a member of "this group of families living in the slums and working in theft and pickpocketing, where women are the ones who are working, while the men stay at home" ("Shaima Saif" 2014). She had been able to "learn a lot," including the "terminology used by thieves." Another article describes the Hanagra depicted in *Women's Prison*: "Hanagra . . . a new slice of the Egyptian society that was never highlighted before! Women are leading the tribe and their skills in pickpocketing define their dowry. They are living in the out-skirts of towns and villages and they speak a secret language that no one understands. They solve their problems in their council and have their own law" (Ashur 2014). The article marvels at this new world and how the series made people curious about it. The fragmented accounts serve to appease the desire to learn about them without engaging in extensive research, or potentially trigger scientific interest. The audience is fed enough to be excited and not enough to become knowledgeable, which could trigger empathy. Of course, the lack of extensive information is also due to the lack of interest in going beyond cliché.

The connivance with the audience also needs to reassure that audience and blame the Ghagar and not society, in order to avoid challenging social order. The Ghagar's crimes are not rooted in poverty and marginalization but in their nature ("they have crime in the blood"). Their crimes are not the results of social failure, but of their own. To further that idea, the media discourse tends to emphasize the Ghagar's or Hanagra's 'wealth': they have money but "enjoy living in tents" (Egypty 2005). Nowhere is it suggested that perhaps they live in tents because that is all they can afford; they appear to live on the edges of towns, not because they have been pushed to the margins of society, but because they choose to exclude themselves, because of their roots in the desert. They are also presented as 'rich' (from all their crimes) but choosing to live in marginalized areas, or hiding their wealth. They are not recognized as belonging to the lower levels of society or as socially marginalized; they are outside the usual social structures, not part of them. Their outsider status creates a kind of moral panic, in which the light is shifted away from society's institutional failures to integrate them and shines instead on their 'hidden wealth.'

Media discourse tends to construct the Ghagar as amoral criminals, conflictual opposites to an honest, moral society. This contributes, in a hegemonic manner, to their apparent status as 'depraved' and asserts the superiority of the dominant non-Ghagar society, which is not only superior but also has the power and ability to describe and assess the Ghagar, and thus to create them. News representations are based on dramatized pieces of information and description of the Hanagra/Ghagar, posing as 'factual' pieces that are more akin to storytelling and sensationalist discourse. Obviously, unlike in many European countries where the 'Roma issue' is a well-recognized phenomenon, Ghagar are still a novelty in the Egyptian context. They are being constructed right now, in the discourse of the media on their criminality. As a result, fragments of stories become the whole story, and the communities are reduced to a category of criminals and a category of matriarchally organized groups (both negative constructs). The rest of this chapter examines how this criminalized identity is negotiated by members of the Ghagar community.

They Can Only Be Criminal: Rigid Boundaries and Confrontation of Perceptions

Abdelrahman explained that typically the gifts he received from Ghagar parents were ranked from the least to the most prestigious: drugs, mostly in the form of Tramadol, a cheap opiate painkiller that ranks among the most commonly used drugs in Egypt; knives; and offers of protection. The latter represents the highest form a gift could take: the Ghagar would offer protection to the social workers of the organization, including repayment of debts or intimidation of 'enemies.' The knives, which Abdelrahman kept in a locked drawer of his office, were large fighting knives. The gifting was perceived as another illustration of the inescapable criminal nature of the Ghagar. Their detractors argue that it is all that the Ghagar can do, and they marvel at the Ghagar's inability to understand that "life is not all about crime" because in their world, life is all about crime and probably always will be—a narrative very close to the 'displayed empathy' presented in the media discourse.

This exclusive essentialist discourse does not allow for alternative explanations for why the Ghagar seek to assert themselves against the organization, which they may have constructed as a representation of power and authority in the only way they can, which is by using the only type of power they have access to. Or perhaps the Ghagar have internalized their criminalized image and therefore act as expected, in order to make sense in the interaction, in a sort of self-fulfilling prophecy, but also to speak the language of the dominant group and play the role ascribed by the dominant group. Furthermore, perhaps Abdelrahman and Shaima are more likely to acknowledge criminally connoted gifts, simply because they are more noticeable than a simple 'thanks' or a freshly baked Umm Ali, and because they are expecting them. Another social worker, Habiba, who did not perceive all of 'her' Gypsies as criminals, but acknowledged that they also engaged in other activities (such as begging, entertaining, or metalwork), displayed the white shell bracelet she had received from a fortune-telling Ghagar.

While many of the 'wise' have clearly stated that Ghagar would not deny their criminal activities, in some instances they have. Uncovering the perspective of the Ghagar regarding crime is difficult. Crime was never addressed directly during my discussions and encounters, but I identified different implicit allusions, or positions that interlocutors adopted, that permitted me to form a fragmentary hypothesis. First, there was a striking contrast between the rigid representation and the impossibility of escaping crime that is depicted in media and outsiders' discourses, and the way in which the Ghagar have positioned themselves toward the criminalized identity of the group. Second, I would argue that crime and begging have been reinterpreted by members of the community: crime became a way to regain social prestige and begging embodied the complexity of a true profession, requiring both skills and the ability to negotiate independence vis-à-vis the non-Ghagar majority. Lastly, different impression-management techniques are utilized to address crime: in other words, the Ghagars' relationship to their criminalized and marginalized identity is based on performativity. They may perform the criminal, in a way that is perhaps linked to regaining prestige, or they may distance themselves from this role, either by attributing it to another group (the

Hanagra), or by disengaging themselves fully from the Ghagar identity. Sometimes they use their language metaphorically, as a code that allows them to be misunderstood, both practically and symbolically. The Ghagar have internalized the criminalized representation and many interlocutors have acted according to various strategies: denying that they were Ghagar themselves; blaming another group, mostly the Hanagra, who seem to be constructed as the 'criminal other' even within Ghagar communities; talking about "someone" they knew about; or talking about their use of the Sim language as a metaphor for engaging in the criminal trade.

Fluid Boundaries: The 'Saved' Ghagar

I met with Abdelrahman and Tarek, the young man he calls the "saved Ghagar." Tarek is a nineteen-year-old Ghagar who was the "only Ghagar" left in Shaima and Abdelrahman's organization. Before our meeting, I spoke with Abdelrahman, Shaima, and a few other social workers from their organization. They were mostly worried that I would ask Tarek questions about the crimes his family committed, which would trigger the family's ire and induce them to take revenge on the organization. I assured them I would not, since I was mostly interested in how Tarek perceived his own identity, and whether the term 'Ghagar' meant anything to him. I had decided that the conversation would mostly be freeflow and I would follow Tarek's lead. I also mentioned that I would be interested to hear what he would say about 'Ghagar traditions,' a term that I often find reassuring and broad enough to allow people to talk about whatever they wanted, which makes them laugh: "Ghagar don't have any kind of traditions . . . aside from being criminals!"

The contrast in the representations of the group by Abdelrahman the 'wise' outsider and Tarek the Ghagar demonstrated how, despite the copious amount of time they spent together, much remained unknown and misunderstood, perhaps on both sides. In previous meetings, Abdelrahman had argued that Ghagar could *only* be engaged in criminal activities and had stopped participating in *mulid*s or in other forms of entertainment. Tarek, on the other hand, explained that occasionally members of his group were still engaged in artistic activities, such as belly dancing and fire-eating during *mulid*s, as well as playing the *rababa* for weddings. He reported seeing Ghawazi performing on many occasions and added that young female Ghagar learned from their mothers how to dance Ghawazi style. He also addressed the impossibility of moving out of the group, another crucial component of the discourse of the workers in the organization, noting that his family allowed him to study at the center and did not ask him questions about what he was doing, nor offered any sort of judgment about his choices. He appeared to have reached an implicit agreement, according to which his family did not intervene in his education while he did not question what they were doing. When asked if he was encouraging his siblings to join him at the center, he said that he was, and explained that he was pushing both his younger brother and sister to continue their education with the center, which his father did not oppose. The contrast was striking compared to the descriptions from the members of the center, who depicted Ghagar families as resisting their work, since children given an education were taken away from the crime and the paid work that the family relied on. Clearly, the concepts of social acceptance and pride need to be taken into account here, and it is very possible that Tarek deliberately described his family in a positive light.

Tarek also addressed the topic of Saudi Arabia, where his mother and aunt live, both married to Saudi men. His mother and father divorced when he was younger. His mother, he explained, went to Saudi Arabia in order to sell clothes and incense and she decided to stay there. His aunt was married and did not work. He added that his mother constantly asked him to join her in Saudi Arabia, "where salaries are better," but he refused, as he wished to continue his education with the center in Egypt. Tarek appeared to have created a managed relationship with his family, living with them but engaging as little as possible and oscillating between pity and shame, mainly because most of the non-Ghagar he interacted with assumed that they were criminals. He reflected on the stereotypes held by his non-Ghagar acquaintances: "Yes, there are criminals among the Ghagar . . . but probably a minority, but people think the majority [of Ghagar] are criminals." When asked if he contemplated doing something to improve the Ghagar's image, he sighed: "Maybe . . . but it is almost impossible. I don't think anyone can do it."

His position on the margins of the community generates a need to negotiate his own identity and allegiances, as well as a potential contestation of perceptions and practices in both territories, the Ghagar and the non-Ghagar ones. He explained that he had been engaged to his cousin, according to the Ghagar tradition. He eventually broke the engagement because of the 'virginity check,' a Ghagar practice according to which the mother and future mother-in-law of the bride check her virginity before the wedding. Tarek described the practice as "awful . . . I did not want to be part of it." He later met another woman whom he wants to marry, but admitted that he had not told her he was a Ghagar, because "she might be . . . scared or something like that."

Shaima and Abdelrahman described Tarek as a "saved Ghagar," implying that he was "different" from other Ghagar, a difference anchored in his ability to study and his willingness to resist the temptation of crime, unlike the other Ghagar students in their organization. Tarek's own narrative, however, established more fluidity in boundaries. His family does not put pressure on him to stop his education and become a criminal, nor do they all engage in crime. They did not force him to marry his cousin and they accepted that he broke his engagement. However, the stereotypes associated with the group affect his interactions with outsiders: he hides his identity from the woman he wishes to be engaged to, he purposely spends as little time in the company of his family as possible (just for sleeping), and he tries to avoid exploring what they do or socializing with them. He also focuses on "things that are important to [him]," such as working out in a gym and studying hard. The boundaries are interpreted as much more rigid by the outsiders who read the 'saving' of Tarek as an accomplishment and something unique, while he simply perceives it as having moved away from the group, which offered the fluidity to do so.

Perhaps one of the most striking elements in the discussion between Tarek, Abdelrahman, and myself was the difference in representations that the two of them had about Ghagar and how important Abdelrahman viewed the 'saving' of Ghagar from themselves as he had done with Tarek. He mentioned that he was hoping that Tarek's brothers and sister would join the center and wanted to "bring them to the center in order to start modifying them and correcting their path," which he explains is very hard because most Ghagar children "are not responsive and prefer the life of their parents." The criminalized activities appeared more inflexible in the narrative of the social worker, who had in previous meetings established the impossibility of the Ghagar to engage in non-criminal activities, while Tarek presented fluidity in the activities of his family, who seemed to adapt to their context, engaging in small temporary jobs as peddlers, musicians, service providers, or drivers. One telling point was their answer to my question about the food that Ghagar eat. Tarek answered that there was no specific Ghagar food, while Abdelrahman explained that Ghagar liked *asida*, a dish made of milk, flour, and sugar or honey, which can be found in Libya, Yemen, and Tunisia and, less commonly, in Egypt. While Abdelrahman presented the 'saving' of Tarek embodied in his acceptance of mainstream Egyptian values, different from the ones he ascribed to the Ghagar, Tarek interpreted his decision in terms of asserting what he, as an individual, wants to achieve, not simply transferring from one group to the other, but reflecting on his own aspirations, as a body-builder and a mechanic, as well as his own marriage, based on free choice.

Begging Skills

Overall, the Ghagar are very destitute and socially abandoned, so crime and begging could be perceived as means of subsistence in an environment that is both hostile and inattentive to the group. While this is definitely true, the essentialization of the group in both its criminality and begging needs to be explored beyond pure materialism.

Begging is interpreted differently by Ghagar. It has the tangibility of a profession that requires skills. In his ethnographic work on the Ghagar of Sett Guiran'ha, Nabil Sobhi Hanna listed begging as a Ghagar profession following "smithing, tinkers, wool-workers, skin trading, dancing and singing, and hawking and haberdashery" (1982, 24–35). He defined begging as "a temporary occupation used to see the family through an economic crisis," and said it was gendered: "men may beg but typically it is the work of women. Sometimes children beg using tortoises as a drawing card, asking for money from the people who watch it crawl." Hanna continues:

Begging can be direct and devious. The women are very clever at weaving fantastic tales of woe in order to extract money, food or clothing. This is why they usually beg far from their native villages. (1982, 34)

Nowadays among the Ghagar, begging has become more than a temporary occupation, and it is exclusively practiced by women and children. It seems to be carried on in different areas of Cairo, particularly in neighborhoods situated far from the areas where Gypsies have settled, not only to avoid being recognized by neighbors who may identify their 'tales,' but also for proximity to high-traffic areas where people may be willing to give them something. Many Ghagar have established themselves near mosques, ATM machines, restaurants, and supermarkets. Like fortune-tellers, they seem to disappear once their begging activity ceases, and reintegrate into their own neighborhoods. Hanna describes female beggars as "devious" in their constructing of tales, or in the form of what he calls "indirect begging," which he defines as "providing a service, not necessarily wanted, in return for a sum of money. A woman will often offer herself as a wet nurse, establishing a relationship with a number of families in different villages to whom she goes regularly to suckle the babies. This is considered a regular source of income" (1982, 36).

The act of begging requires the internalization of specific rules that are culturally and spatially relative. In some parts of Europe, "the shabbily dressed 'Gypsy woman' who presents herself, with children, as a destitute wife and abandoned mother makes a good beggar (and also meets the Gaujo stereotype of Gypsy men as abusive and irresponsible rogues). A Gypsy man making similar demands on the passing Gaujo may well find himself up in court faced with an assault charge. It is important to make clear here that for many Gypsy groups begging in itself is not 'debased,' but the image required to make the operation credible and economically successful has to be" (Clark 2002, 193). In Egypt, any overemphasis of Gypsiness may not necessarily bring any goodwill, perhaps because of the lack of a stereotype of Gypsies as being abused by their husbands and resorting to begging. The role that needs to be adopted is usually that of a conservative Muslim Egyptian. Ghagar typically wear *hijab*, and sometimes *niqab*, for a variety of reasons. One is to look conservative and encourage sympathy by playing by the rules of social modesty. Another (mentioned by both Ghagar and non-Ghagar) is to hide their blond hair or their possible, but rare, facial tattoos. The need for a conservative religious appearance may also be rooted in the religious ethos of Islam that encourages almsgiving to the poor. The other important dimension is the location in which to beg. The Ghagar beg in specific areas (mosques, ATM machines, supermarkets), following a certain structure, often with children, sometimes also selling tissues.

Begging is symbolically intermediary as well, as the beggar relies on the support of the community, evoking charity and perhaps good deeds, as well as occasionally fear. Foucaultian visions of panoptic social control combine with traditional systems of aid to categorize and separate the urban poor, but also to integrate them into the socio-spatial fabric of the city (Foucault 1977). The genderization of the occupation integrates women into the economic system and is yet another means to construct them as intermediaries between Ghagar and non-Ghagar populations, by performing actions that have some sacredness based on religious ethos and fear, somewhat similarly to fortune-telling.

A Ghagar interlocutor explained that he had to borrow money through what Hanna calls *nokoot* from one of his aunts in order to be able to marry his bride, whose price was moderately high (30,000 Egyptian pounds) as she was a successful beggar. While he was himself working as a tuk-tuk driver, it was principally his wife's begging activity that allowed him to reimburse the sum to his aunt within a couple of years. Money that is begged and money that is borrowed have very different meanings; borrowed money needs to be paid back, while the begged money is owned by the beggar. Borrowed money serves to create a reciprocity bond between the lender and borrower and automatically establishes a long-lasting relationship, at least until the sum has been paid back, which is not the case with money obtained from begging. The temporariness and non-bindingness of begging seem to be important components of the inclination to beg. Ghagar receive money from non-Ghagar when they beg (or perhaps steal), but they try to avoid engaging in a loan relation with non-Ghagar. Both social workers and Ghagar mentioned that Ghagar did not like to receive loans from non-Ghagar, as the transaction creates a bond that deprives them of their social and economic fluidity. Many Ghagar explained that they would exclusively borrow money from someone they trusted, which would have to be a person from the community.

Begging, although a traditional symbol of social exclusion, is reconstructed as a form of independence from society. The only dependency in the transaction is rooted in the necessity for the beggar to rely on the goodwill of the giver. It creates a temporary, non-binding type of relation that offers the beggar flexibility: once the money is received, she can walk out and she never has to engage in any relation with the giver again. This controlled temporariness with non-Ghagar can be contrasted with the kind of bonding and lasting, trust-based relation that is created between the lender of money within the Ghagar community and the borrower. Hanna describes the importance of repaying the *nokoot*, "regardless of whatever dispute or quarrels occur between families. Even when they are on the point of avoiding each other, the payment of the Nokoot remains as a standing obligation" (1982, 67).

The dependency on the giver's goodwill is addressed in the form of specific skills that the beggar, like the fortune-teller, can develop to adapt to her 'clients.' Those skills, typically transmitted from mothers to daughters, are perceived to be prestigious because the begging business is constructed as lucrative. Hanna mentions that in instances of Ghagar–Kashana (non-Ghagar) weddings, Ghagar women may tease the Kashana spouse because of her poor begging skills, which suggests that begging skills were explicitly respected in Sett Guiran'ha.

The Language of Crime

While I have not been able to directly discuss crime with Ghagar, because of the sensitivity of the topic, I have compiled partial descriptions and interpretations in different Ghagar narratives, in which criminal activities were consistently addressed through descriptions of the fragmented Ghagar language. I sat in a tiny room in Alexandria, in a neighborhood called Muharram Bek. The first family I talked to denied knowing any kind of Ghagar language and the mother noted that "our grandparents may have had their language, but we have forgotten it. We only speak Arabic now."

That denial was very similar to the one I encountered in the neighbor-hood of Hosh al-Ghagar where the two women I talked with also initially asserted that the notion of a Ghagar language was simply an invention and such a language had never existed, before adding that "only Hanagra speak a different language." However, when I reached the second house, interlocutors had started to warm up to the idea of sharing controlled information about their language. After a few pleasantries, it became clear that there were remnants of Sim, or "Markat" as they called it, that they were ready to share. There were only a few words, the most useful ones, allowing Ghagar to talk without being understood and "go about our busi-ness." After about half an hour, a 'language expert' was brought in, an older lady, dressed in a black *abaya* with a colorful scarf on her head. She quickly got to the point: "You want to know about our language? I can talk about it." She first explained a specific code that is used to talk about someone without saying his/her name, using the term *goodee* for this code, and then started to list the words she knew. These were similar to the ones that had been given to me by the non-Ghagar, and mostly related to descriptions of individuals, their possessions, and public order, such as 'man,' 'woman,' 'necklace,' 'wallet,' 'cell phone,' 'officer,' 'danger,' 'police.'

> *kadja*: woman, similar to the Halebi recorded by Newbold ("kudah")
> *mehmaza*: wallet
> *yahara*: man
> *menis*: move here
> *chili*: cell phone
> *winit*: small bag
> *esban, addo*: money
> *amoha*: government
> *lamu*: officer
> *cub*: gone
> *mznarh*: an hour

When asked if she could articulate constructed sentences in the language, she said she could not; all that had survived were some random words, associated with Ghagar trade. The words have a purpose and serve as a code. The structure, if there was ever one, has been lost. According to other accounts by Ghagar, the language is now almost completely lost and only used very pragmatically: to escape the police or to steal. As a result, the words that have survived are mostly related to these purposes. A few Ghagar noted that many of the Sim words were discarded because Egyptians could understand them.

One Alexandrian interlocutor and her daughter explained that they mostly used other types of languages, for instance, the 'eye language.' When I asked them to elaborate, they demonstrated how their eyes could talk and how some codes could be understood between different Ghagar, and explained the meaning of each of their looks (which to the non-initiated all seemed very similar): 'go away,' 'give up,' 'there is a chance here or there,' 'the police are coming,' 'be quiet,' and so forth. In this case as well, most of the jargon was focused on escaping authorities and looking for potential targets.

Tarek, the 'saved' Ghagar, confirmed that that there was a language used by Ghagar that he had learned as a child. He described it not as a structured language but mostly a series of words used in specific contexts. When I asked him to say some words, he immediately produced a few words that he translated as 'police,' 'government,' and 'officer.' The word 'Sim' did not mean anything to him: "It is just some of the words we know, to say things others won't understand. It does not have a name; it is just the Ghagar language."

One of my Egyptian interlocutors explained that some of the Sim words were also used in specific contexts, by certain categories of individuals. One example is Egyptians who interact with Ghagar and whose ability to recognize a few words could allow them to avoid a planned theft—for instance, those who can identify the Ghagar words for 'wallet' or 'man' on a crowded bus. Borrowings from the language are occasionally used as additions to the Egyptian dialect of Arabic, the Ghagar roots being forgotten. Egyptians would use some Ghagar words, such as those for 'man' or 'woman,' as slang. Third, some words of the language are used by certain groups who are not necessarily Ghagar, but who need a 'code' in order to talk among themselves and deceive the non-initiated. I was given the specific example of jewelers, some of whom are Ghagar, who would use Sim words to communicate in front of a customer and set up a plan. Thus language now follows different paths, sometimes associated with the Ghagar themselves, sometimes with practices that are perceived as intrinsically Ghagar, such as theft or deception, and sometimes by categories of people who may have been predominantly Ghagar, such as jewelers. In Alexandria there may be a rather large community of Ghagar jewelers who brought in their own jargon in an earlier period, and who stayed in the trade even though they no longer compose the majority of the group. Gypsies in general are seen as "loving gold," and many women wear gold earrings or other jewelry. While I have not been able to confirm it with the few jewelers I spoke with in the Khan al-Khalili, the author of an article published in al-Monitor, entitled "The Secret Language of Cairo's Jewelry Merchants," relates this special code to Hebrew.

> "All sorts of groups have secret languages," says Rosenbaum, "religious and ethnic groups, criminal organizations, sportsmen, students. Parents speak a foreign language near the kids so they won't understand them. And there are languages developed for specific purposes such as the language of the professional guild. For the Egyptian merchants the purpose is to set prices or pass information behind the customer's back. Since it's been used for secret oral communication, it's never been written down."
>
> At first, he says, the merchants were not happy to share their code language with him, but after they understood that Hebrew is his native language and he uncovered their code language, they opened up to him. They know that the strange words that got mixed in with their language originates [sic] in Hebrew, from the Jewish merchants. That's why they call their secret language "Hebrew" or the "language of the Jews." (Hugi 2013)

Among Ghagar, Sim is not prevalent but has been reduced to a few useful words. Somehow it truly embodies its Arabic meaning of 'code.' It is not a structured language whose speakers can form complete sentences and engage in conversations, but a series of words. None of the Ghagar I have spoken with in Alexandria or in Cairo could carry on a conversation in Sim,

176 Underground World: Crime in the Blood and Secret Language

or had ever heard anyone do so. They all knew some essential words. New words can apparently be created, such as *chili* ('cell phone'). Some of the words seemed to be close to Arabic, while other were not. They were not necessarily close to Domari, either, as it has been recorded by linguists, and since there is no formal structure that anyone seems to be able to convey, it is hard to connect it grammatically to either Arabic or Sanskrit. Aside from its use in specific actions (stealing, escaping the police), Sim also seemed to be meaningful as a reminder of some lost identity. A few Ghagar said the words with pride and nostalgia, but at the same time seemed satisfied with those few words, and no one expressed any interest in learning more of the language or learning about it. Very much like other aspects of the Gypsy identity, the language itself has disintegrated.

Linguists look at language maintenance or language shift within a linguistic minority after extensive contact with dominant groups, but this was not done for Sim. The language as such is lost. What remains of it is useful for economic activity within the dominant society. The language takes its entire meaning from that relationship, and otherwise seems irrelevant as a cultural marker for the group. It is mostly used to communicate in specific instances and not be understood by the majority, while interacting with that majority. It no longer serves as a vehicle of communication within the group.

This limited use of the Sim language seems to indicate that many Ghagar have internalized the notion that their identity is mostly based on a set of specific relationships with the dominant group, which is what they are also stigmatized for. The relationship is somehow rigidified by the decay of the language that has come to embody this very relationship. The language represents the relationship, in a sense, but also creates it, because it is one way to transmit one group's perception of another. In other words, because much of the relationship between non-Ghagar and Ghagar may have been based on the ability of the latter to steal from the former, the language reduced itself solely to the words useful in that interaction. The fact that these words are the only fragments of the language that are now transmitted automatically indicates that this is indeed the basis of the relationship between Gypsies and non-Gypsies. Being taught specific 'secret' words such as 'wallet' and 'police officer,' children will internalize those as the basis for their identity in the relationship to the majority group. A few young Ghagar listed those words as the only ones they knew. They seem to embody the loss of a time when this may have been the language spoken in the group (although none of them could recall having heard anyone speak it as a language), the language that gave them an identity distinct from the majority.

The term "thievish language" used by von Kremer does, in this case, express a literal meaning. Sim has become a language or a code for theft and has reduced the Ghagar to that very identity, which is why it has been appropriated by jewelers (and possibly other groups, but I mostly heard about the jewelers) to steal from or abuse their customers. In this way, it essentializes even more deeply the characteristics associated with the Ghagar, making them the thieves par excellence.

Sensuality in Crime?

The media discourse creates a rigid, criminalized character that serves not only to describe Ghagar/Hanagra but also, as a conflictual opposite, to inject prestige into the non-Ghagar, who are thereby constructed as moral and honest in contrast to the amoral, depraved, dangerous Ghagar. 'Contrast' is an interesting notion to examine how the Ghagar position themselves within the limited space of criminality. As we saw in the narrative of Tarek, the young 'saved' Ghagar, their identity is, unsurprisingly, more fluid than the uncompromising media representation. What is also of interest is the fact that criminalized activities have gained different meanings. Begging is interpreted as an independent activity that requires unique skills and allows the Ghagar to carve some freedom and strategic control into their relations with the non-Ghagar. The Ghagar rarely talk about crime directly. They mention it either in connection with other groups (the Hanagra in particular seem to embody the 'bad Gypsies') or by reference to the Ghagar language, which has become crystallized into a few terms related to theft and authority. Another interpretation is that crime is a way to inject prestige into a group that is severely deprived of it.

In his seminal 1990 publication, *Seductions of Crime*, Jack Katz challenges the positivist notions that view criminals as intrinsically depraved, but also view crime as mainly about acquisition, materialism, or economic need. He refocuses the debate on the status and prestige associated with criminal activities and the persona of the criminal. The material aspect is present, particularly in an abandoned underclass, but the prestige associated with criminal activities also permits the members of the group to acquire a form of power. Katz specifically talks about the sensual experience that is lived by criminals and the "sacredness" that comes with the power of invading, defiling, and changing moral order. For a group that is intensely disrespected, gang life is a form of empowerment that is obviously transmitted to children, potentially more influential than any type of skill. Gang organization appears to be the deviant form of power that many Ghagar want to portray, perhaps excessively favoring inspiring fear over inspiring disrespect. Inspiring fear to gain respect is also part of the strategy fortune-tellers engage in, by asserting their mental strength in order to establish themselves in a spiritual position.

The turn to crime is not only a way to regain respect. It is also sometimes a defense mechanism when the state is not capable of ensuring the safety of its citizens. In his book on political civility in the Middle East, Frederic Volpi analyzes the negotiations that take place between the power and the citizens, looking at the complexity of relationships and power relations established between the police and individuals.

> It would appear that there are multiple orders of state, with their rules and laws perpetually criss-crossing, contingent and situational ... at the same time the citizens must improvise in the face of ambiguities and fluidities in the orders of state. They may seek the police for protection from a local thug and be told that it is up to them to take care of the problem. They may have to devise means of chasing away drug dealers from their neighborhoods because the police decline to intervene. In such instances it would appear that the thug and the drug dealers are part of the state (the police employ thugs to run the mini-van service in the area in return for serving as informants and are also thought to be somehow implicated in protecting drug dealers). (Volpi 2014, 55–56)

While the criminal role can be empowering, in the sense that it gives one type of power to an otherwise totally powerless group, it is also oppressive, as it keeps the members of the group in a stigmatized environment. Few of the Ghagar I spoke with oscillate between different roles, from the 'tough guy' to the individual trying to resist groupism and assert his or her difference. Ghagar interlocutors have mentioned that it was difficult to find a job, or a house to rent, because of their bad reputation and the attendant lack of trust. They tend to hide their identity, knowing that it has negative connotations. Young Tarek expressed his ambivalence with respect to the group.

> They are not all criminals . . . some are, but people think that everyone is. It is hard for those who are not, and sometimes they have no other choice than to become criminals. I think if you want to work and be respected, it is better to go far from the group.

He goes on to emphasize that the police are very suspicious of Ghagar.

> They always come to our place . . . . I have never had problems with them, the police, but they always come and look for criminals in our neighborhood . . . . I don't want to do anything bad . . . . I would like to change this image of the Ghagar, that we also can have a good and clean life.

Upon reflection, he concluded that he was conflicted. While he wanted to create a good image of the Ghagar, he also tried to disassociate himself from them because of their bad reputation. He had decided to break the engagement with his cousin because he disapproved of the virginity check that the girl had to go through; he had met another young woman that he liked but still had not been able to tell her that he was a Ghagar.

The rigidification of their representation and the creeping preponderance of the criminal category have an impact on the Ghagar, on the non-Ghagar, and on the relationships they construct. There may be a certain glorification of the power that is given to their group, via fear, an internalization of the representation. It is certainly better to be a feared pariah than an ordinary one.

6

MATRIARCHY AND BRIDE PRICE: GHAGAR TRADITIONS?

"What Are Your Traditions?"

In the previous chapters, we looked at how fragments of boundaries have been erected by outsiders, and how the discourse of the media contributed to the genesis of Ghagar as a category, with very specific characteristics, mostly linked to criminal behavior. We also looked at Ghagar strategies for the negotiation of their identity in a hostile environment, and how their identity affected their economic as well as their social relations with non-Ghagar. The groups have been integrated into Egyptian society culturally; as we have seen, the fragments of differentiation are often constructed with a hegemonic goal of domination and hierarchization.

The last question I want to address is, perhaps, a bit simplistic. It concerns the 'traditions' of the Ghagar, and asks if there are indeed some practices that they consider intimately and uniquely theirs. Traditions are not tangible and become such when they are somehow singled out of a set of practices and given the title of norms of a group, or occasionally lost practices that are used to anchor the group identity. I was interested in their vision of what it means to be Ghagar in terms of practices and beliefs, and to what extent those practices and beliefs act as a glue holding the group together. I wanted to find out what they perceive as the "cultural stuff" (Barth 1998, 15) inside of the boundaries, and more importantly, whether these factors are viewed as generating 'Ghagarness.' The question "What are your traditions?" often functioned as an icebreaker. Most Ghagar I spoke with were suspicious of the reasons why I would want to interview them, and assumed I wanted to talk about crime or their relations with the police and the government, all topics they would rather avoid. Asking about traditions de-dramatized the situation by refocusing it on elements they perceived as less threatening—elements belonging to the realm of culture more than the realm of politics or economics. The question also often surprised them. Most of the interlocutors had to think before answering, reflecting on what their 'traditions' would be, what had been transmitted from one generation to the next that made them Ghagar.

Interlocutors felt compelled to find "something" that would make them Ghagar. One of the recurrent responses was the identification of occupational and "personality" differences between the purportedly different tribes. Halebi were described as the gifted fortune-tellers; Ghawazi the dancers and entertainers, free and impetuous; Ghagar the beggars, cunning and resourceful; Hanagra the thieves, dishonest. Some tried to go beyond occupations and mentioned their language, which has been addressed in chapter 5. However, language was mostly linked to occupations, as the few remaining words in use belong to a glossary that involves authorities ('officer,' 'police,' 'government') and certain items that can be stolen ('bag,' 'wallet'). Only words, fragments of the language, seem to still be used.

Some interlocutors tried to display some consciousness of their identity as embodied in nostalgia over lost practices. An older Alexandrian woman identified the "old lost ways" in practices related to cooking. In the past, she explained—without specifying whether that "past" was one that she had known or not—Ghagar would only use coal to cook. They would rarely cook meat, as it was expensive, but now, most Ghagar are able to buy meat and they do not use coal to cook any more. They also had some special pans that cannot be found any more. She also contemplated a more collective past: "We also like to live together as a community. You will never find a Ghagar family isolated, and there are always a few families together." she said. This can be explained by the fact that since preserving the in-group is so important, the population cannot be overly diluted. The nostalgia over lost traditions also morphed into a lament for the loss of unifying factors. As one interlocutor put it: "It was easy to follow our traditions before. Our grandparents lived in villages, and they could have their ways. Now we live in big cities, we are losing many traditions, but we remember them and some of us try to keep them." The traditions seemed to be constructed mostly as 'something' holding the group together, whose disappearance affected the sense of belonging.

However, while conversation about food or language was typically received with hesitation, as soon as the talk turned toward marriage, interlocutors became enthusiastic in sharing some of the easily identifiable differences between mainstream Egyptian practices and theirs. Some interlocutors passionately described how weddings were planned among Ghagar communities, reflecting on past and present practices. In the past, weddings were celebrated in the streets and the whole community participated in the party; there was plenty of food and people were dancing and singing in a collective euphoria. Now, in urban environments, weddings are described as often contained in the space of one room, even if the whole community is invited. One Ghagar woman noted: "Even those who became rich, they come for the weddings. We don't always see them, but we go to their weddings and they come to ours, and they bring us money." The mother of the bride cooks food on three occasions: when the groom comes and asks for the bride's hand, at the mattress ceremony, and on the night of the wedding. They cook 'regular food' but in large quantities, chicken, *mahshi* (typical Egyptian dish, consisting of an assortment of stuffed vegetables). In the past, it was the sole responsibility of the groom's parents to pay for the wedding, which was the case in Egyptian society too. This tradition is usually kept, and the price for the bride depends on how skilled and beautiful she is. The bride receives many presents, among them a set of three or four outfits for belly dancing, as she will "dance for her husband." Being a skilled thief, as well as a skilled dancer, are the two most valuable attributes for a bride.

I would argue that the one area where the Ghagar seem to have a specific habitus is in their marital and sexual practices, as well as in gender relations. These representations of marital and gender differences may be equally anchored in real practices, in perceptions of difference in their practices, and in the external discourse, particularly in the media, which tend to project an image of a matriarchally organized society. Undoubtedly, much of the unified media discourse and the fragmented narratives from non-Ghagar interlocutors emphasize how much Ghagar "give priority" to females: "The women work," "Ghagar prefer having girls instead of boys," "Women are the true leaders of the group," and so on. There is also a notable difference with both mainstream Arab culture and Roma culture in Europe, in the fact that baby girls are prized, often more than boys, a seemingly surprising practice in a society that is surrounded by patriarchy. In all Ghagar narratives about weddings, it appears that women are a "prize"; their value is based on their "beauty and skills," as well as their ability to dance.

This chapter will first present the marriage, gender, and sexuality practices that have been depicted by Ghagar interlocutors and contrast them with the data collected by Nabil Sobhi Hanna in his ethnographic research on the Ghagar of Sett Guiran'ha. I also ask whether there are indeed patterns of matriarchal and gender structures that may apply to Egyptian Gypsies. Finally, similarly to what was done in the chapter on the criminalization of Ghagar, I examine the space left for Ghagar to negotiate their identity amid outsiders' discourse.

Endogamy

The wedding traditions are perceived as a marker of difference with mainstream Egyptians, first of all, because of the taboos around who can or cannot be married to whom. The nineteenth-century Orientalist Newbold saw a caste-like practice in Gypsies' endogamy: "They never intermarry with the Arabs, Copts, or other inhabitants of Egypt. In this respect they are as rigid as the Hindus" (1856, 289). While Hanna, in his study of the Ghagar of Sett Guiran'ha, noted very strong endogamic practices, he nonetheless noted that there were apparently no ritual prohibitions, as had been reported between Europeans and Roma (1982, 46). He also listed specific motives behind unions with non-Ghagar (whom he calls Khashana). In one case, a woman agreed to give her daughter to a wealthy Khashana because of her own inability to support her, combined with the generosity of the suitor. In the case of polygynous marriages, a Ghagar who already has a Ghagar wife might marry a Khashana in order to become closer to the inhabitants of the village and thereby increase his security and social integration within the village. Yet another Ghagar male explained that he would prefer to marry a Khashana who was "green" (inexperienced) and did not know the secrets of the Ghagar, so he could "form her as he wants. She would not be critical of him or argue with him, he says, like a Ghagar woman" (1982, 49). Overall, Hanna's examples of exogamic marriages are mostly anecdotal. In some cases, the Ghagar wanted to become more integrated into the non-Ghagar community; in others, the wealth of the non-Ghagar was a factor; in still other cases, it was because the non-Ghagar was not particularly well off that they would agree to marry within the Ghagar community. His examples also show that there were no gender taboos, and both male and female Ghagar could marry outside of the community. He reports that specific problems arose in exogamic unions, and many resulted in divorce. Many of the depicted problems are rooted in conflict between the Khashana and the Ghagar spouse's family.

> The Ghagar also talk about the non-Ghagar wife who, as soon as her husband leaves for work, goes to her family (in the same village) and does not come back until her husband returns at night. Consequently, she is neither helpful to her mother-in-law, nor has she any close relations with her husband's family. (1982, 51)

In other cases, he describes how members of the Ghagar family laugh at the Khashana for not being able to speak their language, or being unable to beg (1982, 51). He also emphasizes the general feeling in the Ghagar community that Khashana spouses are often perceived as "strangers" (1982, 52).

Occasional exogamic marriages were confirmed by many of my interviewees. A group of Alexandrian Ghagar invited me to a wedding between a Ghagar female and a non-Ghagar male, which they said would be a unique ceremony. They were excited about the party and particularly about showing non-Ghagar how Ghagar organize ostentatious wedding parties with an abundance of food and dancing.

Nowadays it appears that endogamy is still prevalent, particularly for women: the bride needs to be Ghagar, not only for lineage, but more prosaically, according to many interlocutors, for financial reasons, as she embodies the valuable asset in the union, the one who is capable of bringing money into the household, the "skilled one." While many groups have specific taboos on whether a woman or a man can marry outside the group, I could not identify a strict pattern, as different interlocutors offered different explanations. For most interlocutors, however, since the Ghagar woman is considered more precious, it was important that she should be protected and marry only a male Ghagar. One young Ghagar male from Cairo reported the story of one of his cousins, a woman who studied at Cairo University, where she had met a young non-Ghagar Egyptian man who wanted to marry her. The family had first refused, on the principle of endogamy, but eventually one uncle, referred to as a sheikh, had decided that the young woman was free to marry outside of the group. The rationale he gave the cousin to whom she had been promised was that since she had studied in a university, she would not be able to carry on the trade (stealing or begging); therefore, she would not be valuable to the group and he most likely would have to work. In other words, because she was symbolically lost to the group, being educated enough to be unable to fulfill the regular Ghagar duties, she could then be concretely lost and allowed to marry a non-Ghagar.

Cousin marriage is also prevalent, as is often the case in rural Egypt, which obviously reinforces the group's links. Hanna notes:

> Ghagar may marry kinsmen of their village or beyond. However, the prevailing preference is marriage between cousins. This pattern is characteristic of the rural fellahin who also live in the area. While such marriages are most frequent within the given village, nearly all marriage of couples from different villages are also between cousins. The Ghagar do not discriminate between patrilateral or matrilateral cousins. (1982, 40)

Even that tradition was changing when he was writing the book, since "residence in the same place for a long time has led to marriages between non-kin Ghagar working in different professions" (1982, 43). Interestingly, Hanna balances the importance of those two factors, kinship and profession, in the choice of marriage partners (1982, 42). From the different discussions I had with Ghagar both in Cairo and in Alexandria, it appears that cousin marriage is still prevalent, mostly because families live close to each other and cousins are typically raised in the same neighborhoods. The notion of 'cousin' is loose, and often a family would refer to other Ghagar as their 'cousins.' Many Ghagar said that they had married their cousin, who was not, however, their 'first cousin.'

Scholars have recently been revisiting the rural tradition of cousin marriage in general. They have shown that while it clearly embodies patriarchal structures (protection of women, importance of kinship), it is also the basis for political organization, while occasionally leaving space for individualism (Sholkamy 2003). Many Ghagar mentioned that what matters more than kinship is how much money a bride can obtain from her marriage.

Divorce and Separation

Many of the women I interviewed in Alexandria were separated from their husbands, and most of them had more than three children. In some cases, the husband was in prison; sometimes he had simply "gone away"; less frequently, the wife explained she could not live with him because he was "abusive" or "lazy." One very young woman explained that her husband had been jailed for theft one month after their marriage; she was childless and worried about her future, as she was in what she described as "a state of limbo." If you can divorce, she explained, you can get remarried; if you have children, they are the markers of social accomplishment; but being childless with a husband whom she could not rely on for anything (including reproduction) was a burdensome situation. She was living with her mother and sisters and doing small jobs. Her mother herself was divorced, but her husband had left and she did not know where he was: "Well, I know where he is, he is alive, and I know he is not in jail, but it is like I don't know him anymore. We don't talk to each other and he does not give me money."

Two other women had not divorced but their husbands were absent. They explained that they were satisfied with their situation: they both had children and were able to bring enough money home to raise them. None of them elaborated on how they "made money." They explained that were also helped by other family members. Another woman told her story: she had been without her husband for a certain time and had to raise alone a daughter who was sick (she said that her daughter had a "hole in her head"). She felt resentment for her husband who had left her the burden of raising a sick child, while at the same time she admitted that he never brought much home anyway. She was relying on small jobs and the help of her brothers.

Acceptance or desire for divorce was presented differently by different groups. While the Alexandrian Ghagar seemed to accept divorce and prefer it to the state of limbo that prevented remarriage if the husband was jailed or had disappeared, the group in Sayyida Zaynab displayed less tolerance for it. One interlocutor was quite straightforward: "We don't recognize divorce." He and his cousins explained that in the event of marital issues, the wife would typically move back to live with her parents for one year, with her children if there were any, and then return to the marital household, since usually after one year of separation, things were "back on track." The cousins linked that practice to their "Ghagar law," not explicitly written but implicitly known by the members of their community. The return to the family home after temporary separation is also mentioned by Hanna, who reports cases when a wife would go to her father's home for a certain period of time, "some days, months, or even several years," and that separation may or may not lead to a divorce.

> With the Ghagar, separation may happen for a short or a long time. In some cases, separation ended with a divorce and in other cases it ended with the return of the spouses. Separation happens when the wife leaves her husband's house or when the husband orders her to leave and to go back to her family. Separation may extend for some days, months or even several years. (1982, 56)

One of the Cairo interlocutors explained that even when a wife had left the household to go back to her father's home, the husband would nonetheless be entitled to visit her at least once a month, "to take care of his manly needs" and ensure that he would not cheat on his wife during that period of separation. This practice would allow for eventual reconciliation without any complications of adultery. The interlocutor explained that the wife was the one who decided whether she wanted to allow her husband's visits, and when during the month. He added, "Smart wives usually accept that because they know that men have needs and they don't want to take risks, even if they are angry."

Some cases of separation without divorce were also reported. One Cairene Ghagar explained that his mother had left his father to go to Saudi Arabia more than twenty years ago. She was not able to remarry, since her divorce had not been finalized, but was living with her sister and brother-in-law. The husband, meanwhile, had taken a second wife.

Bride Price, Polygyny, and Early Marriage

The Ghagar follow the Egyptian tradition of having the groom's family pay for the wedding. A respondent explained that if they cannot pay for it themselves, they typically borrow from a brother or an uncle and "usually repay when the girl starts to bring some money home." However, a specific feature described by Ghagar as important to their group was a small variation on the concept of the 'bride price.' Tradition in Egypt calls for the husband to pay a dowry. This is given to the bride's family and then transmitted to the bride in various forms, from furnishing the apartment to gifts for the bride, usually gold. Most importantly, it is meant to be the bride's property that she can reclaim in case of divorce. Symbolically, it provides the bride with independence, as she possesses her own wealth. The Ghagar variant is that the money must be given to the parents of the bride and not transferred to the bride herself. The rationale is that a young woman can bring money home because she works, and if she marries, the family needs to be compensated for their loss of income.

It is this variant notion of the bride price, and of taking into account the abilities of the women to work, that serves as the basis for the claim that Ghagar communities present strong matriarchal features. Female Ghagar are not supposed to marry outside of the community, precisely because they are so economically valuable to the group. In many articles focusing on the Ghagar, as well as in the television series *Women's Prison*, the same rhetoric is identifiable: Ghagar parents favor girls because they can marry them off for a good price, which can be exceptionally high for the most gifted girls. According to my interlocutors, a "normal girl" would go for about 50,000 Egyptian pounds, while the price for a very skilled girl could reach about 150,000 Egyptian pounds, which is very high, particularly considering that many Ghagar live in poverty. The determination of the sum appears to depend on the bride's ability to steal or to beg, which has been confirmed by most interlocutors. A girl who is not so gifted as a thief but would mostly beg can go for about 30,000 Egyptian pounds.

Polygyny occasionally occurs. It is often described as a "business decision": the man who marries two wives can guarantee himself an increase in his income. The desire to realize material or financial gain was highlighted by Hanna among the reasons why Ghagar in Sett Guiran'ha may seek an additional wife. He gives the example of men who use their multiple wives as beggars or dancers.

> The desire to realize material or financial gain is seen in the case of one man who declared that he had married two women in order to turn them begging. Another married two dancers and declared that the competition between them leads each to work harder and consequently bring more profit. (1982, 45)

In many current narratives, the increased income based on additional labor is given as the justification for polygyny, along with the notion of protection and the creation of social ties. One woman explained that her cousin had lost her husband and decided to remarry a man who had a wife so she would not be lonely. She gave him some money to take her as his second wife, as she needed to be part of a household, and continued her thieving activities. The arrangement was that she would obtain the protection offered to a married woman and he would receive an additional income. I was also told stories of widows who were offered marriage as a second or third wife but did not want to remarry because the suitor only wanted to marry them "to get their money," as some of them had rather lucrative jobs in entertainment or begging. It is an interesting contrast to the more traditional rationale for polygamy in Egypt, which is based on societal protection of unmarried females, divorcees, or widows. Ahmed from Sayyida Zaynab told the story of his grandfather, who "was a strong and honest man who married twenty-five beautiful Gypsy girls. He was protecting all of them and receiving some money from all the families of the area." Women are thus not represented uniquely as in need of social protection, but also as possessing agency and financial significance.

Many interlocutors noted that polygamy was accepted solely on the condition of acceptance by the first wife. To justify her refusal, however, she needs to demonstrate to her husband that she will consent to work sufficiently so that an additional breadwinner will not be needed in the house. This consideration often leads first wives to agree to a second wife in order to "take a break" from work. Most interlocutors agreed that polygamy usually stopped with two wives, as that was enough money for the household. Ghagar in Sayyida Zaynab explained that the first wife had the right to choose the new bride, usually based on her own needs and taste. Her ability to choose means that her decision is binding: when she accepts the second wife, she is expected not to complain about her, and the two wives are usually expected to work collaboratively in the home and outside. The two wives usually share the education of children, and each is supposed to treat the other wife's children like her own. However, the first wife would be entitled to obedience from the second, and should the two wives enter into an argument, the opinion of the first one would carry more weight.

While early marriage is still a common practice in Egypt, particularly in rural environments, it has decreased since Egypt set the minimum legal age for marriage for girls at eighteen. The reason for early marriage is that education is not regarded as a priority for women, since they are largely confined to a reproductive role. Therefore, as soon as a girl is mature enough to know right from wrong and to be able to carry out the responsibilities of raising a family, she can be married. According to Hanna:

> Most Ghagar prefer early marriage. Typically males marry at about age eighteen, females even younger, although in a few cases marriage may be delayed due to illness or to a man's preference to extend his bachelorhood. It is said that a girl [could be] married before menstruation, according to the will of her mother. (1982, 39)

Marriages are typically arranged, often from a very young age; in some cases, two- or three-year-old children are matched by their parents. The culturally rooted explanations have to do with the girl's protection, particularly from promiscuity. Hanna notes that in the Sett Guiran'ha area, boy and girl cousins in Ghagar families often live in the same homes because the families would share a household, and marrying girls early is seen as a way to ensure that women would not engage in any unsuitable premarital activity.

Youth can be commoditized and younger girls may command a higher bride price, not only because there is a certain social prestige in marrying a youthful bride, but also because the parents can claim a greater financial loss in letting go of their daughter earlier, and therefore demand a higher compensation. The Ghagar sometimes try to circumvent the minimum legal age of eighteen. One of their strategies is to bring an older decoy bride to the authorities to register the marriage, and then marry the groom to his real bride, a much younger girl. The official age of the girl is also often modified, and it is mostly the physical appearance and not the legal age that will suffice to determine whether a girl can be married. However, since identity cards are becoming compulsory among Ghagar, they cannot use that scheme any more, and most of the time they have to abide by the minimum age.

Female Circumcision and Sexuality

Female circumcision has been illegal in Egypt since 2008, but it is still very often deeply entrenched within particular communities (Gruenbaum 2005; Shell-Duncan and Hernlund 2000). According to some estimates by UNICEF, in 2008, 91 percent of married Egyptian women aged between 15 and 49 had been mutilated. There are some wide differences based on rural versus urban environment, and on the socioeconomic level of the families. The practice is often associated with women's purity. Many parents' representations of the procedure construct the moral benefits for their daughters, particularly by preserving their chastity, which enhances the prospects of a good marriage. Circumcision is also associated with a girl's feminity, since the 'masculine' part of her body is removed (Assaad 1979). It is also constructed as a rite of passage and the integration of an important social and cultural norm.

Female Ghagar in Alexandria indicated that many Ghagar women performed 'female circumcision,' but it is not certain that Ghagar women are themselves circumcised. Two centuries ago, Newbold noted that Ghagar women would alter their bodies by tattooing their lips blue, as well as practicing "the operation of circumcision and boring the ear of the nostril" (1856, 292). According to Edward Lane, "Gypsy women" would go around the street crying "Nedukk wa-n'tahir," which means "We puncture, we circumcise" (1871, 98). None of their accounts, however, indicate whether Gypsy women practice circumcision on other Ghagar as well. Some male Ghagar indicated that their wives were not circumcised, as "we believe that our wives have to enjoy the relation at the same time as we do; they need to have the same pleasure."

The sensuality of female Gypsies is strongly anchored in most historical stereotypes, epitomized in the representation of Carmen, a beautiful, free, and independent temptress. In the fantasies of outsiders, Gypsy females are perceived as being less inhibited sexually than non-Gypsies. I collected different narratives regarding the role of women in sexual relationships. According to a group of young Ghagar males from Cairo, women dictate the schedule of marital sexual encounters. One young man explained:

> The relationship between a Ghagar man and his wife is in the full control of the wife . . . especially if she is working and supporting the family with her money. The wife sets the rules of the relation before the marriage, about two weeks before the marriage . . . and that includes how many times they can make love every week. The wife can change everything after the marriage, like say more or less times each week; she decides.

Since menstruation is considered dirty and there is also a taboo around it, to the extent that women cannot speak about it directly, she may also establish a specific code to inform her husband. For instance, she might wear a scarf of a specific color—red in the examples that were given to me—"to show us she is not ready for it right now."

Some couples try to control family size, especially if the wife is the breadwinner—unless she is a beggar, in which case having a child is an asset. One means of control is the spacing of sexual intercourse, as dictated by the woman; it can vary, according to various interlocutors, from one to four or five times a month. One male interlocutor explained that there needs to be control over sexuality because, "If a couple has a lot of sex, we believe they will have a boy, and for us, having a baby girl is the most precious thing, so that is the reason why men should not have too much sex with their wives."

The scheduling of sexual activity seems to lead to the unexpected outcome of drug use. A newly married Ghagar from downtown Cairo explained that his wife had scheduled specific dates for sexual encounters (twice a week), and that in order to make the programmed and limited encounters successful, he had to resort to drug use.

> Our relation is kind of restricted . . . so I need to make sure . . . you know. I don't trust stuff like Viagra. I find smoking grass is best, it makes you stronger, you know. My wife takes some too. But only at that time; we take it together. But my wife, she never uses it alone.

Drug use for sexual performance is common practice in Egypt. Other interlocutors have alluded to the use of Tramadol, either themselves or, more frequently, referring to a friend's use of it. The drug is also widely used by workers and taxi drivers to give them more energy. It would seem that female Ghagar occasionally use the drug with their husbands, in a controlled environment. It is relatively cheap; one pill can be bought for two Egyptian pounds.

One practice described recurrently in difference instances was the execution of belly dance by the wife, for the sole enjoyment of her husband. Karim noted that this had become expensive; his bride had to buy no less than six belly-dancing costumes in preparation for their marriage. The wealthiest brides are able to buy more costumes, and the number of costumes they can afford increases their value as brides. A good bride should be able to dance for her husband. Umm Hamid from Alexandria explained that this is crucial, especially in the first months of their marriage: "If the bride cannot dance, it is a problem. She needs to be beautiful, to have skills in different trades, maybe theft, but also very importantly, she needs to be able to dance." When I asked her if she had to learn the moves, she simply answered: "Of course not, it is in our blood to dance!"

Matriarchal Features and 'Kin Contract'

Women are represented as being the breadwinners and possessing authority in the household. One episode of *Women's Prison* mentioned in previous chapters embodies these representations perfectly: a female Ghagar steals a bag in the bathroom of an expensive hotel where young Egyptian women are talking and not paying attention to their belongings. She then returns home where she is welcomed by another female, who admonishes her for allowing her husband to go out in the streets, as men should stay at home and take care of household chores. The episode then depicts men at home, caring for young children and ironing. The men then subserviently light the women's cigarettes. However, these representations do not embody the reality of the Ghagar, even if they may have internalized some of them.

I was sitting in a room with Alexandrian Ghagar, most of them women, holding small children as I jokingly asked them about 'women's power.' Of course, answered one, "women are so much better; they work outside the home and bring children. There is no better joy than to welcome a girl into a Ghagar family." To what extent do these women indeed believe in 'women's power'—or do they simply want to display that image, to use the Weberian approach to regain a sense of dignity even though they are at the bottom of society? One woman, who had been abandoned by her husband and had to work to raise their three daughters, one of whom had a medical condition, kept smiling and saying how wonderful it was to be a woman, how powerful Ghagar women were, and how delighted she was to have three girls, even a sick one. One man was present, and he said with a smile that he was happy that in his tribe, women were so strong and worked so hard. He added that he did not mind the power of women, unlike Egyptian men, who would get upset about the situation.

However, despite the importance of Ghagar women, their society is by no means matriarchally based. Women are revered as the breadwinners, but decisions in the household, although they are based on negotiation, are often ultimately made by the husband. Some patriarchal practices are still very much ingrained in Ghagar traditions, such as polygyny, early marriage, virginity checks, or female circumcision. The role of female breadwinners is not uncommon in impoverished Egyptian households where the wife engages in paid work, often as a domestic worker, while her husband stays home. However, the husband is still the authority figure who controls the finances of the household. The main difference with the Ghagar may be the presence of shame in the Egyptian males, which is often translated into making sure they demonstrate their inherent superiority and strength by abusing their wives. Still, there is considerable evidence of 'women's power' in Ghagar families. Many interlocutors, male and female, concurred that the female was the breadwinner. For instance, in one young couple from Cairo, the wife works as a beggar and makes enough money to sustain her family. Her husband works in a marble factory and makes a small salary that serves as his pocket money, to pay for coffees he drinks with his friends and for his clothes or cell phone. In another family, the groom had to borrow money from his aunt to pay for the wedding. The wife is now repaying the aunt, as he is unemployed and she is engaged in a variety of activities, mostly begging.

It is striking that the Ghagar, as a group, are represented as feminized, as many of their distinguishing characteristics are associated with the females in the group. This is true not only in the marriage traditions that emphasize the importance of the bride and her skills in order to determine the bride price, but also in their characteristic occupations. In Captain Newbold's description in "The Gypsies of Egypt," we find a strong interest in the women. His article starts with the description of "certain females whose features at once distinguished them from the ordinary Fellah Arabs and Copts of the country. In dress they differ little from the common fellah women, the dark blue cotton *tob* being common to both; but they seldom wear the *shintiyan* (drawers), and are remarkable for going abroad without the *burka*, or veil" (1856, 285). Newbold goes on to describe the males as simple vagrants, while the females are usually rope dancers and musicians (Ghagar) or fortune-tellers (Halebi). A large part of his description focuses on the fortune-tellers' practices and strategies, as well as their lack of chastity, which does not go unpunished, as he also notes that "if discovered, they are punished with death; the women being usually thrown into the Nile, with a bag of stones tied to her neck" (1856, 289). Newbold also remarks that the women are not clean, but love trinkets of brass, silver, and ivory. Nowadays, the main occupations associated with Gypsy groups are begging, stealing, and occasionally entertainment, although Ghawazi have largely disappeared from the Egyptian social and cultural scene. All of these occupations are practiced primarily by women. As we saw earlier, begging is a lucrative activity. It is inferior to stealing in terms of prestige, but is more often practiced, as it requires less skill and is potentially less dangerous.

Movies and television series like *Women's Prison* have reinforced the construction of a matriarchal society where women are dominant, acting as the main breadwinners as thieves, prostitutes, or entertainers, while their husbands stay home, care for the children, or spend their days in coffee-shops. Many articles on the Ghagar or Hanagra delight in depicting the economic role of females, as well as the importance of their criminal skills in commanding a high bride price. These articles also underline the fact that Ghagar families "rejoice" when they have a girl, which is quite con-trary to the traditional preference for boys in Egyptian society. The image portrayed is one of powerful wives and weak husbands, which further mar-ginalizes the Ghagar in the conservative Egyptian society. It implies that Ghagar men are dominated by their wives and that those wives are amoral, very much the opposite of what is expected in Egyptian social norms that value masculine strength and feminine modesty. These norms create a social space where the crossing of normative gender boundaries is not acceptable, and is constructed as threatening to social and moral stability.

This imagery, while representing some fragments of Ghagar social organization, also serves to reinforce the social boundaries and alienate this group whose norms appear irreconcilable with mainstream Egyptian social norms. It contributes to creating that dichotomous other, where the one who should be strong is weak and the one who should be weak is seemingly strong; men appear particularly emasculated in these repre-sentations. Women, in a neo-Orientalist fashion, appear both threatening (they are thieves; they are arrogantly powerful, which destroys social order) and seductive (they are sexual, independent, beautiful, skilled). As in every othering construct, it is the fears and the fantasies of the one who creates those identities that prevail. These constructs seem to encapsu-late what Egyptian society intimately rejects as ruptures in gender roles, which are perceived as intensely socially disruptive.

The fact that women are working and not protected challenges traditional values of control/care: Ghagar women are neither controlled by their husbands, nor cared for by them. This structure presents a twist on what Suad Joseph (2005) describes as the 'kin contract,' which stipulates allegiance from family members to their kin, in exchange for social stability and protection. Joseph conceptualizes the kin contract by describing how people in the Middle East construct rights and responsibilities through their relations to kin; she views the kin-based relation as mediating the relation that citizens have to the state. In parallel to the legitimization of gender inequalities via the kin contract in which males and elders dominate, she identifies a social contract, in which the relationship that citizens have to their state is influenced by the kinship-defined set of social relations and network. For instance, she explains, Egyptian men can transmit their citizenship to wives and children, but women historically could not (although this has changed recently); women are subordinated to men in the legal system and in the political system. As Joseph puts it: "The family as idea and institution does occupy a central terrain in the political and legal landscape and significantly mediates women's relationships to the state and to the laws and practices of citizenship" (2005, 151). As a result, women are often second-class citizens in the Middle East. Since that link to the state based on kin practices is broken for Ghagar, their abnormal family relations translate into non-integration as citizens.

The other dimension Joseph looks at is the private/public sphere binary, which in Western liberal discourse typically situates citizenship in the realm of the public. This is an invention of state societies, but so is the notion of family, according to Joseph. Societies invent their perfect family, and while there is occasionally a separation between the domain of the state and the domain of the family, this is not always the case. In the Middle East, she continues, government, non-government, and domestic spheres are clearly interwoven, "both in imaginative discourses and in reality" (152), while in Western countries, states have managed to consolidate families as a distinct domain (153). These differences, she argues, explain among other things the gendering of citizenship in the Middle East. Therefore, what is important to understand about the emphasis placed on the perverted gender roles (both imagined and real) by outsiders when they represent the Ghagar family is that it not only presents something that is outside of Egyptian social norms, but by extension it perverts the Ghagar's relationship to the state itself, since the legal and political systems are based on kin-inspired models (and at the same time reinforce those models).

By this analysis, the occupations of Ghagar women do not empower them. On the contrary, they serve to distort the state-supported family model that should prevail in Egyptian (and in general Middle Eastern) societies. The kin relation appears distorted, as if seen through a disfiguring mirror, although not fully opposed to the general model. The kin contract being so crucial to Egyptian society, its perversion means an active perversion of the national model. The kin contract reinforces patriarchy inside the family, but also creates a patriarchal state model, reinforcing the notion of the patriarchal bargain that creates certain responsibilities among members, but also certain 'rights,' or what Joseph calls "the pleasures of patriarchy" (155). This is also called the control/care paradigm: the assurance of familial care coupled with submission to familial controls (155).

7

CONCLUSIONS:
THE FRAGMENTED CONSTRUCTION
OF EGYPTIAN GYPSIES

E gyptian Gypsies are constructed in fragments, according to the
perceptions that non-Gypsies have of them, based only on the
small encounters that I have been able to collect. Together with
fragments of perceptions, fragments of boundaries are created, erected
where they are deemed important. Because of the sporadic nature of the
interaction between the Ghagar and non-Ghagar, the differentiation is
typically based on one notion, be it spatial, religious, 'racial,' or cultural.
Fragments are perceptible in popular culture, and even Egyptian folklore
is indebted to parcels of Gypsy imports.

Beyond Western Mimicry
The analysis presented in this book seeks to situate Gypsies within the
Egyptian context, going beyond vague notions of mystery, subjectivity,
romanticism, or superstition. It also seeks to go beyond the Western
understanding of situating Gypsies within the national narratives, which
was very apparent in the search for roots and explanations of origins
in chapter 1. This analysis contrasts the pseudo-scientific racialization
of the European Roma based on linguistic evidence with the different
approaches that are more fruitful in the Egyptian context, where myths
of origins and certain facets of Western analysis are used to look at the
group's history and ancestry with perhaps less rigidity. On this view, the
Ghagar may be associated with Indian origins and may be related to the
Roma and Lom; they may be associated with biblical sins, as sons of Cain;

or they may embody either betrayal or deliverance, as thieves of the largest nails used in the crucifixion of Jesus Christ. The lack of scientific evidence to support the Doms' journey, ancestry, and identity has served, historically, to situate them in a zone of social absence. As a result, they have not been forcefully sedentarized or assimilated. They have not had to display specific social markers. The fragments of boundaries constructed around them and the fragments of imagination associated with them have given the Dom the ability to navigate freely within Egyptian society.

One anthropologist colleague asked me how, in a society that values conformity as Egyptian society does, the Dom had been able to continue leading a differentialized life, without either culturally disappearing, or being stigmatized and discriminated against. The answer is because they have not clearly been identified collectively, and by collectively I mean both as a group and by the collective imagination. Much of the mythology or the fear around the Ghagar seems anchored in individual imaginations, based on singular encounters (with a fortune-teller, for example, or a beggar), idiosyncratic fantasies (belly-dancers, interest in 1950s movies, Gypsy music, and *rababa*), or sensationalistic fears. Consequently, the Dom are not attributed wholeness as a group. Instead, they often become the embodiment of a single characteristic, a single fear, or a myth; they are denied a complete existence, made ahistorical and atemporal. The paradox of that situation resides in the concurrence of societal freedom and a denial of identity.

It is important to look beyond these fragmented representations and focus on the Doms' agency, which is explained in chapter 4. Ghagar-ness is fluid and often based on performativity in 'doing' Ghagar identity: practices and interactions are based on overemphasis, underemphasis, or temporary status. To paraphrase Judith Butler, Ghagar's identity is doing rather than being.

Cultural Performance and Social Failure

The process of 'doing Ghagar' is nonetheless changing. Throughout this research, I have highlighted how notions associated with Gypsies had been shifting from romanticized exoticism to sordid criminality. Movie representations, for instance, are evocative of these shifts. We saw that the

Tamr Hennas of Egypt, like the Carmens of Europe, had morphed into criminals, and that cultural performances have slowly been transformed into social failures. While the criminalization of the Ghagar is inexorably gaining ground, there still exist some fragmented instances where Ghagar are 'doing' more traditional Ghagar things: perhaps their role in *mulids* is the best metaphor for how their ethnic performativity as romanticized Gypsies is still alive, although evolving.

Ghawazi, as we saw in chapter 2, have largely disappeared as such and are mostly identifiable as models within the belly-dancing community. According to many accounts, and particularly in contributions to specialized belly-dancing magazines, the 'last Ghawazi' are the Banat Maazin, or 'daughters of Maazin,' a family from Luxor. In an article published in 1993, Edwina Nearing retraces the story of the daughters of Maazin.

> Yusuf Mazin, a Nawari Gypsy, had wandered the land dealing in livestock, entertaining the villagers with stories, delivering messages and generally making himself useful until his non-Gypsy wife blessed him with five beautiful daughters. Beautiful, talented daughters who could master singing and dancing—the arts of the *ghawazi*, as such women were traditionally called in the countryside—were the best hope for the prosperity of a Nawari family in Egypt. (Nearing 1993)

By the mid-1970s, the daughters of Mazin were famous in Qena. However, in the mid-eighties, Mazin died and "things fell apart" (Nearing 1993). When the author visited the Ghawazi's home in 1993 she saw a sad scene of a dying art. Her 1993 article depicts the Ghawazi art as "on the edge of extinction," suggesting that economic pressures and the rush toward Westernization have induced the people of the Middle East to turn their backs on their own rich cultural heritage. Religious fundamentalism is another explanation Nearing gives, based on her discussions with some villagers.

One place where Gypsy performativity may still be encountered is in *mulids*, which are held for the Prophet Muhammad's birthday and are part pilgrimage, part carnival, and part mystical Islamic ceremony. In Egypt, however, the *mulids* are not limited to the Prophet's birthday (Mulid al-Nabi), but also refer to the celebration of local Sufi saints. *Mulid*s are widely practiced and in some ways similar to Christian carnivals: a time of anarchy and license, where usual norms can be broken, gender segregation is discarded, sexual taboos are forgotten, and people dance and consume drugs in an atmosphere of general hysteria. *Mulid*s embody a temporary relief from the hardship of life, a time where people can let go of all boundaries; they can be said to lead to acceptance of difficult social conditions in the long run, interspersed in this way with short periods of subversive madness. While they can be an occasion of charity, devotion, and fun, they are also often treated as an expression of superstition, or archaic folklore.

*Mulid*s have been the subject of criticism ever since they were first celebrated, but with the rise of Islamic reform and modernism since the late nineteenth century, they have become a symbol of the ignorance, backwardness, and irreligion that are supposedly holding back the nation's progress (Schielke 2003). They are also often associated with Sufism and saint worship, both of which are rejected by the Sunni authorities. The promiscuity between men and women is also considered immoral. As a result, *mulid*s tend to be rejected both by religious authorities and by secular modernists. *Mulid*s also embody the erasure of usually rigid class differences by inverting and relativizing the absolute norms that are set by hegemonic religious discourses (Schielke 2003, 164), but this is done in a festive and irrational way, which the modernist and secular thinkers would not perceive as a real challenge to those norms in the long run.

For the government, *mulid*s represent a kind of dilemma. On the one hand they are conservative, loyal, and politically safe forms of religious practice that should be encouraged. On the other hand they represent a moment of unpredictable disorder, opposed to the public authorities' understanding of festivity, public space, and order (Schiekle 2003, 168). The *mulid*s are perfect spaces for the Ghagar, who also embody archaism, license, and lack of morality. Their performances during *mulid*s have also represented the mood changes of society, sometimes more conservative, sometimes more depressed or jubilant. For many years, Ghawazi performed during *mulid*s, as represented in *Tamr Henna*, but they have gradually vanished from the festivals, in part because of the disappearance of Ghawazi in general, and in part because of the stronger moral constraint applied to the festivals nowadays. Occasionally, male dancers have replaced the Ghawazi. I was provided with a few examples of "secret tents" where Ghawazi were still, almost clandestinely, dancing or "showing part of their bodies" to enthusiastic crowds.

The Ghagar, however, are still essential actors in *mulids*, and their roles have been reinvented according to the moral space they are allotted and the interests of the crowd, as well as the increasing commercialization of *mulids*. For instance, many have become purveyors of children's entertainment: they operate small, colorful Ferris wheels, slides, or toy stands. They also run a variety of contests, and in some tents display "rarities." While I never visited the tents, I was told about the exhibition of "five-legged goats/cows," "levitating women," or "midgets." *Mulids* have taken a strong commercial turn, and some areas of Cairo, normally rather desolate, benefit from them. Shopkeepers can sell small items or coffee, and people rent out spaces in tents for families to rest or eat. Small hostels rent rooms to the visitors coming from neighboring towns. The Ghagar have been able to use their pragmatic fluidity to creatively find new ways to participate in the *mulids*. This remaining occupation is crucial, as it defines the Ghagar in terms of cultural performance rather than social failure.

What Will Happen Next?

To try and answer this question, it is useful to look at Hanna's conclusion about the Ghagar of Sett Guiran'ha, in which he asks whether the Ghagar will be integrated into the majority population of the area. His hypothesis is:

> A major factor contributing to the integration of the Ghagar of Sett Guiran'ha with the rest of the community has been their longevity in the area. Most of the families migrated there many years ago and have long since established a pattern of trust and respectability. Another reason for increased acceptance has been the continual, if gradual improvement and expansion of traditional crafts, as they saw necessary, to keep up with modernization. Willingness to engage in

non-traditional occupations such as shop keeping, not only generate a higher standard of living but leads to greater interaction with the villagers. Finally, the Ghagar of Sett Guiran'ha are very careful to appear as local Egyptian villagers and do not cultivate strong ties in other areas. (Hanna 1982, 109)

He continues to outline the limitations to Ghagar integration:

However, it must be realized that the integration of this Ghagar group has its limitations and is not yet total. There are still many barriers between them and the villagers, with the issue of intermarriage presenting the greatest obstacle. Even in the few cases where mixed marriages have occurred, they have not produced greater social interaction between families. A village girl may leave her family home and be accepted by the Ghagar as a wife but not considered one of their own. (1982, 109)

The last social area that presents difficulties is that their integration is not always readily accepted by their neighbors.

Ghagar find difficulties too and are not accepted on an equal basis. Their attempts to participate in the joys and sorrows of the villagers are often misinterpreted and they are accused of only pretending to share. Again, in certain situations, the Ghagar behavior becomes cautious and withdrawn. Their refusal to interact, to discuss, and their general sensitivity does not create an atmosphere in which relationships can grow naturally. Thus, their integration with the rest of the community, though somewhat successful, is not without limitations and reservations which reduce and restrict its development.

Nevertheless the idea that these Ghagar may achieve an even higher degree of integration is not at all impossible or distant, since this group has already taken large steps in that direction. The matter basically depends on a change in the stereotyped images on both sides. (1982, 110)

We can now, almost forty years after Hanna conducted his study in a rural environment, reflect on his conclusions. He considers that the main obstacles to a successful integration lie in the stereotyped representations on both sides, Ghagar and Kashana; acceptance of the outsider partner in cases of exogamy; and doubts about the sincerity of the Ghagar, "accused of only pretending to share." I would argue that the hopeful direction mentioned by Hanna has not been taken, for a variety of reasons that have been made evident in this research. One of them is the increasing urbanization of Ghagar. While a rapprochement in rural villages may have seemed more hopeful because of social similarities, in new urban environments the distance between Ghagar and non-Ghagar may be greater. They have also lost some of the sacredness associated with their representations, and their social failure has become more evident in the urban setting.

Their rigidification into stereotyped representations is also taking a different turn, mostly because of the mediated discourse that constructs them as threats to security and moral imperatives by turning them into 'folk devils,' who are not only dangerous as criminals but also challenge the normative Egyptian identity because of their matriarchal features. The very term 'Ghagar' has largely come to refer not to cultural practices but to social marginalization, to the extent that there seems to be only a thin boundary between being a Ghagar and simply being a criminal.

National Identity and Gypsies

The last point that is striking and worrisome is the relationship to the state, which has been an underlying theme of this research: the place of the Ghagar within the Egyptian national identity. As Joseph explains, the public and domestic spheres are intertwined: the "kin contract is played out in the administering of the state laws, and especially family law, in the privileged relationship between religion and kin entities, in the everyday practices of citizens and state agencies" (Joseph 2005, 154). Hence the model of the domestic sphere is important, and the kind of structural twist presented by the Gypsies cannot be kept submerged, even if it is often constructed as secret. It has an impact on their national integration as citizens.

Of particular importance is the fact that women are outside of the control/care paradigm. In acting as breadwinners, they are not following the patriarchal model of submitting to their subaltern role. Still, as we saw earlier, this may be more of an illusion of power, since many very patriarchal structures remain: polygamy, early marriage, female circumcision, lack of paternal support in case of divorce, and so on. What matters, however, is the appearance of rejection of the care/control model.

Joseph also shows that the kin-contract model is not limited to family relations but has spread to the national structure, affecting laws as well as political and economic structures. It is also the base upon which citizenship is built. Being outside of that ingrained system alienates the outsiders from the type of belonging that is based on citizenship. In simple terms, deviating family structures damage their potential to belong as citizens, since the very model of civic belonging and citizenship is shaped by normative kin structures. As Joseph says: "Kin are central to social, political, and religious identity, economic and political security, and emotional stability in much of the Middle East" (2005, 156).

Not only are Ghagar/Hanagra alienated, they are also unprotected. As Joseph describes, Middle Eastern states generally set themselves up as the protector of family—that is, the type of family it is shaped by and, in turn, continues to shape, which is not what is represented by the Ghagar/Hanagra. This lack of protection potentially marginalizes them even more than other factors such as nomadism. They are in effect social nomads, in the sense that they are not anchored in social reality and norms.

The fact that Ghagar women are uncontrolled, by their husbands and by the state, renders them unprotected, but does not empower them. In fact, their apparent independence only serves to alienates Gypsies even further. Since states purport to take families into account in their nation-building projects, Ghagar may be excluded from those projects on those grounds.

Umm Khalas: Where Are You?

I had initially planned to name this book "Umm Khalas Moved to the City of the Dead," in reference to a figure that inspired this research. Umm Khalas is a shadow. She inspired my research because somehow, by her name and her occupation, she seemed to embody both desperation and humor. When I started researching the Dom, I was told of a Ghagar woman whose job was to wash the bodies of the deceased. Her name was "Umm Khalas," which means 'Mother of "that's all."' In Arabic, 'Umm' is traditionally used by women to recreate their own name from the name of their first-born son. As we saw in previous chapters, the Ghagar use this tradition defiantly by using the names of their daughters instead of sons. 'Khalas' is a very common term in Arabic, nearly untranslatable in English. It means that something is finished, a discussion is over. It is used all the time and has many connotations, including a certain playfulness. I found her name both funny and tragic. Playful and fatalistic, it perhaps encapsulated some of the 'gypsy identity' that I was looking for.

It also encapsulated the impossibility to grasp that identity fully. When I looked for Umm Khalas in the area of Muqattam where she had been located, I was told, matter-of-factly, that she had moved to the City of the Dead, which seemed somewhat ironic for someone whose occupation made her an intermediary between life and death. I could not find out whether she moved there alive or not. I assumed she was. Of course I looked for Umm Khalas in the City of the Dead, but of course I never found her.

BIBLIOGRAPHY

Acton, T., ed. 2000. *Scholarship and the Gypsy Struggle: Commitment in Romani Studies: A Collection of Papers and Poems to Celebrate Donald Kenrick's Seventieth Year*. Hatfield, UK: University of Hertfordshire Press.

Acton, T. 2006. "Romani Politics, Scholarship, and the Discourse of Nation-Building: Romani Studies in 2003." In March and Strand 2006, 27–39.

Acton, T., and N. Gheorghe. 2001. "Citizens of the World and Nowhere: Minority, Ethnic and Human Rights for Roma." In *Between Past and Future: The Roma of Central and Eastern Europe*, edited by W. Guy, 54–70. Hatfield, UK: University of Hertfordshire Press.

Acton, T., and G. Mundi, eds. 1997. *Romani Culture and Gypsy Identity*. Hatfield, UK: University of Hertfordshire Press.

Aly, S. 2013. "Asl al-ghajar fi Misr." Abwab blog, March 30.

Anderson, B. 1991. *Imagined Communities*. London: Verso.

———. 2011. "Western Nationalism and Eastern Nationalism: Is There a Difference That Matters?" *New Left Review* 9: 31–42.

Aoyama, Y. 2009. "Artists, Tourists, and the State: Cultural Tourism and the Flamenco Industry in Andalusia, Spain." *International Journal of Urban and Regional Research* 33, no. 1: 80–104.

Armbrust, W. 1996. *Mass Culture and Modernism in Egypt*. Cambridge, UK: Cambridge University Press.

"Arrival in Europe." n.d. The *Council of Europe* website, Project Education of Roma Children in Europe, http://www.coe.int/t/dg4/education/roma/default_EN.asp.

Ashur, K. 2014. "Sijn al-nisa': al-sajeen wa-l-sajjan kilahuma fi sijn." *Civic Egypt*, October 18.

Assaad, M.B. 1980. "Female Circumcision in Egypt: Social Implications, Current Research, and Prospects for Change." *Studies in Family Planning* 11, no. 1: 3–16.

Back, L. 1996. *New Ethnicities and Urban Culture: Racisms and Multiculture in Young Lives*. London: UCL Press.

Bains, J., and S. Johal. 1998. *Corner Flags and Corner Shops: The Asian Football Experience*. London: Gollancz.

Barth, F., ed. 1998. *Ethnic Groups and Boundaries: The Social Organization of Culture Difference*. Long Grove, IL: Waveland Press.

Barthes, R. 1970. *Mythologies*. Paris: Editions du Seuil.

Belton, B. 2005. *Questioning Gypsy Identity: Ethnic Narratives in Britain and America*. Walnut Creek, CA: Rowman Altamira.

Benjamin, W. 2008. *The Work of Art in the Age of Its Technological Reproducibility, and Other Writings on Media*. Edited by M.W. Jennings, B. Doherty, and T.Y. Levin. Translated by E. Jephcott et al. Cambridge, MA: Harvard University Press.

Bercovici, K. 1928. *The Story of the Gypsies*. London: Jonathan Cape.

Berger, M. 1961. *A Curious and Wonderful Gymnastic*. Brooklyn, NY: Dance Perspectives.

Bhabha, H. 1994. *The Location of Culture*. New York: Routledge.

Bhopal, K., and M. Myers. 2008. *Insiders, Outsiders and Others: Gypsies and Identity*. Hatfield, UK: University of Hertfordshire Press.

Borrow, G.H. 1846 (2004). *The Zincali: An Account of the Gypsies of Spain*. Digital Antiquaria.

Brubaker, W.R. 1990. "Immigration, Citizenship, and the Nation-State in France and Germany: A Comparative Historical Analysis." *International Sociology* 5 (December): 379–407.

———. 2005. "The 'Diaspora' Diaspora." *Ethnic and Racial Studies* 28, no. 1: 1–19.

Buenaventura, W. 1994. *Serpent of the Nile: Women and Dance in the Arab World*. New York: Interlink.

Burton, R. 1898. *The Jew, the Gypsy and El Islam*. London: Hutchinson and Co.

Butler, J. 1990. *Gender Trouble: Feminism and the Subversion of Identity*. New York: Routledge.

Cabanel, P. 2007. "Patricia M.E. Lorcin, *Kabyles, Arabes, Français: Identités coloniales*." *Archives de sciences sociales des religions* 140: 157–310.

Charnon-Deutsch, L. 2004. *The Spanish Gypsy: The History of a European Obsession*. University Park: Pennsylvania State University Press.

Charrad, M. 2011. "Gender in the Middle East: Islam, State, Agency." *Annual Review of Sociology* 37: 417–37.

Chatty, D. 2006. *Nomadic Societies in the Middle East and North Africa: Entering the Twenty-first Century*. Leiden and Boston: Brill.

Clark, C. 2002. "Not Just Lucky White Heather and Clothes Pegs: Putting European Gypsy and Traveller Economic Niches in Context." In *Ethnicity and Economy: "Race and Class" Revisited*, edited by S. Fenton and H. Bradley, 183–99. Basingstoke: Macmillan.

Clifford, J. 1988. *The Predicament of Culture: Twentieth Century Ethnography, Literature, and Art*. Cambridge, MA: Harvard University Press.

Cohen, R. 1996. "Diasporas and the Nation-State: From Victims to Challengers." *International Affairs* 72, no. 3: 507–20.

Cohen, S. 1972. *Folk Devils and Moral Panics: The Creation of the Mods and Rockers*. Oxford: M. Robertson.

———. 1985. *Visions of Social Control*. Oxford: Polity Press.

Crofton, H.T. 1907. "Borde's Egipt Speche." *Journal of Gypsy Lore Society* 1, no. 2: 157–68.

Dabashi, H. 2009. *Post-Orientalism: Knowledge and Power in a Time of Terror*. New Brunswick, NJ: Transaction Publishers.

"Dabt usra min 'al-hanagraniya' bi-hawzatiha rub' milyun juneh hasilat al-nashl fi-l-'umra." 2012. O News Agency, August 11.

Desiderio, A., and E. Desiderio. 2012. "Constructing Romanies: The Representation of Roma People in News Reporting Discourse." Intersecting Spaces Blog, October 3.

"Domari." 2017. Ethnologue, https://www.ethnologue.com.

"Domari Gypsies of Egypt." 2017. People Groups, www.peoplegroups.org.

Drummond, S. 2011. *Mapping Marriage Law in Spanish Gitano Communities*. Vancouver: UBC Press.

Dundes, A. 1981. *The Evil Eye: A Casebook*. Madison: University of Wisconsin Press.

Durkheim, E. 1997. *The Division of Labor in Society*. New York: Simon and Schuster.

Eickelman, D., and J. Piscatori. 1990. *Muslim Travellers: Pilgrimage, Migration, and the Religious Imagination*. Berkeley and Los Angeles: University of California Press.

Fairclough, N. 2003. *Analysing Discourse: Textual Analysis for Social Research*. London: Psychology Press.

Fairholt, F.W. 1862. *Up the Nile, and Home Again: A Handbook for Travellers and a Travel-Book for the Library*. London: Chapman and Hall.

Fargues, P. 2003. "Family and Household in Mid-nineteenth Century Cairo." In *Family History in the Middle East: Household, Property, and Gender*, edited by B. Doumani, 23–50. Albany: State University of New York Press.

Fisher, J., and A. Shay. 2009. *When Men Dance: Choreographing Masculinities across Borders*. Oxford: Oxford University Press.

Fraser, A. 1992. *The Gypsies*. Oxford, Cambridge: Blackwell.

Fraser, K. 2014. *Before They Were Belly Dancers: European Accounts of Female Entertainers in Egypt, 1760–1870*. Jefferson, NC: McFarland.

Foucault, M. 1972. *The Archeology of Knowledge*. London: Routledge.

———. 1977. *Discipline and Punish: The Birth of Prison*. London: Penguin.

Geertz, C. 1973. *The Interpretation of Cultures: Selected Essays*. New York: Basic Books.

Gilroy, P. 1993. *The Black Atlantic: Modernity and Double Consciousness*. Cambridge, MA: Harvard University Press.

Goffman, E. 1959. *Presentation of Self in Everyday Life*. Garden City, NY: Doubleday.

———. 2009. *Stigma*. New York: Simon and Schuster.

Goldberg, D. 1993. *Racist Culture: Philosophy and the Politics of Meaning*. Cambridge: Blackwell.

Gramsci, A. 1971. *Selections from Prison Notebooks*. London: Lawrence and Wishart.

Gruenbaum, E. 2005. "Female Genital Cutting: Culture and Controversy." In *Gender in Cross-Cultural Perspective*, edited by C. Brettell and C.F. Sargent, 393–404. Upper Saddle River, NJ: Pearson Prentice.

Halbwachs, M. 1992. *On Collective Memory*. Chicago: University of Chicago Press.

Hall, S. 1990. "Cultural Identity and Diaspora." In *Identity: Community, Culture, Difference*, edited by J. Rutherford, 222–37. London: Lawrence and Wishart.

———. 1992. "The Question of Cultural Identity." In *Modernity and Its Futures*, edited by S. Hall, D. Held, and A. McGrew, 274–316. Cambridge: Polity Press.

———. 2006. "Introduction: Who Needs 'Identity'?" In *Questions of Cultural Identity*, edited by S. Hall and P. du Gay, 1–17. London: Sage.

Hancock, I. 1987. *The Pariah Syndrome: An Account of Gypsy Slavery and Persecution*. Ann Arbor, MI: Karoma.

———. 2002. *We Are Romani People*. Hatfield, UK: University of Hertfordshire.

———. 2008. "The 'Gypsy' Stereotype and the Sexualization of Romani Women." In *"Gypsies" in European Literature and Culture*, edited by V. Glajar and D. Radulescu, 181–91. New York: Palgrave Macmillan.

Hanna, N.S. 1982. "Ghagar of Sett Guiran'ha: A Study of a Gypsy Community in Egypt." *Cairo Papers in Social Science* 5, no. 1.

Harkness, G., and R. Khaled. 2014. "Modern Traditionalism: Consanguineous Marriage in Qatar." *Journal of Marriage and Family* 76: 587–603.

Hasdeu, I. 2008. "Imagining the Gypsy Woman." In "Picturing Gypsies: Interdisciplinary Approaches to Roma Representations," special issue, *Third Text* 22, no. 3: 347–57.

Helbig, A. 2004. *Carmen*. New York: The New York City Opera Project.

Herin, B. 2012. "The Domari Language of Aleppo (Syria)." *Linguistic Discovery* 10, no. 2: 1–52.

Hirshman, C. 1986. "The Making of Race in Colonial Malaya: Political Economy and Racial Ideology." *Sociological Forum* 1, no. 2: 330–61.

Holloway, S. 2005. "Rural Roots, Rural Routes: Discourses of Rural Self and Travelling Other in Debates about the Future of Appleby New Fair, 1945–1969." *Journal of Rural Studies* 20: 143–56.

Holmes, K. 2002. "The Dom of Egypt: A DRC Update, May 2002." *Kuri: Journal of the Dom Research Center* 2, no. 3, May 2002.

———. 2004a. "A Videographic Portrait—An Introduction to the Dom Musicians of Egypt." *Kuri: Journal of the Dom Research Center* 2, no. 1, Fall/Winter.

———. 2004b. "The Rababah." *Kuri: Journal of the Dom Research Center* 2, no. 1, Fall/Winter.

———. 2004c. "Visiting with the Dom Musicians of Egypt." *Kuri: Journal of the Dom Research Center* 2, no. 1, no. 1, Fall/Winter.

Hugi, J. 2013. "The Secret Language of Cairo's Jewelry Merchants." al-Monitor, September 25.

Incirlioglu, E. 2006. "Where Exactly Is Cincin Baglari? The Boundaries of a 'Gypsy' Neighborhood in Ankara." In Marsh and Strand 2006, 191–204.

Iordanova, D. 2003. "Introduction." Special edition on Romanies and Cinematic Representations, *Framework* 44, no. 2: 5–14.

Isaac, D. 2004. *The Invention of Racism in Classical Antiquity*. Princeton, NJ: Princeton University Press.

Jackson, M. 2005. *Existential Anthropology: Events, Exigencies and Effects*. New York: Berghahn Books.

Joseph, S. 2005. "The Kin Contract and Citizenship in the Middle East." In *Women and Citizenship*, edited by F. Marylyn, 149–69. Oxford: Oxford University Press.

Kabachnik, Peter. 2009. "The Culture of Crime: Examining Representations of Irish Travelers in *Traveller* and *The Riches*." *Romani Studies* 19, no. 1: 49–64.

Karayanni, S. 2006. *Dancing Fear and Desire: Race, Sexuality, and Imperial Politics in Middle Eastern Dance*. Waterloo, Canada: Wilfried Laurier University Press.

Katz, J. 1990. *Seductions of Crime: Moral and Sensual Attractions in Doing Evil*. New York: Basic Books.

Kenrick, D. 2004. *Gypsies: From the Ganges to the Thames*. Hatfield: University of Hertfordshire Press.

Kenrick, D., and C. Clark. 1999. *Moving On: The Gypsies and Travellers of Britain*. Hatfield, UK: University of Hertfordshire Press.

Kertzer, D., and D. Arel, eds. 2002. *Census and Identity: The Politics of Race, Ethnicity and Language in National Censuses*. Cambridge, UK: Cambridge University Press.

El-Kholy, H. 2002. *Defiance and Compliance: Negotiating Gender in Low-Income Cairo*. New York: Berghahn Books.

Koinova, M. 2010. "Diasporas and International Politics: Utilizing the Universalistic Creed of Liberalism for Particularistic and Nationalist Purposes." In *Diaspora and Transnationalism*, edited by R. Baubock and T. Faist, 149–67. Amsterdam: University of Amsterdam Press.

Kolukirik, S. 2006. "Perceptions of Identity amongst the Tarlabasi Gypsies, Izmir." In Marsh and Strand 2006, 133–40.

Kyuchukov, H. 2009. "Projection Hypotheses in Language and Identity among Muslim Roma." In *Roma Identities*, edited by H. Kyuchukov and I. Hancock, 26–37. Prague: NGO Slovo.

———. 2010. *Essays on the Language, Culture and Education of Roma*. Uppsala: Hugo Valentin Centre, Uppsala University.

Lane, E. 1871. *Manners and Customs of the Modern Egyptians*, vol. 2. London: John Murray.

Leland, C.G. 1874. *English Gipsies and Their Language*. London: Trübner & Co.

———. 1882. *The Gypsies*. Boston: Houghton, Mifflin and Company.

Lieberson S. 1980. *A Piece of the Pie: Black and White Immigrants since 1880*. New York: Academic Press.

Liégeois, J.P. 1986. *Gypsies: An Illustrated History*. Translated by T. Berrett. London: Al Saqi Books.

———. 1987. *Gypsies and Travellers: Socio-cultural Data, Socio-political Data*. Strasbourg: Council for Cultural Co-operation.

Lorcin, P. 2006. *Algeria & France, 1800–2000: Identity, Memory, Nostalgia*. Syracuse: Syracuse University Press.

Mahmood, H. 2009. "Commentary: The Role of Feeling in Intrapersonal and Interpersonal Ethnic Identities." *Culture and Psychology* 15, no. 2: 284–92.

Mamduh, A. 2015. "Hal yumkin an ya'ish mujtama' mutakammil bi-nfisal kamil 'an mujtama'ih al-akbar fi 'adatih w-taqalidih wa-mawruthih wa-qiyamih?" al-Badil, July 27.

Mahmud, Y. 2010. "al-Hanjraniya: al-sariqa sharaf wa-l-i'dam masir man tarfud al-nashl." Masress, April 22.

Mansur, H. 2015. "'Ghagar suriya' yastawtinun shari' Clot Bek." Rosa Maga-zine, March 14.

Marsh, A. 2000. "Gypsies and non-Gypsies in Egypt: the Zabaleen and Ghagar Communities of Cairo." *Kuri: Journal of the Dom Research Center* 1, no. 3.

———. 2006. "'…the strumming of their silken bows': The Firdausi Legend of Bahram Gur in the Context of Narratives of Origin in Romani Histories." In Marsh and Strand 2006, 39–58.

———. 2007. "Research and the Many Representations of Romani Identity." The European Roma Rights Centre, November 20.

Marsh, A., and E. Strand, eds. 2006. *Gypsies and the Problem of Identities: Contextual, Constructed and Contested.* Istanbul: Swedish Research Center in Istanbul.

Marushiakova, E., and Popov, V. 2001. *Gypsies in the Ottoman Empire: A Contribution to the History of the Balkans.* Hatfield: University of Hertfordshire Press.

———. 2006. "The Turkish Gypsies in the Balkans and the Countries of Former Soviet Union." In Marsh and Strand 2006, 179–90.

Matras, Y. 2000. "Two Domari Legends about the Origin of the Dom." *Romani Studies,* 5th series, 10: 53–79.

———. 2012. *A Grammar of Domari.* Berlin: Walter de Gruyter.

———. 2015. *The Romani Gypsies.* Cambridge, MA: Harvard University Press.

Mayall, D. 2004. *Gypsy Identities 1500–2000: From Egipcyans and Moon-men to the Ethnic Romany.* London: Routledge.

Meyer, F. 1994. *Dōm und Turkmān in Stadt und Land Damaskus.* Erlangen: Fränkische Geographische Gesellschaft.

Mitchell, T. 2002. *Rule of Experts: Egypt, Techno-Politics, Modernity.* Berkeley: University of California Press.

Mostyn, T. 2006. *Egypt's Belle Epoque: Cairo and the Age of the Hedonists.* London: I.B Tauris.

Nearing, E. 1993. "The End of the Banat Mazin? Struggles with Religious Fanatics, Real Estate Management, and Other Ghawazi." Gilded Serpant, February.

Newbold, T.J. 1844. "The Chenchwars; a Wild Tribe Inhabiting the Forests of the Eastern Ghautst." *Journal of the Royal Asiatic Society* 8: 271–78.

———. 1856. "The Gypsies of Egypt." *Journal of the Royal Asiatic Society* 16: 285–312.

Nord, D.E. 2006. *Gypsies and the British Imagination, 1807–1930*. New York: Columbia University Press.

Okely, J. 1975. "Gypsy Women: Models in Conflict." In *Perceiving Women*, edited by S. Ardener, 55–86. New York: John Wiley & Son.

———. 1983. *The Traveller-Gypsies*. Cambridge, UK: Cambridge University Press.

———. 2005. *Own or Other Culture*. London: Routledge.

Oprisan, A. 2006. "An Overview of the Romanlar in Turkey." In Marsh and Strand 2006, 163–71.

Özatesler, G. 2012. *Gypsy Stigma and Exclusion in Turkey, 1970*. Basingstoke: Palgrave Macmilian.

Peretz, M. 2006. "Dances of the 'Roma' Gypsy Trail From Rajasthan to Spain: The Egyptian 'Ghawazi' Dance." *Kuri: Journal of the Dom Research Center* 2, no. 4, Spring/Summer.

Piotrowska, A. 2013. *Gypsy Music in European Culture: From the Late Eighteenth to the Early Twentieth Centuries*. Boston: Northeastern University Press.

Polansky, P. n.d. "Original Research on Gypsies." Paul Polansky's Website, http://paulpolansky.net/original-research/.

Pratt, N. 2006. "Identity, Culture and Democratization: The Case of Egypt." *New Political Science* 27, no. 1: 69–86.

"Qabilat al-hanajraniya." 2011. Wasafat Cleopatra website, April 12.

al-Qalb al-Hakim. 2014. "Qabilat al-hanajraniya fi Misr." D-la3 online forum, March 14.

Reed, A. 1997. *W.E.B. Du Bois and American Political Thought: Fabianism and the Color Line*. Oxford: Oxford University Press.

Renard, S., A. Manus, and P.V. Fellman. 2009. "Understanding the Complexity of the Romany Diaspora." Online Proceedings of the Seventh International Conference on Complex Systems, http://necsi.edu/events/iccs7.

Richardson, J., and A.R. Ryder, eds. 2012. *Gypsies and Travellers: Empowerment and Inclusion in British Society*. Bristol: Policy Press.

"Romani, Domari in Egypt." 2017. Joshua Project, www.joshuaproject.net.

Romani Project at the University of Manchester. n.d. "A Brief History of Romani Linguistics."

Roushdy, N. 2010. "Baladi as Performance: Gender and Dance in Modern Egypt." *Surfacing* 3, no. 1: 71–99.

Safran, W. 1991. "Diasporas in Modern Societies: Myths of Homeland and Return." *Diaspora: A Journal of Transnational Studies* 1, no. 1: 83–99.

———. 1999. "Comparing Diasporas: A Review Essay." *Diaspora* 8, no. 3: 255–91.

El Safy, S. 1999. "Raks Sharqi: Cairo's Disappearing Act." *Habibi* 17, no. 4: 32–35.

Sa'id, A. 2011. "Dabt sayyidatayn min al-hanajra qabl safarhuma li-l-sariqa bi musim al-hajj." *Youm 7*, October 27.

Said, E. 1978. *Orientalism*. New York: Pantheon.

Saint John, B. 1853. *Village Life in Egypt: With Sketches of the Said*, vol. 1. Ticknor, Reed and Fields.

Salo, M., and S. Salo. 1977. *The Kalderas in Eastern Canada*. Ottawa: University of Ottawa Press.

———. 1986. "Gypsy Immigration to the United States." In *Papers from the Sixth and Seventh Annual Meeting, Gypsy Lore Society, North American Chapter*, edited by J. Grumet. New York: Gypsy Lore Society.

Saul, N., and S. Tebbutt, eds. 2005. *The Role of the Romanies: Images and Counter-Images of "Gypsies"/Romanies in European Cultures*. Liverpool: Liverpool University Press.

Schielke, S. 2003. "On Snack and Saints: When Discourses of Rationality Enter the Egyptian Mawlid." Paper presented at the Netherland-Flemish Institute of Cairo, January 23.

———. 2012. *Perils of Joy: Contesting Mulid Festivals in Contemporary Egypt*. Syracuse, NY: Syracuse University Press.

Schneeweis, A. 2012. "If They Really Wanted To, They Would: The Press Discourse of Integration of the European Roma, 1990–2006." *International Communication Gazette* 74, no. 7: 673–89.

Sedláková, R. 2006. "The Media as a Tool of Social Exclusion: An Example of Presentation of the Roma in the Czech Media." In *The Challenge of Social Inclusion: Minorities and Marginalized Groups in Czech Society*, edited by T. Sirovátka, 155–81. Brno: Barrister and Principal.

El Shabrawy, C. 2014. "'Women's Prison': A Ramadan TV Triumph." Mada Masr, August 12.

"Shaima Saif: Kamla Abu Zikri ja'alatni haramiya fi sijn al-nisa' wa-l-fil al-azraq mufaj'atan 'id al-fitr." 2014. *El-Mogaz*, July 2.

Shell-Duncan, B., and Y. Hernlund, eds. 2000. *Female "Circumcision" in Africa: Culture, Controversy, and Change*. Boulder: Lynne Rienner.

Sholkamy, H. 2003. "Rationales for Kin Marriage in Rural Upper Egypt." In *The New Arab Family*, edited by N. Hopkins, 62–77. Cairo: Cairo Papers in Social Sciences.

Silverman, C. 1982. "Everyday Drama: Impression Management of Urban Gypsies." *Urban Anthropology* 11, no. 3–4: 377–98.

———. 1988. "Negotiating 'Gypsiness': Strategy in Context." *Journal of American Folklore* 101, no. 401: 261–75.

Smith, D., and M. Greenfields. 2013. *Gypsies and Travellers in Housing: The Decline of Nomadism*. Bristol: Policy Press.

Spivak, G. 1999. *A Critique of Postcolonial Reason*. Cambridge, MA: Harvard University Press.

Strand, E. 2006. "Romanlar and Ethno-Religious Identity in Turkey." In Marsh and Strand 2006, 97–104.

Streck, B. 2006. "Nabil Sobhi Hanna: A Personal Reflection." In Marsh and Strand 2006, 175–78.

Thomas, C.F. 2000. "Dom of North Africa: An Overview." *Kuri: Journal of the Dom Research Center* 2, no. 1, January.

Toninato, P. 2009. "The Making of Gypsy Diaspora." *Translocation: Migration and Social Change* 5, no. 1: 1–19.

Tönnies, F. 2015. *Communauté et Société: Catégories Fondamentales de la Sociologie Pure*. Paris: Presses Universitaires de France.

"Unreached: Domari, Gypsy of Egypt." n.d. Idlewild website, http://www.idlewild.org.

Van Dijk, T.A. 1989a. "Mediating Racism: The Role of the Media in the Representation of Racism." In *Language, Power and Ideology: Studies in Political Discourse*, edited by R. Wodak, 199–227. John Benjamin Publishing.

———. 1989b. "Structures of Discourse and Structures of Power." In *Communication Yearbook 12*, edited by J.A. Anderson, 18–59. Newbury Park, CA: Sage.

———. 1993. "Principles of Critical Discourse Analysis." *Discourse and Society* 4, no. 2: 249–83.

————. 2000. "New(s) Racism: A Discourse Analytical Approach." In *Ethnic Minorities and the Media*, edited by S. Cottle, 33–49. Buckingham, UK: Open University Press.

————. 2012. "The Role of the Press in the Reproduction of Racism." In *Migrations: Interdisciplinary Perspectives*, edited by R.S. Michi Messer and R. Wodak, 15–29. New York: Springer.

Van Nieuwkerk, K. 1995. *A Trade Like Any Other: Female Singers and Dancers in Egypt.* Austin: University of Texas Press.

Volpi, F. 2014. *Political Civility in the Middle East.* New York: Routledge.

von Kremer, A. 1864. "The Gipsies in Egypt." *Anthropological Review* 2: 262–66.

Warner, C.D. 1881. *My Winter on the Nile.* New York: Houghton and Mifflin.

Weber, M. 2003. *Economie et société, tome 1: Les Catégories de la sociologie.* Paris: Poche.

————. 2011. "Class, Status, Party." In *The Inequality Reader: Contemporary and Foundational Readings in Race, Class, and Gender*, 2nd ed., edited by D. Grusky and S. Szelenyi, 56–67. Boulder, CO: Westview Press.

Wehnert, K. 2010. *Passing: An Exploration of African-Americans on Their Journey for an Identity along the Color Line.* Hamburg: Diplomica Verlag.

Wikipedia. 2017. "Ghawazi." March 15.

Willems, W., and L. Lucassen. 2000. "Gypsies in the Diaspora? The Pitfalls of a Biblical Concept." In *Social History*, no. 6: 251–69.

William, A. 2000. "Dom of the Middle East: An Overview." *Kuri: Journal of the Dom Research Center* 1, no. 1, January.

————. 2005. "Dom Ethnic Identity." *Kuri: Journal of the Dom Research Center* 2, no. 3, Fall/Winter.

————. 2006. "The Current Situation of the Dom in Jordan." In Marsh and Strand 2006, 205–12.

Winant, H. 2000. "Race and Race Theory." *Annual Review of Sociology* 26: 169–85.

Young, I.M. 1992. "The Five Faces of Oppression." In *Rethinking Power*, edited by T. Wartenberg, 174–95. Albany: State University of New York Press.

Zaki, A. 2004. *A History of Theatre in Africa*. Edited by M. Banham. Cambridge, UK: Cambridge University Press.

Zeidel, R. 2014. "Gypsies and Society in Iraq: Between Marginality, Folklore and Romanticism." *Middle Eastern Studies* 50, no. 1: 74–85.

INDEX